Gnosticism and the History of Religions

Scientific Studies of Religion: Inquiry and Explanation

Series editors: Luther H. Martin, Donald Wiebe,
Radek Kundt and Dimitris Xygalatas

Scientific Studies of Religion: Inquiry and Explanation publishes cutting-edge research in the new and growing field of scientific studies in religion. Its aim is to publish empirical, experimental, historical and ethnographic research on religious thought, behaviour and institutional structures. The series works with a broad notion of scientific that includes innovative work on understanding religion(s), both past and present. With an emphasis on the cognitive science of religion, the series includes complementary approaches to the study of religion, such as psychology and computer modelling of religious data. Titles seek to provide explanatory accounts for the religious behaviours under review, both past and present.

The Attraction of Religion, edited by D. Jason Slone and James A. Van Slyke
The Cognitive Science of Religion, edited by D. Jason Slone and William W. McCorkle Jr.
Contemporary Evolutionary Theories of Culture and the Study of Religion, Radek Kundt
Death Anxiety and Religious Belief, Jonathan Jong and Jamin Halberstadt
The Impact of Ritual on Child Cognition, Veronika Rybanska
Language, Cognition, and Biblical Exegesis, edited by Ronit Nikolsky, Istvan Czachesz, Frederick S. Tappenden and Tamas Biro
The Learned Practice of Religion in the Modern University, Donald Wiebe
The Mind of Mithraists, Luther H. Martin
Naturalism and Protectionism in the Study of Religion, Juraj Franek
New Patterns for Comparative Religion, William E. Paden
Philosophical Foundations of the Cognitive Science of Religion, Robert N. McCauley with E. Thomas Lawson
Religion Explained?, edited by Luther H. Martin and Donald Wiebe
Religion in Science Fiction, Steven Hrotic
Religious Evolution and the Axial Age, Stephen K. Sanderson
The Roman Mithras Cult, Olympia Panagiotidou with Roger Beck
Solving the Evolutionary Puzzle of Human Cooperation, Glenn Barenthin
Understanding Religion Through Artificial Intelligence, Justin E. Lane

Gnosticism and the History of Religions

David G. Robertson

BLOOMSBURY ACADEMIC
LONDON • NEW YORK • OXFORD • NEW DELHI • SYDNEY

BLOOMSBURY ACADEMIC
Bloomsbury Publishing Plc
50 Bedford Square, London, WC1B 3DP, UK
1385 Broadway, New York, NY 10018, USA
29 Earlsfort Terrace, Dublin 2, Ireland

BLOOMSBURY, BLOOMSBURY ACADEMIC and the Diana logo are trademarks of
Bloomsbury Publishing Plc

First published in Great Britain 2022
This paperback edition published 2023

Copyright © David G. Robertson, 2022

David G. Robertson has asserted his right under the Copyright, Designs and Patents Act, 1988, to be identified as Author of this work.

For legal purposes the Acknowledgements on p. vii constitute an extension of this copyright page.

Cover image © Shutterstock

All rights reserved. No part of this publication may be reproduced or transmitted in any form or by any means, electronic or mechanical, including photocopying, recording, or any information storage or retrieval system, without prior permission in writing from the publishers.

Bloomsbury Publishing Plc does not have any control over, or responsibility for, any third-party websites referred to or in this book. All internet addresses given in this book were correct at the time of going to press. The author and publisher regret any inconvenience caused if addresses have changed or sites have ceased to exist, but can accept no responsibility for any such changes.

A catalogue record for this book is available from the British Library.

Library of Congress Control Number: 2021938958

ISBN: HB: 978-1-3501-3769-1
PB: 978-1-3502-5859-4
ePDF: 978-1-3501-3770-7
eBook: 978-1-3501-3771-4

Series: Scientific Studies of Religion: Inquiry and Explanation

Typeset by Newgen KnowledgeWorks Pvt. Ltd., Chennai, India

To find out more about our authors and books visit www.bloomsbury.com and sign up for our newsletters

Contents

List of Figures		vi
Acknowledgements		vii
Introduction: A strange charm		1
1	Against all heresies: Gnosticism before modern scholarship	11
2	The era of gnosis restored: Nineteenth-century Gnostics	25
3	The alien god: Gnosticism as existentialism	39
4	A crack in the universe: Jung and the Eranos circle	51
5	No texts, no history: Nag Hammadi	65
6	A revolt against history: Gnostic scholarship, after Nag Hammadi	77
7	Tongues and misunderstandings: Messina 1966	89
8	Takes a Gnostic to find a Gnostic: Contemporary gnostic groups	105
9	The third way: Gnosticism in Western esotericism	123
10	Knowledge of the heart: The gnostic New Age	137
11	The greatest heresy: Jeffrey Kripal's gnostic scholarship	151
12	Elite knowledge: Gnosticism and the study of religion	157
Notes		163
Bibliography		197
Index		221

Figures

1. Jung and Corbin at Eranos in 1950 — 60
2. Corbin (right) and Scholem at Eranos, 1977 — 62
3. Puech, Quispel and Michel Malinine examining the Jung Codex — 73
4. The delegates of the VII International Congress on the History of Religions, 1950 — 90
5. Delegates of the Messina Congress, 1966 — 102
6. The Besant Lodge, Los Angeles, in April 2019 — 108
7. Gilbert Durand (another Centre International du Recherche Spirituelle Comparée member), Henry Corbin and Antoine Faivre at Eranos in the 1970s — 126

Acknowledgements

Thanks to those who helped me access research material at the British Library, the Scottish National Library, the Freemasonic Library in London, the Jung Archive in Zurich, Satoko Fujiwara of the IAHR committee, the Philosophical Research Centre Library in Los Angeles, the Ritman Library in Amsterdam, Scott Donaldson at the library of St Andrews University and Suzanne Newcombe at INFORM. Thanks too to those who allowed me to research among them – Bishop Hoeller, Winston Wiggins and the other officials and congregants of the Ecclesia Gnostica, John DiGilio and Jordan Stratford of the Johannite Apostolic Church, Jesse Folks, and Nomita and Gareth of the Edinburgh Gnostic Centre. Some of this fieldwork and research was supported by the Open University through a grant from the Strategic Research Investment Fund, for which I am most grateful.

Thanks to all those whose discussions helped to shape or hone the arguments here: Jonathan Tuckett, Steve Sutcliffe, Leonardo Ambasciano, Wouter Hanegraaff, Egil Asprem, Luther Martin, Einar Thomassen, Chris Cotter, Ann Taves, Russell McCutcheon, Michael Stausberg, Paul-François Tremlett, Fryderyk Kwiatkowski, Paul Middleton and the anonymous reviewers of the proposal and manuscript. Special thanks to Richard Bartholomew for indexing it, and catching several proofing errors in the process. A project of such breadth would be simply impossible without such knowledgeable friends.

Thanks to Lalle Pursglove and Lucy Carroll at Bloomsbury for all their help, encouragement and patience, and to Don Wiebe and Luther Martin for inviting me to publish it as part of the Scientific Studies of Religion: Inquiry and Explanation series. Thanks to my colleagues at the Open University, the Religious Studies Project, the committee of the BASR and the network of critical scholars of religion around the world – my own Pilgesh Club. These collaborations are what I like most about this career. Finally, love and gratitude to Aileen, Teddy and Rex for all their support – especially through the long, strange holiday of Lockdown 2020.

Chapter 10 contains elements of 'A Gnostic Study of Religion', published in *Method and Theory in the Study of Religions*. Chapter 12 contains elements of '"When the Chips Are Down": A Response to Ambasciano', published in *Religio: Revue pro religionistiku*.

Figures 1, 2 and 7 are reprinted with the permission of Association des amis de Henry et Stella Corbin (AAHSC) (www.amiscorbin.com). Figure 3 is reprinted with the permission of Lemniscaat Publishing House, Rotterdam. Figures 4 and 5 are reprinted with the permission of the International Association of the History of Religion. Figure 6 was taken by the author.

Introduction: A strange charm

As I was beginning work on this book, a colleague raised the question of whether scholars could still refer to new religious movements as 'neo-gnostic'. I responded by asking why they would want to, given the term's vagueness and the increasing consensus that no such religion ever existed in Antiquity. What would be gained by doing so?

Their response, and that of some others who joined in, was illuminating. Paraphrasing (because the comments were not intended for publication), they told me that they were drawn to the term because of its particular strange charm. It could be a wicked distortion of scripture that seeks to slander the goodness of God or the exhilaration of an experience of heroic, antinomian awakening. They talked of a moment of sudden recognition of their own soul trapped in a prison of the material and a romantic yearning for freedom.

Such sentiments would not sound out of place in the writing of Joseph Campbell, Paulo Coelho or other writers who blend Jungian psychology, New Age self-development and various mythologies together. And it struck me that they were not uncommon in writing on Gnosticism in Religious Studies. Consider the following extracts:

> Something in Gnosticism knocks at the door of our Being and of our twentieth-century Being in particular. Here is humanity in a crisis and in some of the radical possibilities of choices that man can make concerning his view of his position in the world, of his relation to himself, to the absolute and to his mortal Being.[1]

> Gone is the God of damnation. Gone is the focus on sin and retribution. In its place is the God of Love that the Gnostics claimed to know. Separation from God and reunification with the sacred has become the story of salvation. Behind it all is the individual as the divine human agent empowered to do great things. The demand is for therapy, for religion that is useful. To be successful, religion

today must promote personal well-being, health, and spiritual wholeness. It must be attuned to a raising of consciousness, to global awareness, to life that is linked with the transpersonal or transcendent.[2]

The first, by Hans Jonas, was written in 1973, though it reflects research carried out before the Nag Hammadi corpus was discovered. Jonas was primarily a philosopher, though his existentialist definition was endorsed by the International Association for the History of Religions (IAHR) in 1966. The second, by April DeConick, was written in the twenty-first century, after the category had all but collapsed in Biblical Studies. The strange charm of Gnosticism isn't going anywhere, and scholars are in no way immune.

I get it, though. I have felt that strange charm too. *The Nag Hammadi Library in English* was on my shelf, alongside Philip K. Dick novels and *The Matrix* on VHS, long before I started studying religion at university. I even wrote my master's dissertation on contemporary gnostic religions. But the subject turned out to be bigger and more complex than I had realized, and I put it aside for a few years while I got my doctorate and eventually a job. When I returned to the subject of contemporary Gnostics in 2016, I began by trying to set out the background, but like a cartoon sweater, when I pulled at the loose threads, they just kept coming and coming until the whole thing unraveled.

This, then, is not a book about Gnosticism per se. It is in part history of an idea, part disciplinary history and part reflection upon the current field. It tells the story of how the idea of Gnosticism moved from a specific, historical religious tradition to an ahistorical type of salvific experience. Its characters are scholars of religion and members of gnostic religions, and sometimes both at the same time. Crucially, both camps claim access to elite knowledge.

Our story begins when a polemic category of heresy was taken up by liberal Protestant theologians. Later, it was transformed into an ahistorical religious type by philosophers and psychologists. Then, in 1945, a body of previously unknown sectarian texts from the fourth century CE was discovered in the Egyptian desert near Nag Hammadi, which revolutionized our understanding of the early Christian period and fundamentally challenged Gnosticism as a historical category. The contents would not be fully published until 1975, and in some ways the dust is still settling.

Comparative scholars of religion take this work and use it to make ahistorical assertions, although sometimes it is the opposite way around – a textually trained biblical scholar steps into a comparative frame of reference, again, without the necessary methodology or caution. More specifically, I am concerned with a particular History of Religions school which came to dominate the field in the post-war years and to a large degree remains dominant in the classroom and in popular discourse. History of Religions (1950s–80s) was the inheritor of the Victorian comparative Science of Religion school (1850s–1910s). Institutionally speaking, History of Religions was a lab-created Frankenstein's monster of different European approaches which had emerged in the intervening decades, including Dutch phenomenology (1870s–1950s), German/Austrian *Kulturkreislehre* (1890s–1950s), Italian Historicism (1910s–50s), Romanian hermeneutics (1920s–40s) and esoteric perennialism (or Traditionalism).[3]

Despite considerable internal debate regarding the details, the History of Religions school can be identified by several shared assumptions. As identified by Ambasciano, these are a methodological commitment to diachronic and synchronic comparison; a tendency towards classification through the identification of similarities and, less often, differences; religion seen as a motive and generally beneficial force in the evolution of human culture(s); a stress on the uniqueness and independence of religious phenomena, and the resulting need for a unique discipline; and, despite the name, a primarily phenomenological rather than historical method.[4] This is merely a rough schema, and I will discuss its development, and the methodological and theoretical debates within and without, in later chapters.

But it is also a book about how scholars construct ideas and then lose control of them again. These ideas also pass into the religious sphere, and today a number of sizable groups identify as Gnostics – indeed, they may be the only people ever to do so – who, in every case, trace their ideas back to the same sources as our scholarly understandings. In some cases, they have actually informed the scholarly models.

Thus was Gnosticism as we think of it today born – an ahistorical and *sui generis* category ultimately derived not from historical or textual analysis, but from the preconceptions of Carl Jung, Hans Jonas and various phenomenologists. Although the radical anti-cosmic dualism and the more orgiastic claims have largely been dropped, Gnosticism continues to be presented as heretical, experiential, transformative and salvific. A unique and irreducible special knowledge reached through transformative experience, Gnosticism is sui generis religion par excellence. Which is why it has been so closely tied to the development of the History of Religions and, indeed, continues to be so.

Introductory books on Gnosticism typically begin with some variation on the question, 'Why is Gnosticism so hard to define?' The existence of Gnosticism is presumed even in the wording, and the problem becomes finding a definition for *a very complex but nevertheless real thing*, rather than acknowledging that the category was a chimera produced in the interface of scholars, religious entrepreneurs and heresiologists from the very beginning. I won't do that here. To quote Hanegraaff while invoking J. Z. Smith, we might say, 'There is no such thing as "gnosis" until we start talking about it, and even after we start talking about it the gnostics still only exist in our minds, if indeed they exist anywhere at all'.[5] But Henry Green puts it best:

> We have only a variety of statements made with words by a variety of different writers with a variety of different intentions and as such, there is no history of an idea to be written, but only *a history of various people who used the idea and of their varying social situations.*[6]

This book is my attempt to write that history.

My interest in presenting an archaeological investigation of the term is not to argue that it is useless or meaningless, however. Rather, I will argue that it is a loaded, and often polemical, term. My starting point is the position argued by Michael Williams in *Rethinking 'Gnosticism'* (1996); no such religion as Gnosticism existed historically, and the groups then and now considered gnostic have no one thing in common except that they were considered heretical in the early days of the church. The modern category Gnosticism is defined neither doctrinally nor through self-identification, but theologically, and this agenda has informed the category from the start. The catalogue of groups presented by *Adversus Haereses* in the second century CE was concerned only with identifying *heresy*. The Nag Hammadi corpus, however, whatever it was, demonstrated to scholars – or at least it should have – that the picture was a little more complicated than how Irenaeus's polemic presented it.

Williams convincingly challenged, one by one, the 'clichés that have come to be almost routinely invoked at any mention' of Gnosticism and certainly the 'family resemblance' definitions usually presented in modern primers on the subject.[7] Rather than practicing 'protest exegesis' – that is, the systematic and deliberate reversal of conventional scriptural interpretation, as often claimed by those who present Gnosticism as fundamentally heretical or countercultural – Williams shows that in fact these unconventional exegeses were of passages that proved equally problematic to orthodox Christian interpreters and therefore represent innovative problem-solving rather than systematic reversal. Williams shows that the claim that Gnostics were 'anticosmic' (world-rejecting) pessimistic isolationists was certainly not always the case, nor did they all hate their bodies. Similarly, the charge that Gnostics were either ascetics or wild libertines is an oversimplification of a diverse range of ethical agendas. Williams even challenges that they were elitist, suggesting that their deterministic soteriology – that is, the doctrine that only some were capable of receiving gnosis and salvation – was not a prescription against evangelism, but rather an explanation of why the teachings were resisted or ignored. In other words, it was a reaction to the hostility from wider society that some groups may have experienced. Williams concludes that the category Gnosticism be replaced with more transparently heuristic second-order categories, and presents 'biblical demiurgical traditions' as one possible alternative.[8]

A quarter of a century after Williams's critique, this position is unremarkable in Biblical Studies. That is not to say that all scholars accept that the category can have no heuristic value or empirical validity, but it is used with more reservation and defined with greater care.[9] Yet in contemporary Religious Studies, these critiques are given little more than lip service. Indeed, here, Gnosticism is positively thriving. For example, consider the following excerpt from Roelf van den Broek:

> Michael Williams has convincingly shown that the popular view of Gnosticism as a monolithic religious movement is untenable. He concluded that it would be better to dismantle the whole category of 'Gnosticism' altogether, and that terms such as 'gnosis' or 'Gnosticism', 'gnostic' and 'gnostic religion' are so vague that they have lost any specific meaning and should be avoided as well. Elsewhere I have argued that while Williams' analysis is convincing, his solution is too radical. The terms 'gnosis' and 'gnostic' are perfectly applicable to all ideas and currents, from Antiquity to the present day, that emphasise the idea of a revealed secret gnosis (spiritual knowledge) as a gift that illuminates and liberates man's inner self. The term 'Gnosticism', however, should better be restricted to the mythological gnostic systems of the first centuries.[10]

Van den Broek here is 'convinced' by Williams's argument, but apparently not convinced enough to stop using gnosis and gnostic phenomenologically as an ahistorical essentialist category in language clearly drawn from Jung. Jung was many things, but a trained scholar of religion was not one of them. Tellingly, in a later comment on Williams, van den Broek's objection is boiled down to 'avoidance of the terms "gnosis" and "gnostic" does not contribute to a better understanding of the spiritual movement usually characterized by these words' – missing completely that Williams's point is not which signifiers we use, but that no such signified 'movement' ever existed.[11]

I will therefore offer no definition of Gnosticism. As a critical historical analysis, my criterion for inclusion here is simple: when an individual or a group refers to someone or something as gnosis, gnostic or Gnosticism. Rather than seeking to define Gnosticism or gnosis, this study is concerned with how others have defined these terms, and the strategies they have used to legitimize Gnosticism – historically, experientially, phenomenologically or otherwise. My questions are, first, how this person understands Gnosticism and/or gnosis, and second, how that understanding relates to broader trajectories in the discourse on religion more broadly.

Other scholars have written in detail about certain aspects of this story, particularly Steven Wasserstrom and Hans Thomas Hakl on Eranos and the History of Religions, Willem Styfhals and Benjamin Lazier on post-war German thought, Michael Williams on the polemical roots of Gnosticism and Karen L. King on the term's adoption by Protestant theologians.[12] My contribution is to show the threads connecting these and bring them together to show the larger narrative behind Gnosticism and the History of Religions. Historically speaking, this book picks up where King and Williams stopped: where they are concerned primarily with a process of historical reification or essentialization, my focus is a second stage of essentialization, where this (imagined) historical entity is transformed into an *ahistorical* essence. In this sense, then, Gnosticism can be seen as a case study in the process of *essentialization* in Religious Studies. It is this sui generis essence – this 'transcendent quality that stands above history and resists reductive analysis'[13] – which has come to be regarded as perhaps the most problematic legacy of the History of Religions school.

Chapter 1 outlines what was believed about the Gnostics from the heresiological writings of Irenaeus and other 'church fathers' in the second century CE up until the beginnings of the Science of Religion during the nineteenth century. This chapter concerns the first stage in the essentialization of Gnosticism, in which 'a historical term [is] confused with a historical entity'.[14] This is followed by a chapter showing how these ideas were picked up by new religious entrepreneurs in France, Germany and Great Britain, who would in turn influence later scholars and instigate lineages that would result in today's gnostic religions – a tautological loop in which the scholar becomes the actual 'initiator to the mysteries they have themselves invented'.[15]

The next two chapters focus in more detail on the second stage of this process of essentialization, in which a historical entity is transformed into an *ahistorical* category. The first is concerned with an existential interpretation of Gnosticism which culminates in Hans Jonas's *Gnosis und Spätantiker Geist* in 1934. The second is centred on Carl Jung, whose psychological interpretation directly influenced many scholars who took part in the Eranos meetings and continues to indirectly influence scholars today. These lineages come together in the central section of the book – Chapters 5 through 7 – which concern the period from the discovery of the Nag Hammadi corpus at the very end of the Second World War until the Messina Congress of the IAHR, twenty-one years later.

The remaining chapters look at the fallout from the essentialization process. Chapter 8 looks briefly at some contemporary self-identifying gnostic religions, focusing on how they use these same sources and ideas in their (re)construction of gnostic religion, reaching the same conclusions about a suppressed alternative to contemporary Christianity and the existence of transformative, salvific elite knowledge. Next, Chapters 9 through 11 focus on different approaches to Gnosticism in contemporary Religious Studies: gnosis as the epistemological and experiential essence of Western Esotericism in the work of Wouter Hanegraaff and others; Gnosticism as antecedent of the contemporary New Age, focused on the work of April DeConick; and a new gnostic approach to the study of religion in the work of Jeffrey Kripal.

The concluding chapter collects my thoughts on how this tangled history reflects on the broader history of the study of religion and the shape of Religious Studies as a field today. Some of these observations are merely methodological – such as how Gnosticism shows interdisciplinary work can perpetuate problematic categories or that scholarship is too frequently driven by personal religious quests. But some of the issues raised in the conclusion cut to the very theoretical core of the discipline. The confusion of first- and second-order categories and the continuing claims of special knowledge are moves in a battle over the place of theory in the study of religion and the place of religion in the academy. In short, in contemporary Religious Studies, Gnosticism has become a dog whistle for a phenomenological approach that is at best essentialist and crypto-theological and at worst openly anti-scientific.

In the following, I have striven to strike a balance between historical detail and readability. I have focused on narrative over encyclopedic detail, and it is not exhaustive. That would be a very different book, if indeed it were possible. There are a few places where I go into more fine-grained detail, however; these are periods which have received less attention from scholars previously, such as Mead's work, the connections between Eranos and the IAHR, and the contemporary case studies. Elsewhere, secondary sources are indicated in the notes, which provide higher resolution. I assume that readers are coming to this book with some idea about Gnosticism already, so I haven't spent too much time outlining texts, explaining cosmologies or practices. It is also the case that from about 1950, and the emergence of the History of Religions as a distinct discipline, Biblical Studies scholarship on Gnosticism fades into the background. This is in part because my argument concerns how it has been dealt with in Religious Studies specifically and in part because that is where my expertise lies. But it is also because the two disciplines have taken very different paths since then and have handled Gnosticism very differently. This book is written for Religious Studies scholars primarily, and where it engages with Biblical Studies scholarship, I have striven to outline the terms, theories and scholars in a succinct but accurate way, but I have assumed a certain level of familiarity with the contemporary social-scientific study of religion.

The chapters on fin de siècle and contemporary gnostic groups are mere sketches, however, which I intend to fully develop in a future work. What is presented here is focused on the issues of relevance to the broader arguments of the book – their appeals to special knowledge, their claims of restoring an authentic, pre-Catholic Christianity and their entanglements with scholars in 'reconstructing' a religion that in all likelihood never existed in Antiquity. I have increasingly come to realize that these contemporary Gnostics cannot be completely separated from the scholarly history. They share many of the same ancestors and at the same time are just as much the inheritors of the History of Religions school.

To keep it readable, I have streamlined terminology in a few places. I have organized the many different groups following some version of Colombian esotericist Samael Aun Weor's (1917–1977) teachings under the rubric of the Gnostic Movement, in order to avoid the many, confusingly similar acronyms. Religious Studies is used to refer to all non-confessional social-scientific studies (in the broad sense of seeking some sort of explanation, rather than a specific methodological approach) of religious groups, traditions, ideas and practices, simply because it is the most widespread in Anglophone scholarship. I do not posit its superiority over other variations or linguistic formulations, nor am I presenting it as a clearly boundaried movement or methodology. Same goes for the History of Religions, for that matter.

Gnosticism and gnosis require a little more justification, perhaps. As explained above, I have not imposed any definitions onto the various actors in the story – beyond standardizing the capital-G 'Gnosticism' and 'Gnostics', and lower-case 'gnosis' and 'gnostic'. The words mean no more and no less than the person using them means by them, and I want only to present *their* definitions as clearly as possible. Until the 1930s, gnosis and Gnosticism were more or less interchangeable, but particularly following Jonas's *Gnosis und Spätantiker Geist* in 1934, the two have taken on distinct meanings – Gnosticism signifying a historical religion and gnosis its ahistorical essence or source. I have followed this convention when making a distinction between historical and ahistorical understandings is necessary, which is often. But when I refer to just Gnosticism in my own voice (such as in the title of the book), you can assume that I am referring to the whole set of terms, as though 'and/or gnosis, gnostic, etc.' follows in parenthesis. As well as streamlining the prose, this avoids me being read as making the same first-order historical Gnosticism/ahistorical gnosis distinction.

A note on sources. I have presented sources in English throughout, as I want the book to have the largest possible audience. Nevertheless, I have favoured the original publication, in the original language, using my own translations (and providing the original as an endnote) wherever possible. Due to a paucity of sources for contemporary gnostic groups – primary and secondary – Chapter 8 additionally draws on my own fieldwork.

Finally, I am aware that I am sticking my thumb into a hornet's nest with this book. I could not cover everything, and some will feel I have missed important sources, misrepresented a particular scholar, not learned enough languages. I cross disciplinary boundaries, even as I warn others of the dangers of doing so. Nevertheless, something draws me on, some strange charm …

1

Against all heresies: Gnosticism before modern scholarship

The first appearance of Gnostics in history is in the work of Irenaeus (*c.*130–*c.*202 CE), a Greek-speaking Christian from Smyrna in modern Turkey.[1] He was a fierce defender of the primacy of the Roman church and the earliest surviving source to stress the primacy of the four canonical Gospels we know today. He became the bishop of Lyon around 177 CE and is regarded with such importance that he is a saint for both the Catholic and Eastern Orthodox churches. Shortly after his ordainment, Irenaeus wrote the 'Unmasking and Overthrow of So-Called Knowledge', more commonly known by the title of a later Latin translation, *Adversus Haereses*.[2] The Greek original is now lost, but the complete Latin translation dating from around 380 CE exists in three manuscripts, the earliest of which is from the tenth or eleventh century.[3] *Adversus Haereses* may have drawn from earlier works, including a no-longer-extant work by Justin Martyr, but regardless, its impact on later heresiologists, and on the category Gnosticism, can still be felt today.[4]

Irenaeus was writing at a time when Christianity was entering a period of consolidation and systematization. The establishment of an ecumenical hierarchy was only just beginning, and the formalization of Christian theology in the Nicene Creed was still a century and a half in the future. Irenaeus was an advocate for a systematic theology out of the developing canon of texts – the four Gospels, as well as Acts, the Pauline letters and Revelation. While it is common for Irenaeus to be presented as a staunch defender of an established orthodox tradition, John Behr argues that Irenaeus was rather representing an emerging, if unarticulated, self-understanding among Christian leaders and establishing a unity in belief, even where there was still diversity in practice.[5] Indeed, his presentation of orthodoxy and its others in *Adversus Haereses* was rather innovative – as the need for five volumes to argue for it might suggest.[6]

Yet in forcefully presenting orthodoxy, Irenaeus also constructed all others as heresy.

Hairesis was then generally used in Greek to refer to different schools of thought – Platonism, for example – but early Christian writers, lacking the institutional might that their fourth-century counterparts could rely upon, turned this neutral term into a negative by applying it to any interpretation other than what they understood to be 'true' Christianity. Therefore, a heretic became a 'false Christian'. These debates over heresies were coeval with the enshrining of many of the theological and doctrinal factors considered fundamental by Christians today.[7]

The English word 'gnosis' is derived from the Greek γνῶσις, usually translated as 'knowledge', and was in common usage among Christians, Platonists and those identified as Gnostics alike in Antiquity. Its fine-grained meaning shifted over that period, however. For Platonists, gnosis was the original knowledge of the human condition, now lost, but potentially recoverable. But in many philosophical schools – *haireses* – of Late Antiquity, such as Neoplatonism, Hermeticism and some Jewish and Christian groups – including, but not exclusively, those we now refer to as gnostic – gnosis came to signify divinely revealed knowledge, exclusive to initiates.[8]

The idea that faith and gnosis make up a dialectical pair, with conformist Christians having one and 'true Christians' the other, is present in these early writings, but is by no means the only or even the predominant dialectic – righteous/unrighteous, pure/defiled, blind/enlightened all also feature.[9] For example, Pauline Christians, who particularly stressed the importance of faith, frequently employed gnosis too – the author of the Epistle of Barnabas sought to give his readers gnosis as well as faith,[10] and for Clement of Alexandria, gnosis was the aim of the Christian life.[11] Both of these are considered examples of what would later become mainstream Christian theology.

In 1 Timothy 6:20, on the other hand, we see evidence of schisms emerging and perhaps even new revelation being claimed under the term 'gnosis', here with the familiar accusatory 'falsely so-called' epithet:

> Turn a deaf ear to empty and irreligious chatter, and the contradictions of knowledge (*gnosis*) so-called, for by laying claim to it, some have strayed far from the faith.[12]

Clement and others use the term to refer to 'spiritually mature Christians who had attained an advanced philosophical understanding of Christianity'.[13] So Irenaeus's 'gnosis falsely so-called' should be read as a mocking rejection of such claims, functioning something along the lines of the way that 'pseudoscience' or 'fake news' does today. Gnosis was not the problem, but rather the illegitimacy of these *particular claims* to gnosis.

The first volume of *Adversus Haereses* is a catalogue of heretical schools, and the four subsequent volumes argue against specific heretical positions. Theologically speaking, Irenaeus's charges were threefold:

1. That the heretic so-called Gnostics rejected the Hebrew God as the creator and ruler of the cosmos;
2. That they rejected the physical suffering of Jesus (were docetics, in other words);
3. That they rejected the need for morally good works, as a spiritual elite would be saved regardless.[14]

Irenaeus uses the term *hoi gnostikoi* (the Gnostics) to refer to them throughout the first volume, though not exclusively. He does not use *hoi gnostikoi* consistently, however. Only once, in 1.25.6, does he refer clearly to a self-designation: the followers of one Marcellina, who 'call themselves Gnostics', though this could be a general description – and a rather mocking one at that – rather than the name of the group (as, e.g., 'Robertson, who calls himself a historian'). These Marcellina Gnostics created images of Jesus which they worshipped alongside Pythagoras, Plato and Aristotle. Elsewhere are a number of references to 'a group (*hairesis*) called gnostic', which might indicate self-designation, designation by others or, again, a more general description.

Significantly, in 1.11.1, Valentinus (*c.*100–*c.*160 CE) is described as adapting the ideas of this hairesis called gnostic and formalizing them into a school. Valentinus's ideas were popular in Rome, and there were Valentinian communities in Syria, Egypt and southern Gaul.[15] Valentinian theology – known to us only through fragments and the developments of his students – posited that humans were divided into three groupings: the spiritual, the psychical and the material.[16] Those of a spiritual nature could receive gnosis, enabling them to return to the *pleroma* (fullness; here understood as the totality of the various emanations from the unknowable god), while those of a psychic nature (i.e. non-Valentinian Christians) would receive a lesser form of salvation. There was no hope for those of a purely material nature. Valentinus also developed an emanationist cosmogony – that is, in which the cosmos emanates outwards in a series of levels from the unitary Godhead – similar to that of the Neoplatonic writer Plotinus. Irenaeus tells us this cosmogony, replete with the now-familiar Aeons (lower deities) Sophia (Wisdom) and the demiurge (or Yaldaboath), was shared with 'falsely-called Gnostics' of whom he will later speak. Note that here the problem again is not with gnosis per se, but rather with gnosis 'falsely so-called'.[17] In fact, Irenaeus equates 'true Gnosis' with Catholic Christianity:

> True Gnosis is that which consists in the doctrine of the apostles, and the ancient constitution of the church throughout the whole world, and the character of the body of Christ according to the succession of bishops, by which they have handed down that which exists everywhere.[18]

Irenaeus may be describing the group who inspired Valentinus in 1.29–30, where he describes a 'multitude of Gnostics' who have arisen from the followers of Simon Magus and who worship an Aeon and its spirit, named Barbelo. At other times, however, he seems to be using *gnostici/gnosticorum* to refer to any or all heretical groups.[19] Here then, Irenaeus's charge is not to do with knowledge, but rather legitimacy. The problem is not that they are Gnostics; the problem is that they are the wrong kind of Gnostics, because their lineage is illegitimate. In contrast to the genealogy of the bishops of Rome, Irenaeus sets out an alternative genealogy back to Simon Magus. Irenaeus's basic strategy continues to underpin historical scholarship on Gnosticism to this day:

> Describing various texts and teachings, emphasising their differences from one another, while at the same time and despite clear recognition of their manifold differences connecting them in a linear genealogy to a single origin and a single essential character.[20]

Later heresiological works drew heavily from *Adversus Haereses*. Hippolytus of Rome's third-century *Refutatio Omnium Haeresium* adds many groups to Irenaeus's list of heresies, two of which he states identify themselves as Gnostics.[21] These are the Naassenes, who worshiped a snake and called themselves 'the only true Christians';[22] and the followers of Justin, who claimed to have discovered 'the Gnosis of the perfect and the good'.[23] Actually, it seems less like this is the name the group used, but rather a quality they ascribed to themselves. Elsewhere, Hippolytus used 'Gnostics' more vaguely, apparently referring to a subset of heretical groups, but including some that are today seldom included in the category, including the Ebionites and the school of Theodotus of Byzantium.[24]

By the late fourth century, Epiphanius of Salamis's *Panarion* refers to only one group as '*the* Gnostics', who he adds go by different names in different regions, including the Phibionites, Borborites and Barbelites, the latter suggesting that this is the same group referred to in 1.29–30 of *Adversus Haereses*.[25] But elsewhere Epiphanius identifies a number of groups as Gnostics, such as the Valentinians,[26] who refer to themselves that way. Williams suggests this ambiguity is caused by his use of earlier sources such as Irenaeus and adds that if self-designation really were so widespread, then its complete absence from the Nag Hammadi corpus is even more surprising.[27]

This assumption is supported by the paucity of references to Gnostics in other writings of the time. Tertullian, writing in the third century, mentions them only thrice and not at all in his *Prescription against the Heretics*;[28] Clement of Alexandria says only that the followers of Prodicus called themselves Gnostics;[29] and Origen mentions that there were some 'who call themselves Gnostics', though he is talking about Christians and separates them from both Valentinians and Simonians.[30]

One text known as *Against the Gnostics* is worth examining in more depth, as it is the only contemporary account we have not written by Christians, but rather coming from a Hellenic philosophical perspective.[31] It was written around 263 CE in Rome by the Neoplatonist philosopher and mystic Plotinus, though it was edited and titled by his student Porphyry after his death. Porphyry introduces the text thus:

> There were in [Plotinus's] time many others, Christians, in particular heretics who had set out from the ancient philosophy, men belonging to the schools of Adelphius and Aculinus – who possessed many texts of Alexander the Libyan and Philocomus and Democritus of Lydia, and who produced revelations of Zoroaster and Zostrianos and Nicotheus and Allogenes and Messos and others of this sort who deceived many just as they had been deceived, actually alleging that Plato really had not penetrated to the depth of intelligible substance. Wherefore Plotinus also often attacked their position in his seminars and wrote the book which we have entitled 'Against the Gnostics'. He left it to us to judge what he had passed over.[32]

This account shows that there were individuals known as Gnostics (even if they didn't always call themselves that) mixing in Platonic circles in Rome in the third century. Moreover, we may actually possess some of these 'revelations', as texts matching some of these titles were found at Nag Hammadi in 1945, meaning that we potentially have actual examples of their philosophical position which Plotinus argues against – a tradition now known as Sethian Gnosticism, due to its focus on the role of Adam and Eve's third son, Seth, as a saviour figure. Dylan Burns has argued that this text, in fact, records the moment when Hellenic and Christian philosophy began to see each other as incompatible and indeed to denounce each other.³³

We must remember that when we read the work of the heresiologists, we are reading one side of a debate, and that these documents were not intended to convey facts but to demonize and ridicule their subjects. Thus, it should not be surprising that we recognize the accusations as like those leveled polemically against minority religions today and in the past. Hugh Urban calls this *mimesis* – the projection of repressed or taboo behaviours onto perceived Others, be they women, ethnic minorities or, in the second century CE, heretics.³⁴ The accusations likely tell us more about the technologies of control of the dominant regimes than anything else.

Nowhere is this clearer than in the accusations of various forms of sexual impropriety levelled by Irenaeus and later heresiologists. For example, Epiphanius accuses the Borborites of practicing a variation of the Eucharist in which semen and menstrual blood replace bread and wine. He reports that their book *The Greater Questions of Mary* (unknown to us except for this report) tells that this practice was taught by Jesus himself.³⁵ He also reports that if a female member accidentally became pregnant, they would cook and consume the aborted foetus.³⁶

Epiphanius is far from a reliable scholar, but there are external suggestions that his account is not completely without historical value. In fact, *Pistis Sophia*³⁷ and the *Second Book of Jeu*³⁸ have Jesus specifically refuting practices such as those Epiphanius mentions, which shows at least that such charges were widely believed at the time. Valentinians did regard sex, and procreation in particular, as sacred,³⁹ and there are elsewhere symbolic representations, for example in the Coptic translation of *Asclepius* from Nag Hammadi, where the privacy of sexual intercourse is used to demonstrate the need for secrecy in the mysteries.⁴⁰ On the other hand, we might see this as a deliberate polemical reflection of the pure apostolic lineage of the church. King (citing Denise Buell) notes that by couching the doctrinal lineage in language invoking biological lineage, Irenaeus invokes powerful notions of miscegenation.⁴¹

Where this becomes more complicated, however, is that these accusations are picked up and détourned by nineteenth- and twentieth-century gnostic groups, building directly from early scholarship who took the accusations of the heresiologists literally. We will return to this in Chapters 2 and 8.

Neoplatonic ideas were largely forgotten about by Western scholars until the Renaissance, when some philosophers began to challenge the dominant narrative that all authentic philosophy – all capital-T 'Truth' – came exclusively through biblical and Hebrew sources.[42] Following the ascent of Protestantism in the sixteenth century, however, theologians were deeply interested in separating Christian Truth from the mythology of the Bible and especially the Old Testament. It is through these debates that the Gnostics remerge and Gnosticism becomes an increasingly important category in the discourse over 'true' Christianity.

Indeed, Gnostic*ism* itself appears during this time and signifies a shift into presenting Gnostics as possessors of a relatively cohesive, if heretical, philosophical or theological system. 'Gnosticism' itself first appears in the work of Cambridge Platonist and rationalist theologian Henry More in the 1660s, though it seems unlikely that he actually coined the term.[43] More's *An Exposition of the Seven Epistles to the Seven Churches; Together with a Brief Discourse of Idolatry, with Application to the Church of Rome* (1669) famously describes Catholicism as 'a spice of the old abhorred Gnosticism', the latter being considered the epitome of false Christianity by Protestants.[44] Likewise, Jacob Thomasius (1622–84), a philosophy teacher who numbered Leibniz among his students, and a pious Lutheran, sought to extricate Christianity from its pollution by pagan error – by which he meant Catholicism. Here, the Gnostics – via Simon Magus, the Magi and Zoroaster – were one of the many examples of Christian teaching syncretizing with Paganism. Indeed, for Thomasius, gnosis was specifically identified as a defining feature of pagan heresy.[45]

Isaac de Beausobré's 1734 *Histoire Critique de Manichée et du Manicheisme* describes the Gnostics as sects descending from Simon Magus who deny the unity of the divine, the eternity of the world and the redeemability of the body.[46] By 1750, Johann David Michaelis's *Introduction to the Divine Scriptures of the New Testament* suggested that the use of 'the Word' for the divine Jesus in the fourth Gospel was taken from the Gnostics. Even Edward Gibbon used the Gnostics (as he understood them) as grist for his critique of religious institutions – again, particularly the Catholic Church – in his *Decline and Fall of the Roman Empire* (1776–88). They 'blended with the faith of Christ many sublime but obscure tenets, which they derived from oriental philosophy, and even from the religion of Zoroaster', but unfortunately, 'as soon as they launched themselves out into that vast abyss, they delivered themselves to the guidance of a disordered imagination'.[47] A few years later, Henry Longueville Mansel (1820–1871), Regius Professor of Ecclesiastical History at St. Paul's, Oxford, gave a series of lectures in which he presented Gnosticism as antithetical to free will and therefore to

Christian morality.⁴⁸ The threat posed to Christianity by Gnosticism in Late Antiquity was repeating itself in his time, he argued:

> The transcendental metaphysics of the Gnostic philosophy and the grovelling materialism of our own day join hands together in subjecting man's actions to a natural necessity, in declaring that he is the slave of the circumstances in which he is placed. ... Merged in the intelligible universe by the Gnostic of old, man is no less by modern 'science falsely so called' merged in the visible universe; his actions or volitions are moral effects which follow their moral causes 'as certainly and invariably as physical effects follow their physical causes'. Under this assumption the distinction between moral evil and physical entirely vanishes. ... How long, we may ask, will it be before the personality of God disappears also, and the vortex of matter becomes all in all?⁴⁹

Around the turn of the eighteenth century, however, the script starts to flip, and some Protestant theologians began to interpret Gnosticism in a more positive light. In these constructions, the Gnostics were seen as an alternative, pure early Christianity which could be separated from Catholic accretions. Rather than heretical pagans, Gnostics were presented as intellectual proto-Protestants, with the gnostic spark as the presence of God within each believer. The poet and mystic Abraham von Frankenburg's *Theophrastia Valentiniana* (published in 1703, though written earlier) was perhaps the first apologia for Gnosticism, suggesting a continuity between Valentinian Gnosticism and Platonism. Frankenburg was a Lutheran, albeit an unorthodox one, and an acolyte of Jakob Böhme.

Gottfried Arnold's *Unparteyische Kirchen- und Ketzer-historie* (1699–1700) constructs a tradition of gnostic heresy running from Antiquity to Arnold's day. Yet the impartiality in the title belies that Arnold is employing the Gnostics to legitimize the Protestant Pietist movement, of which he was an impassioned advocate. Like many later writers, he saw the Gnostics as exemplars of the personal experience which for him, as a pious Protestant, was the essence of religion. Nevertheless, this thesis that heresy is made as a reaction to innovation by those in power will reemerge in twentieth- and twenty-first-century authors like Elaine Pagels and April DeConick, who similarly are perhaps less impartial than is sometimes recognized.

Most influentially perhaps for the development of later scholarship was *Die Christliche Gnosis oder die christliche Religions – Philosophie in ihrer geschichtlichen Entwicklung* (1835) by Ferdinand Christian Baur (1792–1860). Baur was the central figure of the Tübingen School, whose radical insistence that the books of the New Testament had to be examined in their historical context was groundbreaking and dominated biblical scholarship for a generation.⁵⁰ Drawing from Hegel, Baur's central idea was that second-century Christianity was the synthesis of Jewish Christianity (i.e. that deriving from the followers of Peter and James) and Gentile Christianity (i.e. that deriving from the teachings of Paul).[51] In *Die Christliche Gnosis*, Baur presents a history of gnosis as various attempts to construct a religious philosophy that could reconcile Judaism, Christianity and 'Paganism' in various ways – though he also acknowledges an essence of gnosis separate from Gnosticism per se:

> Therefore, if Gnosis is not already understood within its own sphere as a historical phenomenon in the true sense – even if the individual systems do not emerge as the necessary, self-contradictory moments in which the concept, in its inner life movement, separates itself – then the same movement must also emerge in the wider sphere to which it extends, the polemic that was directed against Gnosis.[52]

Die Christliche Gnosis also introduces the leitmotif of Gnosticism paralleling modern thought, through the comparison with the historical dialectic of Hegel's thought – the absolute differentiates itself into antithetical Aeons which become alienated but eventually synthesizes into wholeness again.[53] He traces a lineage from Late Antiquity to the sixteenth-century mystic Jacob Böhme to German idealism, including the philosophy of Hegel, Schleiermacher and Schelling.[54]

But Baur was writing with only the heresiologists as sources. During this period, the pool of sources began to grow, as several previously unknown texts from the early centuries of the Christian era came to light through the nineteenth century. The Bruce Codex, dating from the fifth century, was uncovered in Egypt in 1769 by a Scottish traveler.[55] It wasn't published until a century later, in 1892, in a translation by the German coptologist (and student of Harnack) Carl Schmidt. It is in fact two manuscripts: the first contains the first and second Books of Jeu,[56] which appear to be magical tools to guide the souls of the dead through the heavens, along with a number of untitled Coptic fragments, while the second contains an untitled treatise that has generally since been referred to pragmatically as the *Untitled Treatise*.

The Askew Codex, containing a version of *Pistis Sophia* somewhat different from the version later discovered at Nag Hammadi, was found in a London bookshop in 1773 by a London physician, Anthony Askew, from whom it takes its name. Its provenance beyond that is unknown; it was acquired by the British Library in 1785.[57] An edition in Coptic with Latin translation by M. G. Schwartze was published posthumously in 1851, followed by a French translation by Amélineau in 1885 and a German translation by, again, Carl Schmidt in 1905.

In 1896, a manuscript was brought back to Germany from Cairo (thus becoming known as the Berlin Codex) which contained four texts: the Gospel of Mary, the Apocryphon of John, the Sophia of Jesus Christ and the Acts of Peter.[58] However, the Berlin Codex was not published until 1955, so while its contents were known of, they were not so formative on the study of Gnosticism in this period. Today, these are frequently included in editions of the Nag Hammadi texts, notably including the important *The Nag Hammadi Library in English* (1977).

Lastly, it is worth mentioning that some fragments of the Gospel of Thomas were discovered in the cache of papyri discovered in an ancient rubbish dump near Oxyrhynchus in Egypt by Bernard Pyne Grenfell and Arthur Surridge Hunt at the end of the nineteenth century. However, they were not recognized as such until an almost complete Coptic version was discovered at Nag Hammadi in 1945. After that, Thomas would become (along with *Pistis Sophia*) the most famous 'gnostic gospel'.

Far more influential in pre-war scholarship, however, were the large collection of Manichaean texts assembled by German archaeologists between 1902 and 1914 from the Turfan region of Central Asia and the first translations of Mandaean texts in the nineteenth century, originating from the still-surviving communities in Iran and Iraq.[59] Although they were not mentioned in the heresiological texts, these groups were increasingly drawn into the category of gnostic religions, despite a number of clear differences. Both Mandaeans and Manichaeans were formalized religious systems, composed predominantly by one individual, and existed in a specific place and time, and while both draw from some texts typically regarded as gnostic, they draw as much from Zoroastrian and other traditions.[60] However, the tendency of including Manichaeism in the catalogue of gnostic groups has likely led to an overstatement of dualism as a common feature among gnostic texts.

The *religionsgeschichtliche* scholars of the Tübingen School generally interpreted the Bruce and Askew codices as containing 'a late and degraded form of Gnosticism' and disregarded them.[61] In other words, they rejected the only primary data as it didn't fit their existing conclusions – something which will happen again after Nag Hammadi. Sixty years later, German church historian Adolf von Harnack would write:

> Baur's classification of the Gnostic systems, which rests on the observation of how they severally realised the idea of Christianity, is very ingenious, and contains a great element of truth. But it is insufficient with reference to the whole

phenomenon of Gnosticism, and it has been carried out by Baur by violent abstractions.[62]

Harnack was able to draw from the Bruce Codex and the *Pistis Sophia*, as well as the heresiological sources, for his influential 1885 work, *Lehrbuch fur Dogmengeschichte*. In it, he famously described Gnosticism as 'the acute Hellenisation of Christianity ... ruled in the main by the Greek spirit and determined by the interests and doctrines of the Greek philosophy of religion', which became paradigmatic for a generation of scholarship.[63] Harnack uses Hellenization in a historical sense; he means the cultural context in which Christianity emerged, and as such, all the texts of the New Testament are Hellenized to some degree and show the influence of their Greco-Roman context. These influences begin to supplant their Jewish influences in the second century, Harnack argues, as Christianity began the transformation from a Jewish sect to a universal religion. But this also brought an intellectualizing tendency, Harnack argues, that turned piety and faith into dogma and creed, and spirit into law. Eventually this would lead to a degeneration of Christianity into mythology and saint worship – by which, of course, he is implying Catholicism.[64] For Harnack,

> The epoch-making significance of Gnosticism ... is the transforming of the Gospel into a doctrine, into an absolute philosophy of religion, the transforming of the *disciplina Evangelii* into an aesceticism based on a dualistic conception, and into a practice of mysteries.[65]

In the revolutionary mood of the early Weimar period, Harnack's later *Marcion: Das Evangelium vom fremden Gott* (1921) stirred controversy with his argument for separating the 'new wine' of the later Christian teaching from the 'old wineskin' of the Old Testament as the necessary fulfillment of Luther's unfinished revolution. The foremost task facing Protestantism, Harnack maintained, was to liberate the Christian message of ultimate hope and the everlasting love of the good God from its ties to the law-giving deity of the Old Testament. Harnack concluded that the Old Testament deserves recognition as a crucial historical document but not as a sacred canon, noting with apparent naiveté that das Volk were falling away from Christianity in protest against the church's continuing allegiance to its Jewish heritage.[66]

Harnack focused on the *haireses* (in both senses) of Basilides and Valentinus, but included all other heretical groups under the rubric Gnosticism; thus, he follows More and the heresiologists in using the terms 'Gnosticism' and 'heresy' for all purposes interchangeably. Yet unlike More, Harnack is not entirely critical or condemnatory; rather, he portrays both Gnosticism and Catholicism as attempts to rationalize and Hellenize Christianity, with the latter merely being less radical in its rejection of Judaism because it retained the Old Testament. For the radical Protestant Harnack, the essence of Christianity was the immanence of the Kingdom of God and Jesus's teachings were concerned with how to live one's life in that immanence. The essence was also ahistorical, and so he was able to separate the Hellenized Gospels from the eternal Gospel truth.[67] This *demythologization* – that is, separation of the narrative framing from the theological meaning – was to inspire the next stage of gnostic scholarship (particularly the work of Rudolph Bultmann, who we will meet in Chapter 3) as were his set of typical gnostic features:

1. A distinction between the demiurge (identified as the God of the Old Testament) and the Supreme God;
2. Matter is not created by either God, but is independent;
3. The world we live in was the creation of a lower deity, not the Supreme God;
4. Evil is a force which is inherent in matter;
5. The Supreme God (or their power) is fractalized out into Aeons;
6. Jesus the man and Christ the Aeon were not identical;
7. There were different spiritual classes of humans, and not all were capable of salvation;
8. There was no Second Coming – immortality is achieved by escape from the sensual world;
9. The ethical position that matter and spirit were separate meant Gnostics could be either ascetic or libertine, but nothing in between.[68]

Moreover, Harnack's insistence that the theological meaning could be separated from the historical text allowed for Gnosticism to be taken up by the emerging discipline of the 'Science of Religion'. The German philologist Friedrich Max Müller is often cited as the founder of this school through his publication of translations of various Vedic and Buddhist texts in the Sacred Books of the East series. However, the Dutch universities were particularly important in the emerging discipline's institutionalization, with professorial chairs founded in the 1870s for Pierre Daniël Chantepie de la Saussaye at Amsterdam and Cornelis Petrus Tiele at Leiden.[69] Their students would later be important in establishing the phenomenology of religion as the de facto method of the History of Religions. With the classificatory zeal that epitomized the Victorian period, they attempted to categorize language groups (and thus racial groups) evolutionarily – although according to the prejudices of the period. As many have noted, this school had an implicit colonial imperative, as the classification of races helped one not only to 'know thy enemy' but also to place them lower down the evolutionary tree than oneself, thus justifying their domination.[70] This was often encoded as an obsession with locating origins, whether construed as 'the true meaning, the essential being, the real thing, or the genius of the author-creator'.[71] The search for origins and the search for essences are coterminous.

A concern with origins and essences fitted Gnosticism well. In keeping with the Science of Religion's reliance on philology, such scholars tended to see Gnosticism as a combination of 'Oriental' and Christian influences, rather than Jewish or Greek, so they turned to the Manichaean and Mandaean texts which began publication in 1904. Although of a later composition, these were regarded less as a degraded form, but rather as the 'flowering' of Gnosticism – a move which allowed them to explain away the clear differences. This strategy continues in scholarship today – for example, to equate Gnosticism and the New Age movement (see Chapter 10).[72]

At the centre of these Eastern constructions of Gnosticism was the myth of the *Redeemed Redeemer*. It originated with the German philologist Richard Reitzenstein (1861–1931), who in 1910 equated the Mandaean saviour figure Manda d'Hayje with the Primal Man, thus creating a composite figure who was both saviour and in need of salvation – a 'redeemed redeemer'.[73] Reitzenstein's identification of the origin of the New Testament's 'Son of Man' epithet in the Iranian myth was radical stuff – his Mandaean Gnosticism was no longer a degraded cousin of Christianity, but actually an independent tradition, even a formative influence on Christianity. Wilhelm Bousset's *Hauptprobleme der Gnosis* (1907) developed this argument further, tracing the origin of the Son of Man in a Primal Man mythology going back to the Rig Veda and ancient Persia. The problem was, however, that this narrative only ever existed in the minds of scholars.[74] While various elements are to be found in different (decontextualized) literary and historical sources, no single historical source gives the Redeemed Redeemer narrative as Reitzenstein, and those who followed him, presented it.[75]

Underlying all this was the implicit aim of Science of Religion scholars to demonstrate an Eastern – or Aryan – origin for Western institutions and ideas. Iranian Zoroastrianism was posited as the source of Gnosticism, and thus, the dualism of that system was perceived in the writings of the classical Gnostics. These assumptions were the received wisdom of the institutions and individuals from whom these scholars gained their academic training.[76] Later, the distrust of Christianity and strongly scientific agenda in the German academy during the Weimar Republic would encourage scholars of religion to adopt a phenomenological approach in which religious 'truth' was removed ('bracketed') from the analytical table. It allowed them to posit a 'meta-religion' – such as Rudolf Otto's *Religioser Menchheitsbund* – of which earthly religions were versions.[77] It also implicitly allowed them to immunize their own religious beliefs against criticism.[78]

Charles William King's *The Gnostics and Their Remains, Ancient and Medieval* (1864) also argued for an Asian origin for Gnosticism, but rather than originating in Iran, he conceived of it as a bridge between Vedic teachings and Christianity – Gnosticism could be 'traced up to Indian speculative philosophy, as its genuine fountain-head'.[79] To do this, he innovatively used his sizable collection of carved gemstones as source material, rather than relying entirely on the heresiological sources, attempting to connect the symbolism of 'Mason's Marks' and Hinduism 'backwards through Gnostic employment and Gothic retention, through old Greek and Etruscan art to their first source, and thus attest convincingly what country gave birth to the theosophy that made, in Imperial times, so large a use of the same *siglæ*'.[80] Nevertheless, King – picking up the thread from Baur – understood this synthesis to have continued into the Knights Templar, Rosicrucianism and eventually Freemasonry. Such pseudo-histories naturally had a great legitimating appeal for esoteric thinkers, although they also played into the hands of their conservative detractors. Nevertheless, this thesis – that Gnosticism, like a spiritual version of the A-Team, survived underground, available to the needy if you know where to look – would be picked up by G. R. S. Mead of the Theosophical Society, and through him to Carl Jung and Gilles Quispel, and through them to Religious Studies scholars today. But that is getting ahead of myself.

Religionsgeschichtliche scholars saw Gnosticism as deriving from a synthesis of Jewish and Hellenic influences, whereas the Science of Religion saw it as deriving from 'Eastern' sources. Nevertheless, both posited Gnosticism as existing to some degree before the encounter with Christianity. This allowed for a dramatic shift to take place in the construction of Gnosticism: it could now be seen as a religion in its own right, influencing Christianity, perhaps, but not beholden to it or reliant upon it. Thus, the first stage of essentialization was complete, just as Gnosticism was being encoded into the genealogical family tree of the History of Religions school.

2

The era of gnosis restored: Nineteenth-century Gnostics

In the gaslit parlour of Lady Caithness's flat on the Avenue de Wagram in Paris, a bearded man with a shock of grey hair channels messages from long-dead heretics. Caithness (born Maria de Mariategui, in London), a wealthy widow who supported the Theosophical Society in France financially and later became president of her own independent Theosophical lodge, has been hosting these seances throughout 1888 and 1889. The bearded man, an Orléans librarian named Stanislas Jules-Benoît Doniel du Val-Michel (1842–1903) – Jules Doniel to his friends – is attempting to contact the spirits of Cathars, Templars and Gnostics after having a vision in which Jesus consecrated him 'Bishop of Montségur and Primate of the Albigenses'.[1] In another vision, he is contacted by what he took to be the Paraclete of John 14.16 and 24, who says:

> I address myself to you because you are my friend, my servant and the prelate of my Albigensian Church. I am exiled from the Pleroma, and it is I whom Valentinus named Sophia-Achamôth. It is I whom Simon Magus called Helene-Ennoia; for I am the Eternal Androgyne. Jesus is the Word of God; I am the Thought of God. One day I shall remount to my Father, but I require aid in this; it requires the supplication of my Brother Jesus to intercede for me. Only the Infinite is able to redeem the Infinite, and only God is able to redeem God. Listen well: The One has brought forth One, then One. And the Three are but One: the Father, the Word and the Thought. Establish my Gnostic Church. The Demiurge will be powerless against it. Receive the Paraclete.[2]

In Caithness's parlour, these communications culminated with the manifestation of the spirit of the bishop of Montségur, Guilhabert de Castres, who charged Doniel with establishing the gnostic church, 'an assembly of the Paraclete ... through which the gnostic doctrines could be taught'.[3] Doniel declared 'the Era of Gnosis Restored' inaugurated and appointed himself Patriarch Valentin II. The Église Gnostique was founded in 1890.

Unorthodox churches, Christian and otherwise, flourished in nineteenth-century France. Catholicism had been violently suppressed during the Revolution of 1789, and though it regained much of its status following Napoleon's downfall in 1815, its monopoly on the religious milieu was lost. A wide variety of unorthodox groups competed for capital, including the atheistic Cult of Reason and a number of nationalistic Gallican churches who rejected the pope's authority over the monarchy.[4] Some, such as the *Église Johannite des Chrétiens Primitifs* of Bernard-Raymond Fabré-Palaprat (1777–1838), sought to undermine the authority of Rome by appealing to native French heresies like the Knights Templar and the Cathars.

The Cathars – etymologically, 'the clean ones' – were a dualistic and somewhat ascetic Christian movement in France and Germany between the twelfth and fourteenth centuries CE. They were declared heretical by Rome, who launched the Albigensian Crusade against them. The Crusade ended when 244 Cathar Perfects were burnt in a pyre in front of their stronghold at Montsegúr in the Languedoc region of Mediterranean France. They were then, and are indeed now, frequently described as Gnostics, although no historical link can be established, and there are significant theological differences.[5] Nevertheless, their dramatic martyrdom at the hands of the Catholic Church resonated in the French imagination, as does the similar history of the Templars, also seen as inheritors of the Gnostics ideas. Encyclopedic volumes like Ferdinand Denis's *Tableau Historique, Analytic et Critique des Sciences Occultes* (1830) describe the Templars picking up Asian magical writings during the Crusades and passing this on to the Moors.[6] Gnosticism – here a mixture of Christianity and 'high oriental kabbalah' – was presented as having passed through medieval secret societies and eventually to the Freemasons and Rosicrucians.[7]

This motif of a heretical transmission became an important strategy of legitimation for nineteenth-century Freemasonry, enshrined in works such as Giovanni de Castro's *Il Mondo Secreto* (1864) and Charles William Heckethorn's *The Secret Societies of All Ages and Countries* (1875), and continues to be articulated by contemporary gnostic groups and even some scholars.[8] Freemasonry developed from medieval guilds of stonemasons in seventeenth-century Britain into an initiatory body using the symbols of stonemasonry to expound moral principles. This 'Craft' masonry had three degrees – levels of initiation – each accompanied by its particular ritual, teachings and symbolism.[9] Freemasonry had long had an ambiguous status in France – officially forbidden by the pope, but patronized by the royalty. Following the restoration of the monarchy in 1814, French Freemasonry was generally associated with radical and progressive ideas, in politics perhaps even more so than in religion.[10] Beginning in the eighteenth century, a number of Masonic groups began to offer additional degrees that elaborated upon the Craft degrees, notably 'the Ancient and Accepted Scottish Rite'. Many of these included 'esoteric' teachings, and these groups became important loci for the transmission and development of such ideas.[11] Indeed, the most prominent esoteric orders for twentieth-century magic – the Ordo Templi Orientis (OTO) and the Hermetic Order of the Golden Dawn – were founded by members of these esoteric Masonic orders.

Doniel presented the liturgy of the Église Gnostique as being drawn from the Cathars (although the gnostic Mass, known as the *Fraction du pain*, 'Breaking of Bread', was a new composition).[12] His bishops took names prefixed with the title Tau, representing the Egyptian cross, a practice which continues in some gnostic churches to the present day.[13] The first bishop to be consecrated was Gérard Encausse (1865–1916), a successful doctor of French and Spanish background, better known to history by his occult *nome de guerre*, Papus.[14] Papus was a member of the Golden Dawn, having joined the Parisian Ahathoor Temple in March 1895, but his vocal interest in ritual magic led lodges of the Grand Orient and Grand Lodge to refuse him admission. His response was the creation of his own initiatory order, Martinism, a Christian mystical order based on the writings of 'The Unknown Philosopher', Louise-Claude de Saint-Martin (1743–1803).[15]

A schismatic group, the Église Gnostique Universelle, led by Jean Bricaud (1881–1934), a former trainee Catholic priest, became the official church of the Martinist Order in 1911 and dropped most of the Cathar material.[16] Indeed, providing a liturgical space for members of orders that the Catholic Church discouraged may have been one of the major appeals of these gnostic churches; many Martinists were also Catholics and faced excommunication if their membership of a gnostic church became public knowledge. Their salvation – and good social standing – was ensured, however, when Bricaud was consecrated as a bishop in 1913.[17]

Over the centuries, a number of schismatic Catholic churches have raised bishops who do not represent any diocese, for various reasons; it is a great honour for the bishop, and it helps small churches to attract new members and to actively participate in formal activities, like the Parliament of World Religions. Most importantly, though, the doctrine that sacramental and ecclesiastical authority is passed down in an unbroken lineage that originates in the original apostles, and thus ultimately conferred by Christ himself, confers considerable capital upon the claimant.[18] These bishops have become known as *episcopi vagantes*, or 'wandering bishops', and it is from them that many gnostic groups today claim their authority (see Chapter 8). Many Anglican Roman Catholic authorities were condemned by French bishops, and the Church of England was especially concerned about these *episcopi vagantes* (see, e.g., Bishop Lewis Radford's *Ancient Heresies in Modern Dress* from 1913). The lineages were by no means confined to esoteric bodies, however, and continue to the present in dissident but comparatively orthodox Anglican and Catholic groups, such as the Polish Mariavites.[19]

Bricaud was consecrated into the lineage of Bishop Joseph René Vilatte (1854–1929), who had taken the name Mar Timotheos after persuading the archbishop of the Independent Catholic Church of Ceylon to consecrate him.[20] In 1908, Papus and Bricaud consecrated Theodor Reuss[21] (1855–1923), the principal architect of the OTO, who founded a German branch of the Église Gnostique Universelle, directly transliterating it as *Die Gnostiche Katholische Kirche*, under the auspices of the OTO.[22] The OTO was founded in 1896 by three German Freemasons,[23] but under Reuss's leadership, it became a grand esoteric order, modelled on Freemasonry's initiatory structure. What separated the OTO from other initiatory orders of the day was its interest in sexual magic techniques. In standard accounts, these techniques were drawn from the teachings of Paschal Beverly Randolph (1825–1875) and the accounts of Tantra that were beginning to emerge from India. Urban describes Reuss's knowledge of Tantra as '"nebulous" at best', understanding Tantra as simply 'sexual religion'.[24] This was fairly typical of the time; when Western accounts described Tantric traditions, it was the hedonistic and transgressive aspects that were picked up and amplified, the sexual aspects in particular.[25] Importantly, Reuss identifies Tantra and Gnosticism as identical:

> The secret teachings of the Gnostics (Primitive Christians) are identical with the Vamachari rites of the Tantrics. ... Phallicism is the basis of all theology and underlies the mythology of all peoples. ... The Phallus as a divine symbol received divine veneration for thousands of years in India.[26]

Urban points out, however, that sex magic's supposed forebears are largely imaginary – that is to say, they 'drew upon a long tradition of fantastic narratives about wild orgies, bizarre ritual, and obscene occultism that had little basis in reality but a lasting impact on the popular imagination'.[27] As shown in Chapter 1, this included the writings of the Church Fathers on the so-called Gnostics.

In 1919, Reuss renamed the Gnostiche Katholische Kirche the Ecclesia Gnostica Catholica, which had been suggested to him by Edward Alexander 'Aleister' Crowley (1875–1947), who had joined the OTO around 1910. Crowley was already a practicing Tantrika and had considerable knowledge of yoga for the period.[28] Crowley rewrote the gnostic Mass in line with his own religious system, Thelema, in 1918, producing a 'creative reimagining of the secret rites alleged to have been practiced by the early Gnostics and later corrupted by the Catholic Church', rife with sexual imagery.[29] Reuss devoted the OTO and the Ecclesia Gnostica Catholica to Thelema in 1919, and upon Reuss's death in 1922, Crowley assumed leadership himself.[30]

The French and German gnostic churches regarded themselves as guardians of a universal tradition that would restore (Catholic) Christianity to its original purity.[31] Here, Gnostics stress that their teachings are the *original, pure, uncorrupted* Christianity. In the United Kingdom and other majority Protestant countries, however, where Christianity has been historically associated with power regimes and (rightly or wrongly) oppression, new religions have tended to distance themselves from Christianity, sometimes antagonistically, and have tended to stress connections with either Asian religion (e.g. Theosophy), pre-Christian religion (Paganism and Shamanism) or heresy (Satanism). Gnosticism has been constructed in all of these ways at one time or another.

Gnosticism was one of the many motifs that Helena Petrovna Blavatsky (1831–1891) absorbed into her exhaustively syncretic system, Theosophy.[32] Blavatsky was already forty-two when she travelled steerage from France to New York in 1873 and began performing spiritualistic seances in which she channelled messages from Tibetan 'Ascended Masters'. In 1875, she formed the Theosophical Society with journalist Henry Steel Olcott and W. Q. Judge to promote her ideas. Theosophy – a term taken from the tradition of Christian mysticism associated with Jacob Böhme and Emanuel Swedenborg, and meaning 'knowledge of god' or 'divine knowledge' – was based on the idea that secret knowledge, a 'secret doctrine', lay at the core of all religions and mystical traditions. With all the taxonomic zeal of the age, the Theosophical Society set out to 'scientifically' systematize this knowledge for the benefit of humanity. Theosophy continued to be popular after Blavatsky's death in 1891, reaching an apogee of 45,000 members in 1928,[33] and directly contributed to many of the twentieth century's new religions, particularly the New Age movement, Anthroposophy and many others, as well as the UFO Contactee movement of the 1950s and the Indian independence movement.

With themes of elite knowledge and an underground perennial tradition, Gnosticism was a good fit with Theosophy. Blavatsky's knowledge of Gnosticism was initially drawn from King's *The Gnostics and Their Remains* (1864), as he himself acknowledged in the foreword to the revised second edition.[34] King argued that Gnosticism was a bridge between Vedic teachings and Christianity, leading through the Templars to Freemasonry. In Blavatsky's account, this 'primitive pure Oriental gnosticism', though 'corrupted and degraded by different subsequent sects', was the antecedent of the Theosophical Society.[35] Indeed, it formed the esoteric core of all religions:

> But if the Gnostics were destroyed, the Gnosis, based on the secret science of sciences, still lives. ... The ancient Kabala, the Gnosis or traditional secret knowledge, was never without its representatives in any age or country. The trinities of initiates, whether passed into history or concealed under the impenetrable veil of mystery, are preserved and impressed through the ages.[36]

The Esoteric Section included a 'Gnostic path', among other training programmes,[37] and there was an American Theosophical magazine called the *Gnostic*.[38] Jean Darlés's *Glossaire Raisonné de la Théosophie du Gnosticisme et de l'Esotérisme*, published in 1910, notes:

> A great number of Orientalist and Theosophist readers, who are not familiar with the Sanskrit terms Theosophy, Gnosticism and Esotericism, have repeatedly expressed to us the desire to own a work that gives them the exact meaning of many terms in use today in Theosophical works. This is why we decided to publish this glossary, to which we have added the explanation of the terms of Gnosticism, because many people today are interested in the Gnostic Church and its ceremonies.[39]

The claim that the Gnostics were suppressed – or destroyed – allowed Blavatsky to separate the Gnostics from the Christian institutions she despised. Moreover, she could separate the God of the Bible from the transcendent true God of the Gnostics by identifying the 'subordinate and capricious Sinaitic Deity' with the Demiurge.[40] Not all Theosophists were antagonistic to Christianity, however. William Kingsland, president of the Blavatsky Lodge in London, published *The Gnosis or Ancient Wisdom* in 1937. It was

> written mainly for a class of readers and students who find themselves altogether out of touch with 'Christianity' in any of its current doctrinal or sacerdotal forms, but who, notwithstanding this, have some more or less clear apprehension that behind those forms, and in the Christian Scriptures themselves, there lies a

deep spiritual truth, a real *Gnosis* (Gr. *knowledge*) of Man's origin, nature, and destiny which has simply been materialised by the Church in the traditional interpretation of those Scriptures based upon their literal acceptation.[41]

Kingsland follows Baur and other Protestant theologians in inverting the argument of the heresiologists: Gnosticism is not a corrupt, heretical version of Christianity, but *Christianity is a corrupt, heretical version of Gnosticism*. Kingsland later stresses that the most recent putting forth of this original Christianity, of these 'principles', is none other than Theosophy, only this time 'in much greater detail' by Madame Blavatsky.[42]

The most important link in this chain, however, is George Robert Stow Mead (1863–1933). Mead, a colonel's son, became a teacher in a public school after receiving his BA in Classics from Cambridge in 1884. That same year he joined the Theosophical Society. When Blavatsky settled in London in 1887, Mead became a regular visitor during school holidays, until 1889 when he gave up teaching to become her private secretary, a role he would hold until her death in May 1891.[43] During this time he was one of her closest allies, handling her correspondence and editing her writing, even giving the speech at her funeral. He was general secretary of the European Section from 1890 until 1897, became joint editor of the Theosophical Society's journal *Lucifer* in 1893 and declined the offer of the presidency in 1907, which would go to Annie Besant instead. He continued to work on Blavatsky's posthumous works, including the third volume of *The Secret Doctrine* (1897). Even his marriage was alleged to have been motivated by a desire to keep Blavatsky's circle together during the leadership tussles which followed her death.[44]

His interest in Gnosticism seems to have stemmed from Blavatsky, initially at least. Despite his interest in Hinduism, Mead was to a large degree at odds with 'neo-Theosophy' – the shift towards Vedic or 'Eastern' sources over esoteric sources, spearheaded by Besant. As shown by his 1891 article, 'The Task of the Theosophical Scholars in the West', Mead advocated for the use of sources from Hellenistic cultures. He published the first English translation of the *Pistis Sophia* – regarded as the gnostic text par excellence by pre–Nag Hammadi scholars – in *Lucifer* in 1890–1.[45] It was published as a book in 1896, subtitled *A Gnostic Gospel*, thus setting the pattern for future popular works, and Blavatsky's commentary was published posthumously.[46] In this work, Mead was working from Schwartze's and Amélinieu's translations, though he would revise this for the 1921 second edition as a result of Carl Schmidt's more accurate 1905 translation.

He examined the Bruce Codex himself in the Bodlean Library in May 1900, and his notebook contains the ideas regarding its composition, which he would repeat in *Fragments of a Faith Forgotten* (1900).[47] In it, Mead dismisses King's Indian/Buddhist thesis, stating arrogantly that his work 'lacks the thoroughness of the specialist', instead describing Gnosticism as the product of the synthesis of 'Greece, Egypt, and Jewry'.[48] *Fragments* supports Blavatsky's assertion that Gnosticism is the precursor of Theosophy by tracing a line through Simon Magus, to Menander, Ophites and Sethians, and onto later schools like Valentinus, Marcion and Basilides. Indeed, Mead considered *Pistis Sophia* to have been written by Valentinus himself, an idea he got from Adolf von Harnack.[49]

The book begins by summarizing his interpretation of *Pistis Sophia*, before presenting the 'Untitled Text' from the Bruce Codex, despite considering the latter to be the earlier text. He regarded *Pistis Sophia* as an introductory text, and the *Untitled Treatise* to be 'a series of visions of some subtle phase of the inner ordering and substance of things, taken down, at different times as the seer described the inner working of nature from different points of view'.[50] This was because he wanted to present them 'roughly in such a sequence that the reader may be led from lower to higher grades of the Gnosis'.[51] In keeping with Theosophical comparative perennialism, Mead seems to regard this highest grade of gnosis to be 'nirvana'.[52] In other words, *Fragments of a Faith Forgotten* was composed as an initiatory text.

In the later *The Gnosis of the Mind* (1906), the connection is made even more strongly: Theosophy *is* the gnosis:

> But as for us who are hearers of the Gnosis, of Theosophy, wherever it is to be found ... whether we call it the Gnosis of the Mind with the followers of Thrice-greatest Hermes, or the Gnosis of the Truth as Marcus does, or by many another name given it by the Gnostics of that day, it matters little; the great fact is that there *is* Gnosis, and that men have touched her sacred robe and been healed of the vices of their souls.[53]

This was part of the Echoes of the gnosis series of short books, the description of which makes clear that Mead had both a scholarly and a religious purpose in his writing:

> There are many who love the light of the spirit, and who long for the light of gnostic illumination, but are not sufficiently equipped to study the writings of the ancients first hand, or to follow unaided the labours of scholars. These little volumes are therefore intended to serve as introduction to the study of the more difficult literature of the subject; and it is hoped at the same time they may

become for some, who have, as yet, not even heard of the Gnosis, *stepping-stones to higher things*.⁵⁴

Mead's interest in both Gnosticism and Theosophy, however, was driven by a desire to restore Christianity and establish it as a universal religion:

> Our present task will be to attempt, however imperfectly, to point to certain considerations which may tend to restore the grand figure of the Great Teacher to its natural environment in history and tradition, and disclose the intimate points of contact which the true ideal of the Christian religion has with the one world-faith of the most advanced souls of our common humanity – in brief, to restore the teaching of the Christ to its true spirit of universality.⁵⁵

In this, he was not alone. The death of Blavatsky in May 1891 brought the competing ideas about the direction of the Theosophical Society into focus. While Olcott and Blavatsky tended to focus on the East, many wanted to return that focus to the West or at least broaden it to include both. In particular, many wanted to roll back some of the anti-Christian stance it had inherited from its former leader and had cost the Society the departure of both Alice Bailey and Anna Kingsford, capable women who many had wanted to see in leadership roles.

Eventually, Annie Besant (1847–1933) succeeded Blavatsky, becoming co-leader of the Theosophical Society in Adyar with Colonel Olcott, with William Judge leading the American Section. Besant would have been a remarkable woman in any age; she left her husband, Reverend Frank Besant, in 1873 to become a suffragette, journalist and Fabian socialist, campaigning on issues ranging from atheism to vivisection to birth control, before meeting Blavatsky in 1888 and becoming her student. Her first few years as co-leader were uneventful, but by 1894, Olcott and Besant were involved in a bitter battle for authority with Judge, accusing him of having forged letters from the Mahatmas. At their 1895 convention, the majority of the American Section declared their independence from the Adyar Section.

That same year, Besant began to collaborate with Charles W. Leadbeater (1854–1934). Leadbeater was an Anglican priest in Hampshire in 1883 when he read Alfred Sinnett's *Occult World* and quit to devote himself to Theosophy.⁵⁶ The following year he met Blavatsky and followed her to Adyar. There, he described how, over many weeks of difficult work, he learned astral sight and how to awake his *kundalini* (a form of immanent divine energy) from several Ascended Masters.⁵⁷ Blavatsky did not like him,⁵⁸ but with Besant he began an extensive project of astral research that would eventually diverge from Blavatsky's ideas enough that it later earned the label 'Neo-Theosophy' from its detractors. Besant and Leadbeater claimed to be able to access past lives and, indeed, the history (and future) of the whole universe, by accessing the 'akashic records' – something which even Blavatsky never claimed for herself.[59]

In January 1906, Besant received a letter from the corresponding secretary of the Esoteric Section of the United States, Helen Dennis, alleging that Leadbeater had taught two teenage boys masturbation, telling them it was 'occult training' and demanding secrecy. Besant reluctantly accepted his resignation,[60] but Olcott, the last of the founders, died on 7 February 1907, and in June, Besant was elected president of the Theosophical Society. She was back working with Leadbeater by August, and he was formally readmitted in December 1908.[61] The following February, Mead and around seven hundred other British members resigned in protest (although Mead seems to have been motivated by this demand for blind obedience to the edicts of the Mahatmas, rather than Leadbeater's behaviour per se).[62]

Mead formed the Quest Society later that year with one hundred and fifty former Theosophical Society members and some one hundred new members.[63] They organized public lectures (at Kensington Town Hall in London) and published the *Quest: A Quarterly Review* (edited by Mead) from October 1909 until 1930. The tone is markedly more scholarly than those of *Lucifer*, with a focus primarily upon comparative religion, especially early Christianity. Contributors included the Austrian Jungian biblical scholar Robert Eisler, translator of the Bruce Codex Charlotte Baynes, theologian F. C. Burkitt and a young Rudolf Bultmann on 'Mandaean and Other Saviour-Lore Parallels to the Fourth Gospel'.[64] Although A. E. Waite, W. B. Yeats, Arthur Machen and Algernon Blackwood of the Golden Dawn were all contributors, the *Quest* featured little to no 'occult' material, as Mead was now of the opinion that '"Esotericism" and "occultism" were to be eschewed as corrupting rather than helpful'.[65] It also featured a good deal of psychoanalytic material, which was not unusual for an 'occult' periodical of the time – the compatibility of (certain) psychological theories (particularly Jung's) with esoteric ideas and fringe science was seen as a significant tool in the legitimization of psychical research as a proper science.[66]

Beginning in 1913, Mead began a series of articles on the history of 'the gnosis', drawing from and critiquing Reitzenstein and Bousset's Iranian-origin theory. Beginning with 'The Meaning of Gnosis in Higher Hellenistic Religion', in which he presents 'the ground-idea of gnosis' as 'transmutation into spiritual being', Mead drew widely from the Hermetica and other sources, and claimed:

> What has previously been called gnosticism is thus seen to be a department only, though an important department, of the history of the gnosis, and should preferably be referred to as the Christianised gnosis, if not the Christian gnosis. … Gnosticism as a whole must be made to enter into the general history of religion.[67]

This was followed by a translation of 'A Gnostic Myth' from Hippolytus and 'The Gnosis in Early Christendom'.[68] It is clear that Mead has stayed very much up to date with scholarship, but it is also clear that away from Besant and Leadbeater, Mead is more interested in how gnosis might legitimize esoteric Christianity, rather than the Theosophical Society. Interestingly though, Mead is ahead of his time in making a deliberate separation between an ahistorical gnostic current and Gnosticism as a specific gnostic religion, a distinction which will become a standard feature of the discourse on Gnosticism, ultimately being codified by the IAHR at the Messina Congress in 1966.

But with Leadbeater as President Besant's right-hand man, his Neo-Theosophical innovations became central to the development of the Theosophical Society in the early twentieth century, particularly the divisive promotion of Jiddu Krishnamurti as the World Teacher.[69] Despite her refusal to take communion and devotion to India, the former vicar's wife Besant's writing was increasingly steeped in Christian language too.[70] Leadbeater – an Anglican priest – saw Anna Kingsford's ideas as a potential blueprint for a synthesis, or realignment, of Christianity and Theosophy. Kingsford had split with the Theosophical Society in 1884 over her insistence in seeing Christianity recognized as the highest form of spiritual truth in Theosophy.[71] With Besant in charge, however, Leadbeater felt empowered to push for this synthesis again.

By 1914, Leadbeater was conducting monthly 'church services' for members of the Star of the East who 'missed the pleasant warmth of Sunday morning church-going they had sacrificed for the more intellectual activity of Sunday night lecture-attending'.[72] One of those attending was James Wedgwood, a scion of the famous bone china family who intended to train for Anglican ordination before hearing Besant at a public lecture in 1904. He became general secretary of England and Wales between 1911 and 1913, as well as supreme secretary of the Co-Masonic Order, another Theosophical offshoot. Wedgwood visited Leadbeater (now living in Sydney, Australia) in June 1915, initiated him into Co-Masonry and told Leadbeater about his involvement with the Old Catholic Church in England.[73]

In 1724, an isolated group of Catholics in Utrecht in staunchly Calvinist Holland broke with Rome. They were Jansenists: Cornelius Jansen, a Dutch theologian had stressed a particular interpretation of Augustine of Hippo's teachings on predestination – the doctrine that only certain individuals are predestined to be saved – and the justification by faith. This was a problem for the Church of Rome, as the catechism insisted that 'God's free initiative demands man's free response'. The authorities of the Dutch Republic actively supported Jansenism, as it was seen as more compatible theologically with Calvinism, and the group began to attract Jansenist refugees from France and elsewhere. Under pressure from Rome, in April 1723 a breakaway group raised their own archbishop, and later became known as the Dutch Old Catholic Church.[74]

Arnold Harris Mathew (1852–1919) – a former Roman Catholic priest and Anglican curate – was raised to bishop in Utrecht in 1908, specifically to establish an English Old Catholic mission. Both Mathew and the Utrecht bishops had been misinformed about the numbers of prospective Old Catholics in England, however, although there were some enthusiastic converts, including Wedgwood, who became a priest in 1913.[75] In August 1915, however, Mathew decided Theosophy was heretical and instructed all Theosophists in the OCC to 'withdraw' immediately, and Wedgwood found himself leader of a breakaway OCC.[76] Soon it became the only OCC when Mathew threatened to return to the Catholic Church (which he never did), and OCC bishop Frederick Willoughby raised him to bishop on 13 February 1916[77]. Wedgwood offered the OCC to Leadbeater as a Christian vehicle for the World Teacher and a Theosophical church, raising Leadbeater to bishop on 22 July.[78]

Over the next year, the two rewrote the liturgy 'in consultation with Maitreya and the Masters', incorporating many Theosophical principles – for example, referring to the Christ rather than to Jesus.[79] It was renamed the Liberal Catholic Church in September 1918, as it was felt that the word 'Old' distracted from its mission with the New. The church was not large, with clergy and members in Britain, Australia, New Zealand and the United States meeting in private homes. Four hundred and eighty-six people were baptized in the Sydney Church in the first four years, fifty-one of them children.[80]

Shortly after, four Liberal Catholic priests, including Wedgwood, were accused of paedophilia and sodomy, leading to a police investigation in 1919.[81] Leadbeater had also been under investigation by the New South Wales police since 1917, though they felt they had insufficient evidence to convict him.[82] Wedgwood resigned from the Theosophical Society and the Liberal Catholic Church in March 1922, though Besant continued to defend them both.[83]

Besant's ongoing support for Leadbeater might be explained by evidence uncovered by Tillett that Leadbeater was privately teaching a simple form of sexual magic, which Besant had full knowledge of. He taught one student, Oscar Köllerström, that the state of ecstasy the orgasm induced could be used to advance one's spiritual development and develop psychic powers. The release of energy was to be focused upon the Logos, including, at times, in group masturbation rituals. This teaching was told only to select pupils who were sworn to secrecy, as the secret was too dangerous for ordinary people. In fact, some of Leadbeater's critics accused him of teaching 'Tantra' – which, we know, was essentially shorthand for sex magic – in internally circulated documents, including the claim that he was using the boys' semen to catalyse his clairvoyancy.[84] Tillett even suggests that Leadbeater joined the OTO in Sydney around 1915, inducted by Wedgwood, who was not only a member of the OTO but also a personal friend of John Yarker.[85]

Wedgwood was readmitted to both organizations in 1924, but with Krishnamurti's abrogation of his role as World Teacher in 1929, Besant's death in September 1933 and Leadbeater's five months later, there were few in the Theosophical Society to actively support the connections with the Liberal Catholic Church. When George Arundale succeeded Besant as president of the Theosophical Society soon after, Wedgwood resigned his duties in the Liberal Catholic Church.[86] He continued as bishop, still frequently claiming visions and channelled messages, but increasingly mentally unstable, probably as a result of syphilis.[87] He died in 1951, but the Liberal Catholic Church continues, most successfully in the United States, where theosophical beliefs are supported, though not required, for clergy.[88] The Theosophical–Christian synthesis, however, continues in the Ecclesia Gnostica, who we will meet in Chapter 8.

This chapter has illustrated how much these groups were involved in a discourse with Christianity. The tension between, on the one hand, the critique of mainline religion as exemplified by Christianity and, on the other, its converse, the continuing influence of Christian symbolism, epistemology and ritual within new religious movements in the West, is resolved when both are seen as parts of a narrative of a return to a 'purer' form of religion. These gnostic churches, then, do not challenge Christianity itself; rather, they challenge how the churches have sought to monopolize the capital of the religious field. Gnosticism is here, as in many later cases – etic and emic – constructed as a more authentic form of Christianity, foregrounding notions of individuality and direct experience. This of course slides easily into spiritual elitism. It also directly foreshadows the critique of 'organized religion' in the New Age movement and the contemporary 'spiritual' milieu. In popular religious discourse in the late nineteenth century, gnostic functioned primarily as an indicator of experiential and non-institutional religious identification, in precisely the same way that it would in inter-war esotericism, the New Age movement and, ultimately, today's 'spiritual but not religious' cohort.[89]

There is a direct lineage between the gnostic churches of fin de siècle France and contemporary gnostic religions, though not perhaps the one that they themselves would choose to promote. Less known, however, is the influence these groups had on scholarly understandings of Gnosticism, which this chapter has introduced, and the following two will tease out more fully. Looking forward, their essentialist and ahistorical interpretations would be transmitted into academia through the Eranos conferences and enshrined at the Messina Congress of 1966.

3

The alien god: Gnosticism as existentialism

Hans Jonas's existential reading of Gnosticism is, along with Jung's psychological reading (the subject of the next chapter), foundational to contemporary constructions of Gnosticism, and if scholars are no longer convinced by the details of his argument, few resist acknowledging the motif that Gnosticism was (and often, still is) grounded in alienation. Jonas's view of Gnosticism, and indeed, existentialism, shifted dramatically after the Second World War, and we will consider the reassessment in Chapter 6. Even so, Jonas played an active role in organizing the 1966 Messina Congress of the IAHR, and the definitions it produced (and indeed, which he co-wrote) enshrined his thesis of Gnosticism as estrangement from the alien god.

In this chapter, though, I want to go a little further back, as Jonas is only two links away from Edmund Husserl, the founder of the philosophical school of phenomenology. Phenomenology in Religious Studies – often referred to as 'the phenomenology of religion', a convention I will maintain here to differentiate it from philosophical versions – is generally presented as a methodology in which our own beliefs (implicitly, religious) are supposedly 'bracketed off' to allow us to engage with and describe the religion empathetically. However, this methodological description obscures that the phenomenology of religion is predicated upon a sui generis religiosity. The development of Gnosticism as an essentialized category of sui generis religion is deeply entangled with the regency of the phenomenology of religion as a methodology. This is one of the central themes of this book, so I want to show where this relationship began. This entanglement culminates in the enshrining of an essentialized category at the 1966 Messina Congress of the IAHR, a body founded by and for many years controlled by phenomenologists (although it must be recognized that not all phenomenologists are essentialists). But to get to the essentialists and Mircea Eliade – generally recognized in the field as 'the most influential historian of religions of the twentieth century and, notably, the only one to have an audience among the public'[1] – we must start with Husserl.

Edmund Husserl (1859–1938) was born to a middle-class Jewish family in Moravia, in Austria-Hungary, in 1859. By the age of twenty-three, he held a doctorate in mathematics from Vienna. Shortly after that, however, in 1884 he attended lectures by Franz Brentano, a brilliant young philosopher who was becoming known for his ideas about 'intentionality'. In a striking parallel to later History of Religions scholars, Brentano sought to reserve a specific domain for philosophy, by distinguishing between mental acts and physical reality. Mental acts are intentional, meaning that they are always directed towards an object; they contain other objects, and this constitutes the break between the physical and mental worlds. Under Brentano's influence, Husserl undertook his habilitation in philosophy in 1887, later published as *The Philosophy of Arithmetic* (1891).

For the next ten years, he worked on the project which would make his name: *Logical Investigations*, the first volume published in 1900 and the second the following year. In it, Husserl adapted Brentano's theory of intentionality significantly. Husserl noted that intentions never contain *complete* representations, but only the aspect that is perceivable to us. The upshot is that our perception of, say, a cat is not fully 'a cat'; rather, 'a cat' is something that unites our various perceptions of the said cat. This formed the basis of a methodology that Husserl named *phenomenology*. Phenomenology was revolutionary because

> it does not interpret or explain but tries to describe what the phenomena are 'in themselves' and what they reveal. This attention to the consciousness processes themselves at one stroke eliminates the dualism of 'being' and 'appearing', or, more accurately, we discover that to make such a distinction is simply part of the operation of that consciousness. Consciousness is aware, in a strange way, of what it misses in perception. And because phenomenon is everything that enters consciousness, this invisibility, too, is a phenomenon of consciousness. Essence is not something hidden 'behind' the phenomenon; it is itself phenomenon to the extent that we think of it or the extent that we think that it evades us… Consciousness is always consciousness of something. The fact that consciousness is not 'inside' but 'outside', alongside what it is conscious of – that is observed as soon as one finally begins to raise consciousness to the level of consciousness. That is what phenomenology is.[2]

The book's success led to his appointment as an assistant professor at Göttingen in 1901, where a small phenomenological circle – they called themselves a 'movement' – formed around him, dedicated to the reform and restoration of both philosophy and of life in general.³ Their motto was 'Towards the things' – preconceptions and abstractions were to be forgotten and phenomena experienced anew.⁴ His reputation was such that he went to Freiburg as a full professor in 1916, where he met a young philosophy privatdozent named Martin Heidegger.

Martin Heidegger (1889–1975) was a small athletic man with serious eyes and an olive complexion, who came from the southern German village of Messkirch, where his father was a sexton at the Catholic Stadtpfarrkirche. The young Martin seemed very pious and conservative; his early career was supported by scholarships from the church, and his first publications were reviews in the conservative and Ultramontane (i.e. emphasizing the primacy of papal authority) Catholic journal *Der Akademiker*, in which he argued in defense of both Pope Pius X and the First Vatican Council.⁵

He entered the Jesuit novitiate in Tisis, Austria, at the age of twenty. However, a heart condition quickly led to him being discharged and focusing instead on philosophy and theology at the University of Freiburg. His interest in philosophy had been sparked by Brentano's *Von der mannigfachen Bedeutung des Seienden nach Aristoteles* (1862), and the meaning of being remained Heidegger's foundational question throughout his long career. His reading of Brentano led him to Husserl's *Logical Investigations*, and he became a disciple of phenomenology. He received his doctorate in 1913 and his habilitation in 1915 with a phenomenological reading of the medieval philosopher Duns Scotus. He had wanted to write it on Husserl's work on mathematics, but was persuaded to change it in exchange for a grant from the church.⁶

When Husserl arrived at Freiburg in April 1916, Heidegger did everything he could to form a relationship with his intellectual hero. At first, Husserl was suspicious of Heidegger, who was then deputizing for the professor of Catholic Philosophy. Husserl was by no means an atheist, however, commenting that his phenomenology was intended to 'find the way to God' and a pure life.⁷ Nevertheless, he believed that Heidegger's Catholicism would be a bar to the bracketing required by phenomenology. But when Heidegger was passed over for the chair on a permanent basis, which was given unexpectedly to Josef Geyser instead, he began to openly discuss his conversion to Protestantism. When Husserl learned of this, their relationship began to warm. Heidegger married Husserl's student Thea Petri (a Protestant) in the spring of 1917 and – after a brief spell on the Western Front in 1918 – became Husserl's assistant in January 1919.⁸ Husserl soon came to see Heidegger as his heir, declaring, 'You and I are phenomenology!'⁹

Husserl had hoped that Heidegger would produce a phenomenology of religion – at least, until he read Otto's *Das Heilige* (1917).[10] Rudolf Otto (1869–1937) drew on the Protestant theologian Friedrich Schleiermacher (1768–1834) for *Das Heilige*, famously describing religion primarily in terms of experience, an encounter with a 'mysterium tremendum et fascinans' identified with the 'numinous' itself.[11] Placing this encounter with the *numinous* as the *sine qua non* of religion, Otto stressed a non-reductive, sui generis approach in which there is an essential aspect to religion – an approach which would become central to later phenomenology of religion.[12] Otto never considered himself a phenomenologist, but rather a theologian, though he has certainly been considered one retrospectively. He asserts, 'at the beginning and with the most positive emphasis', the superiority of Christianity over religions of other 'types and levels'.[13] He rails against the 'rationalism' which he sees as prevalent in theology and in the study of religions in general ('allegemeinem Religionsforschung').[14] For Otto, religion is utterly experiential and sui generis – 'if anywhere in a field of human experience there is something peculiar to said field and so only to be found there in it, it is in the field of the religious'.[15] Husserl was impressed, writing to Otto that 'your book on the Holy has affected more powerfully than scarcely any book in years'.[16]

Despite his rejection of first Catholicism, and later all religion, Heidegger retained a fascination with religion. He was deeply influenced by Barth's influential version of Protestant neo-Orthodoxy, and his existential analysis was itself inspired by his analysis of New Testament texts and medieval philosophy.[17] His *Vorlesungen zur Phanomenologie des religiosen Lebens* ('Lectures on the Phenomenology of Religious Life'), given in Freiburg in 1920–1, dealt with phenomenology of religion. He even identified himself as a theologian to his student Karl Löwith in 1921.[18]

In February 1919 Heidegger began lecturing at Freiburg, quickly gaining a reputation as an original and engaging lecturer.[19] These early lectures already contain remarks to the effect that Husserl does not go far enough, that his phenomenology is not radical enough. For Heidegger, phenomena are not merely appearances in human consciousness; they are events. Where, for Husserl, things are how they appear in consciousness, Heidegger is interested in what they are to us before explicit awareness. Husserl remained largely unaware of these criticisms at the time, however.[20]

In 1923, Heidegger accepted an offer of an assistant professorship at Marburg, then regarded as a centre of progressive Protestant theology. Rudolf Otto and the theologian (and later Eranos attendee) Paul Tillich would be colleagues, as well as Rudolf Bultmann, with whom Heidegger soon established a close professional and personal relationship. Heidegger was nominated for a full professorship in 1925, but this was ruled out by the Ministry of Culture in Berlin on the grounds that he had not been sufficiently published – still nothing since 1916. Marburg nominated Heidegger again the following year, this time including the proofs of 'Sein und Zeit' (still unpublished), but they were again denied. In 1927, Husserl came to the rescue and published 'Sein und Zeit' in his journal, *Yearbook for Phenomenology and Phenomenological Research*. Heidegger was immediately raised to full professor.

'Sein und Zeit' takes Husserl's work as a starting point and is dedicated to him, 'with due respect and friendship'.[21] It sets out to address ontology – the question of being – which Heidegger claims has been ignored since the Greeks. It centres on the *there-ness*, the *Da*, of Dasein – which is a being that is *ontological*, having concern for its own *beingness*, and which he uses essentially interchangeably with 'the human being'. The analysis of Dasein is what Heidegger calls *existential analysis*. Yet to understand *being*, we have to understand *time* – indeed, that time is the *ground* of being.[22] Dasein is absorbed in the world, fallen (*verfallen*) or even thrown (*geworfen*)[23] into it, remaining unaware of its authentic self, but rather absorbed with the Others, its 'Being-among-one-another' (*zusammenvorhandenseins*).[24] The realization of authentic Being causes the world and Others to fall away, leaving a state of angst, which is the true state of Dasein. Yet, as Safranski writes, it is through angst 'that Dasein experiences the uncanniness of the world *and its own freedom*':[25]

> If *Dasein* discovers the world in its own way and brings it close, if it discloses itself to its own authentic Being, then this discovery of the 'world' and this disclosure of *Dasein* are always accomplished as a clearing away of concealments and obscurities, as a breaking up of the disguises with which *Dasein* bars its own way.[26]

Rudolf Bultmann helped Heidegger to draft 'Sein und Zeit' because in it he saw a realization of his own hermeneutic project – *demythologization*, an interpretation of 'the very structure of religious and Christian existence but without the ontico-mythical worldview that was an idiosyncratic feature of first-century cosmologies'.[27] In fact, Bultmann adopted and adapted the method from Jonas, which he freely admitted in 1948's 'Neues Testament und Mythologie'.[28] And while Bultmann was already well known for his work on the sources of the Gospels, after the Second World War, demythologization would make him one of the leading theologians of his day.

Bultmann argued that the mythological worldview of the Bible was so different from the modern scientific worldview that the underlying meaning – or *kerygma* – is lost to modern readers, but that existential philosophy offered a hermeneutical key to re-accessing it. Where Heidegger attempts to remove preconceptions from our experience of the world, revealing the things themselves, Bultmann attempts to remove preconceptions from our understanding of the biblical message, revealing Christian truth itself.[29] Interestingly, Bultmann thought that the mythological worldview that obscured the kerygma of the New Testament was dualistic and Gnostic, and so to demythologize the New Testament is effectively to 'de-Gnosticize' it.[30] The idea that truth and ultimate being lies outside of time, separate from human experience, is what existential phenomenology rejected, and it is the basis of Bultmann's demythologization. The truth of the Bible, for Bultmann, is a phenomenon which must be experienced in the here and now.[31]

In Marburg, Heidegger had attracted a group of brilliant philosophy students around him. Many were Jewish, including Emmanuel Levinas, Karl Löwith, Hannah Arendt and Hans Jonas. Jonas (1903–1993) grew up in a secular Jewish home though clearly had a keen interest in questions of religion and Jewish identity, becoming a life-long Zionist at a young age. Despite undeniable racial anti-Semitism, there was something of a 'Jewish cultural renaissance' during the Wilhelmine period in Germany.[32] Jonas was involved in the Zionist youth movement in Berlin, variously undertaking Jewish Studies at the Berlin Hochschule für die Wissenschaft des Judentums (Academy for the Science of Judaism), philosophy at the Friedrich Wilhelms University, vocational agriculture (with the intention of emigrating to Palestine) and philosophy and art history at the University of Freiburg, under Husserl and Heidegger. He was clearly profoundly impressed by Heidegger, enough to follow him to Marburg in 1924. Heidegger, though, was not yet Heidegger the Great Philosopher, which came only after the publication of *Sein und Zeit* in 1927. Its earliest version was a lecture delivered to the Marburg Theology Faculty (at Bultmann's invitation) in 1924.[33] We don't know if Jonas was in attendance, but he was soon attending Bultmann's New Testament seminars, where he and Arendt were the only Jewish students.[34] The two became close; he was in love with her, although their relationship never became physical. In fact, Arendt was in a relationship with the married Heidegger at the time.[35]

On 23 July 1925, Jonas presented a paper entitled 'Die Gnosis in Johannesevangelium' at the seminar. Realizing that the scope extended beyond the Gospel of John, Bultmann suggested that the gnostic texts might prove fertile ground for his doctoral thesis.[36] Jonas protested that he had no intention of becoming a New Testament scholar, so Bultmann took the idea to Heidegger.[37] Jonas submitted his thesis, 'Über den Begriff die Gnosis' ('On the Concept of Gnosis'), three years later, in 1928. Although it was primarily written under Bultmann, it was submitted as a philosophy thesis with Heidegger as supervisor, as it was not then permitted for non-Protestants to formally complete studies in Protestant theology. Heidegger was not as enthusiastic about the results as Bultmann was, however.[38]

This was surprising, as the thesis was based on parallels Jonas perceived between gnostic texts and Heidegger's existential philosophy. Jonas had begun to conceive of Gnosticism as a sort of spiritual existentialism, 'the original form in which the rational intelligibility of the cosmos was ... first radically challenged'.[39] My understanding is that Jonas interprets the Gnostics as the first Daseins – the first humans to experience the angst of being and therefore experience the possibility of freedom. The anticosmic rejection of the physical world that Jonas identified in his gnostic texts is the falling away of the physical world and the Others of Heidegger's angst, in which the authentic self experiences itself as homeless, alone and alien. For Jonas, gnostics are fundamentally alienated, alone and acutely aware of the gulf between their individual existence and the rest of the universe. They seek to bridge this gulf, to reconnect their individual being with that of the true God – or, to put it in Heideggerian terms, to 'exist authentically'. Contemporary existentialism was, for Jonas, simply an expression of this perennial anticosmic Gnosticism.

Anticosmic – a term which Jonas introduced and which remains in common usage[40] – refers to the motif that the cosmos is in some way inherently *bad* – whether flawed, or actually malevolent, by accident or design. Jonas's Gnosticism, then, is fundamentally, essentially anticosmic – this was the revolutionary aspect of the *Dasein* position of Gnosticism.[41] Indeed, Jonas would later go on to state that 'the radical dualism that governs the relation of God and world, and correspondingly that of man and world' is the 'cardinal feature of gnostic thought'.[42]

Like the Science of Religion approach to Gnosticism, he casts his net wide, drawing in Mandaean texts, the Hermetica (including the Poimandres) and some New Testament apocrypha. He also takes from them the assumption of a pagan or Hellenic influence. Jonas was, in part, directly addressing Adolf von Harnack's description of Gnosticism (and Late Antiquity more generally) as 'the acute secularization or Hellenization of Christianity'.[43] He was also deeply indebted to Bultmann's demythologization. Jonas referred always to the gnostic *myth* – that is, a narrative, focused on the Redeemed Redeemer. By uncovering its symbolic meaning of the gnostic myth, he would reveal the essence – *wesensbestimmung* – of Gnosticism.[44]

Jonas took the idea that Gnosticism somehow paralleled his own time from the 'violent abstractions' of Baur and the Tübingen school. Yet Jonas had quite legitimate reasons to feel alienated. Heidegger remained as professor at Marburg only one full year. In 1928, Husserl retired, and Freiburg offered Heidegger the vacant chair. He accepted. Now he was Husserl's successor institutionally as well as intellectually. His thought moved away from theology, instead becoming fascinated with Nietzsche, Schopenhauer and the eighteenth-century poet Friedrich Hölderlin. Heidegger joined the National Socialist Workers Party on 1 May, having become intoxicated by Nazism, as his friend Karl Jaspers put it, as many other academics had following Hitler's appointment as chancellor in January 1933.[45]

His relationship with Husserl – who was still teaching regularly, despite retirement – became increasingly strained. Heidegger presented Husserl with a Festschrift to mark his seventieth birthday on 8 April 1929, but they had little contact otherwise. Finally, in April 1933, the Jewish Husserl was suspended from teaching at Freiburg. Husserl wrote of his feelings of betrayal to a Marburg colleague a few days later:

> The final case (and it hit me the hardest) being Heidegger: hardest, because I had come to place a trust (which I can no longer understand) not just in his talent but in his character as well.[46]

Later the same month, Heidegger assumed rectorship of the university, which involved him giving his public support for the Nazi Party under the *Gleichschaltung* (ideological coordination) project, despite the large circle of Jewish students with which he was associated.[47] As his involvement with Nazism increased, he became increasingly hostile to Christianity, eventually refusing to take Jesuits as doctoral students.[48] In August, Jonas went to London to finish his research on Gnosticism.

Heidegger lasted one year as rector, during which he openly propagandized for the Fuhrer, secretly acted as informant on his colleagues and acted to block the paths of Jewish colleagues and students.[49] He resigned from rectorship in April 1934, after refusing to dismiss a dean who was one of the few members of staff supportive of the sweeping changes he was hoping for.[50] He remained openly Nazi until the end of the war.[51]

Gnosticism remained available as a topic of research under National Socialism. While some theologians managed to reconcile their work with

National Socialism, scholars were more likely to find employment by studying non-Christian religious traditions. Even better, study Persia and India, so your research might be used to bolster the Nazi ideological claims of a pagan Aryan descent. An early (i.e. pre-Christian) Asian (and, therefore, Aryan) origin for Gnosticism would have serious implications for the legitimacy of Christianity and the legitimacy of National Socialist Paganism.[52]

Walter Bauer published *Rechtgläubigkeit und Ketzerei im ältesten Christentum* in 1934, while he was professor of theology at Göttingen. In some ways, Bauer's work was a continuation of the work of the previous century's scholarship: Baur and the Tübingen school, and Harnack's *religionsgeschichliche*.[53] What was revolutionary, however, was the challenge to the primacy of orthodoxy – that is, that the Roman Church represented the earliest form of Christianity, with heresies as later, corrupt developments. Not only was what we now know as 'orthodoxy' just one version of Christianity among many, but it had also actively suppressed its competitors and rewritten history to suggest that it had always been the true version.[54] This idea, known as the Bauer Thesis, was to be highly influential – though not uncontroversial – and later scholars have repeated the dramatic and empowering force of his argument and often his errors. Hartog writes:

> The Bauer Thesis was a bold, provocative understanding of Christian origins. On the one hand, even Bauer's critics acknowledge his fascinating suggestions and erudite contentions, as well as his dismantling of simplistic, ahistorical views of 'monolithic dogma'. By examining data from specific geographical locations with careful attention to localized details, he rightfully persuaded other scholars to mistrust sweeping generalizations. He motivated theologians to consider the role of sociological and political forces within theological debates. Furthermore, he helped to renew interest in forgotten movements that had been swept away by history. On the other hand, Bauer overlooked, ignored, or manipulated historical data, and he often resorted to unfounded conjectures, special pleading, or arguments from silence.[55]

Jonas published the first volume of *Gnosis und Spätantiker Geist* (Gnosis and the Spirit of Late Antiquity), developed from his thesis, in 1935. The second volume was apparently complete and typeset already, but before it could be published, he fled to Palestine.[56] He stopped to bid farewell to Bultmann, but not to Heidegger.[57] He pledged only to return to Germany as part of a conquering army – and he did, as part of the British army's 'Jewish Brigade' in 1945.[58] His mother had already been murdered in Auschwitz, however.

In Palestine, Jonas reconnected with Gershom Scholem (1897–1982), whom he had known in the Berlin Zionist youth movement. Scholem had emigrated in 1923 after receiving his doctorate in Semitic philology from Munich and was now the first professor of Jewish Mysticism at the Hebrew University of Jerusalem, a post he held until his retirement in 1965. Scholem was a skilled historian of the Kabbalah and a committed Zionist, and these themes intertwined in his work, which sought to reform how *religionswissenschaft* dealt with Judaism. He argued that it treated Judaism as a fossil, whereas it should be studied as a living thing and the stages of its ongoing theology historicized.[59] Drawing from Heinrich Graetz's thesis in *Gnosticismus und Judenthum* (1846) that a gnostic influence had corrupted Judaism, and Nachman Krochmal's work on the parallels between Gnosticism and the Kabbalah, Scholem's *Major Trends in Jewish Mysticism* (1941) used Gnosticism as the connective tissue linking disparate traditions of Jewish mysticism through history. Arguing against the consensus of the time, which placed the development of non-Talmudic mystical literature until well after the completion of the Talmud, Scholem argues that the development was concurrent. He contends that they originated from a Jewish Gnosticism that was independent of and earlier than its Christian counterpart. Jewish Gnostics, he argued, saw the vision of God's throne from the Merkabah literature and the gnostic *pleroma* as the same thing but attempted to harmonize its dualism with monotheism in various ways.[60] This concept would later reemerge in thirteenth-century Europe in the *Sefer ha-Bahir*, which was formative in the tradition we now call Kabbalah.[61] Scholem's later *Jewish Gnosticism, Merkabah Mysticism and Talmudic Tradition* (1960) furthered his argument, positing Gnosticism – 'this convenient term for the religious movement that proclaimed a mystical esotericism *for the elect* based on illumination and the acquisition of *a higher knowledge* of things heavenly and divine' – as the mythological connective tissue of Jewish mysticism.[62] But unlike these earlier scholars, Scholem saw this mystic gnostic tradition as a revitalizing force, an existential, primordial, mythic upspring of human consciousness, suppressed by Rabbinic law.

The friendship between Jonas and Scholem would be lasting and productive, though not especially close, and they would have several fallings-out.[63] The two were part of a group of Jewish scholars with an interest in Gnosticism who used to meet at Scholem's home until the mid-1940s, called either the 'Gnostic sect' or the 'Pilegesh Club', drawn from the initials of the members.[64] They were also both parts of a larger network of Jewish émigré scholars which also included Karl Löwith, Martin Buber and Hannah Arendt. Scholem was clearly influenced by Jonas's work; for example, his idea that Gnosticism is alienated[65] and libertinist[66] and perhaps, most influentially, that Gnosticism might be a motif that was not constrained to a specific historical period (although Scholem does not seem to regard Gnosticism as ahistorical, as Jonas does). Importantly, however, Scholem did not internalize or psychologize Gnosticism; it was a mythic cosmology, with a revolutionary potential which fed into – and was fed by – his Zionism.

The connection reminds us that ideas are the product of their time. Arguably, Jonas's and Scholem's arguments project the pessimism of Germany in the 1930s as much as, if not more than, they reflect pessimism or world rejection in the communities of Late Antiquity. That so many influential theorists of Gnosticism – both before and immediately after the Second World War, as Chapter 6 will discuss – were Jewish is highly significant:

> The alien god's occultation of immanent power, in a crudely Durkheimian reading, could be constructed as a collective representation of alienation. But 'The Alien God', so it tautologically appears, is not Alien for nothing. *The Alien God is the aliens' god.*[67]

With *Gnosis und Spätantiker Geist*, Gnosticism was transformed a second time. After having been reified into a heretical religion in the eighteenth and nineteenth centuries, it was essentialized into a religious essence in the years following the First World War and even more so after the Holocaust. Jonas's work directly influenced later biblical scholars like Kurt Rudolph and Birger Pearson in constructing Gnosticism as 'a dualistic religion of alienation, protest, and transcendence, which, though multifarious, adapted itself readily to other religious traditions, perhaps in a parasitic manner'.[68] Yet as we have seen, his construction of Gnosticism is based upon an essence, and by insisting on the sui generis nature of Gnosticism, he was, along with Jung (who we will examine in the next chapter), the predominant influence on the reification of Gnosticism as a sui generis religious type.

4

A crack in the universe: Jung and the Eranos circle

In fact, it was not only Jewish intellectuals who had 'rediscovered' Gnosticism in Germany in the interwar years. The Theosophical Society produced cheap books on occult-related material through Leipzig's Eugen Diederichs Publishing Company between 1903 and 1910. As well as subjects such as astrology, mythology and archaeology, they included several on their perennial interpretation of Gnosticism, derived ultimately from Blavatsky – which also served the publisher's agenda to undermine the church.[1] These proved popular in the emerging *völkische* movement. Meaning 'of the common people', but with connotations of both 'folksiness' and racialism, this was a loose affiliation of populist conservative groups in the German-speaking countries of Europe, typified by a mixture of agricultural romanticism, an interest in folklore and a pan-Germanic ethnic nationalism.[2] This slipped easily into racially charged esoteric ideas, and völkische polemicists like Guido List and Jörg Lanz von Liebenfels interpreted 'Gnostic' texts like the *Pistis Sophia* as allegories of their racial politics – a Manichaean struggle between Aryan light and Jewish darkness, the Fall as the result of mingled blood.[3] The prominent Nazi Ernst 'Putzi' Hanfstängl would later write in his memoirs of Adolf Hitler's 'uncanny gift of coupling the gnostic yearning of the era for a strong leader-figure with his own missionary claim'.[4] That both Hitler's supporters before the war and his critics afterwards could interpret Nazism as a gnostic movement is striking.

Artists were also drawn to these anthologies. Hugo Ball referred to Dada as a 'Gnostic Sect',[5] and Franz Kafka owned a copy of Wolfgang Schultz's 1910 anthology, *Dokumente der Gnosis*, from which Stanley Corngold traces a gnostic theme in his works.[6] Gnostic themes were prominent in Herman Hesse's fiction. His short novel *Demian* (1919) climaxes with the appearance of Abraxas, identified as the supreme gnostic god and a figure of great importance in Jung's interpretation of Gnosticism. Hesse's later *Steppenwolf* (1927) concerns a character described as 'homeless' in 'this alien world', who sees 'the whole of human life as an ill-fated abortion of the primal mother, a savage and dismal catastrophe of nature'. *Steppenwolf* admonishes those with 'a longing to forsake this world and to penetrate a world beyond time': 'Only within yourself exists that other reality'. While the alienation theme echoes Jonas, this admonition suggests the influence of the psychological interpretation of Carl Jung. In fact, Hesse had been through psychoanalysis with Joseph Bernhard Lang between 1916 and 1917. Lang had been one of Jung's student, and it was Jung himself who possibly transmitted him an interest towards Gnosticism.[7]

Thomas Mann's novels of the 1930s and 1940s – the *Joseph and His Brothers* novels (1933–43) and particularly *Doktor Faustus* (1947) – show sustained engagement with interwar scholarship on Gnosticism. Grimstad argues that Mann and his contemporaries saw Gnosticism as a parallel of the European Aestheticism movement, in which the artist sought to shut themselves off from the world and find redemption through an escape into the world of pure Art.[8] Thomas Mann was an effusive supporter of Hesse's work and was similarly influenced by Carl Jung's gnostic 'channelled' book, *Septum Sermones ad Mortuos* (1917), which he possibly received through his friend, Jung's colleague and co-author, Károly Kerényi.

During this period, a number of *lebensreform* communities appeared in Germany (and throughout Europe) which attracted *wandervogel* – young people with a romantic back-to-nature ideology – who were looking to retreat from the world and find new ways to live. Here, theosophical publications, völkische nationalism and a critique of contemporary society blended with interests in vegetarianism, various alternative health practices and art, as well as drugs of various types. Some of these communities developed a more directly millennial leaning and were the direct ancestors of the New Age movement. In this milieu, Gnosticism seems to have functioned as a marker for 'alternative' religion, including a critique of religious and social institutions.

Ascona, in the Swiss Canton Ticino, was home to one such community, called Monte Verità (Mount Truth) and established on Monte Monescia.[9] Theodor Reuss, patriarch of the OTO, founded the Grand Lodge there in 1917.[10] By 1928, however, Ascona had become popular with the artistically-inclined wealthy, and *wandervogel* were rare.[11] One such was Olga Fröbe-Kapteyn (1881–1962), an independent widow of Dutch parentage with an interest in history, philosophy, the arts, Theosophy and Indian religion. She first visited Ascona between 1919 and 1920 to cure her gastritis in the community's sun-bathing sanatorium.[12] Her father[13] bought Casa Gabriella – a large estate on the shore of Lake Maggiore, near Ascona – in October 1920, and after inheriting it from him in the mid-1920s, Olga Fröbe-Kapteyn began inviting artists and intellectuals there, even having a two-hundred-seat conference hall built.[14]

In 1928, she travelled to Connecticut to meet with Alice Bailey and her husband, Foster. Bailey was by now working independently of the Theosophical Society, continuing to publish her channelled communications from the Tibetan and other Ascended Masters about the coming New Age. Fröbe-Kapteyn told them of her plan to establish a 'spiritual centre' at the Casa Gabrielle, 'open to esoteric thinkers and occult students of all groups in Europe and elsewhere'.[15] This was instituted in August 1930 with 'a Summer School for the study of Theosophy, Mysticism, the Esoteric Sciences and Philosophies and all forms of spiritual research', starting 3 August and lasting three weeks, led by the Baileys. These became an annual event in 1933, although by then the Baileys were no longer involved.[16] Instead, she invited Carl Jung to lecture, and despite initial reservations about the connections to Bailey, he accepted.

Carl Gustav Jung (1875–1961) is hyperbolically described by Noll as ranking 'with Julian the Apostate … as one who significantly undermined orthodox Christianity and restored the polytheism of the Hellenistic world in Western civilization'.[17] Nevertheless, behind the tightly controlled public face of Jung as a distinguished, if heterodox, psychologist, it is certainly also true that Jung was a mystic and hierophant who tasked himself with restoring direct experience of extramundane realities to the modern world. It would not be an exaggeration to state that he, along with Blavatsky and perhaps Crowley, was among the most influential figures in twentieth-century religious discourse, particularly in terms of the language of 'spirituality'.

Jung was born in Kesswil, Switzerland, to parents from bourgeois but no longer wealthy families. His father, Paul, was a pastor with a doctorate in theology; his mother, Emilie, came from a family in which stories of clairvoyant abilities and congenital insanity were commonplace. The family identified as Swiss for political reasons but had German roots and a strong connection with German culture. Jung's paternal grandfather was a well-known playwright and rector of Basel University, converted to Protestantism by Schleiermacher himself and – according to rumour – was the illegitimate son of Goethe, the paragon of the heroic German intellectual.[18]

Jung began a medical degree at Basel in May 1895, completing it in late 1900, although his thesis would not be submitted until 1902. His thesis, on mediumistic phenomena at seances, demonstrates that he already had an interest in spiritualism and in pushing at the limits of psychiatry's remit. By then, he was two years into stint as an assistant staff psychiatrist at the Burghölzli, where he would be employed until 1909. The Burghölzli was both the Zurich Canton's insane asylum and the Psychiatric Clinic of Zurich University, and the experimental work on word-association diagnostics that he and his colleagues carried out between 1902 and 1909 established his career in the international field.[19] Jung treated several former residents of the Monte Veritá community at the Burghölzli, including psychoanalyst and anarchist Otto Gross.[20] One case in particular would point towards his later work, that of the institutionalized patient E. Schwyzer, later known as 'the Solar Phallus Man'. Jung interpreted Schwyzer's hallucinations as a Mithraic ritual, and as Schwyzer was not a scholar, Jung concluded that, therefore, it must have come to him through the 'collective unconsciousness'.[21]

This period also saw the beginning of two of his most significant long-term relationships. He married Emma Rauschenbach in February 1903, and the two would remain married until the end of her life in 1955, despite Jung's numerous and sometimes long-standing affairs. Emma came from a family of considerable wealth, and the money she brought to the marriage allowed Jung to sever ties with the Burghölzli and devote himself to writing, lecturing and private practice from 1909.[22]

Jung's relationship with Sigmund Freud is well known. The two men were close colleagues and had an intense friendship, and by 1911, Jung was Freud's nominated successor, president of the International Psychoanalytic Association and editor of the *Jahrbuch*. But Freud was increasingly unhappy about the direction Jung's work was taking, as psychological interpretation of mythological material had become increasingly central. Jung publicly rejected Freud's libido theory in November 1912; Freud responded by accusing him of anti-Semitism, and that was the end of that.

In fact, Jung had begun to perceive of psychoanalysis – as he constructed it – as a functional replacement for religion. 'New Paths in Psychology' (written in 1911, though published after his death) can be read as a manifesto for psychoanalysis as a new religion: individual psychoses are the result of 'the great problems of society. … Neurosis is thus nothing less than an individual attempt, however unsuccessful, to solve a universal problem'.[23] Not only psychoanalysis as religion, however, but religion as psychoanalysis. Many of Jung's best-known ideas – including the collective unconscious, archetypes and synchronicity – are all metaphysical concepts dressed in scientific nomenclature.[24] Noll suggests that Jung's 'confusing but somewhat poetic pseudoscientific vocabulary' was in fact a code to obscure that he was talking about mystical experiences to all but his analytic initiates[25]. Today, Jungian psychoanalysis is largely (though not universally) ignored by the academic psychological community, maintaining its own independent journals and training programmes, and it seems that 'spirituality' is a significant appeal for the majority of participants in the movement – as well as scholars of religion and the general public.[26] Indeed, in a book specifically defending Jung against Noll's criticism, Sonu Shamdasani admits that 'the one academic field in which Jung's work has been most engaged with is that of religious studies.'[27] This is because his theories are based in esoteric and religious ideas, rather than scientific research.[28]

Jung's own spiritual biography is well known, particularly from *Memories, Dreams, Reflections*, a hagiography mostly written by his acolyte Anelia Jaffé. Following the break from Freud, Jung increasingly isolated himself, resigning as lecturer at Zurich University, as president of the International Psychoanalytic Association and as editor of the *Jahrbuch*, and began a period that has been romanticized by his later followers as his 'confrontation with the unconscious'.

During October 1913, he had several visions of Europe being flooded with blood, which he took as indicating a great social revolution, and began to communicate with a female voice he interpreted as an archaic mother goddess. This visionary activity continued through to August 1914, causing Jung much distress and depression.[29] He was analyzing his own memories of his childhood as well as deliberately inducing visionary experiences through 'active imagination' and recording the results in his diaries (including the famous *Red Book*, or *Liber Novus*, published in 2009). In these he interacted with several mythological figures, and by 1916, an elderly figure called Philemon had become Jung's spiritual teacher. Philemon and the others insisted that they were independent beings, as they laid out to Jung the ideas that would constitute his later work. At the same time, Jung began to interpret his role as that of prophet, even perhaps a messianic figure.[30] Indeed, the influence of the *völkische* mystical streak which drives Jung's work up until the Second World War can still be detected in his later, better-known work – for example, that one's soul or even physiology was spiritually connected to the land of one's ancestors or that members of a particular race share a common racial consciousness.[31] In the writings of the Gnostics, he wrote, 'I had suddenly found a circle of friends who had shared my experiences and could sympathize with me and understand the whole realm where I had been so lonely and isolated'.[32] In 1916, he attributed authorship (via channelling) of *Septum Sermones ad Mortuos* (*Seven Sermons to the Dead*, a set of mystical writings which was the only part of his larger *Red Book* he circulated during his life) to Basilides.

Gnosticism played an important part in how Jung reconciled his psychological and increasingly spiritual agendas. Already Jung's doctoral thesis had used the term 'Gnostic' to describe the medium's visions.[33] Around 1909, however, he began to engage more systematically with Gnosticism, with the work of G. R. S. Mead as his primary source.[34] Mead is largely ignored in studies of Jung and Gnosticism, in favour of his later contacts with Eranos scholars such as Gilles Quispel, but Jung had been engaged with Mead's work on Gnosticism for more than twenty years before meeting them.[35] Jung's personal library contained eighteen publications by Mead, including *Pistis Sophia, Fragments of a Faith Forgotten* and *A Gnostic Miscellany*.[36] In fact, Jung's interpretation of the Bergholzli's 'Solar Phallus Man' vision as being based in Mithraic liturgy was drawn from Mead's translation in *A Mithraic Ritual*, published in 1907.[37]

Jung certainly knew Mead personally and possibly much earlier than has previously been thought.[38] In *The Quest* in 1918, Mead notes that his interest in psychoanalysis dates from 'my reading for review some months ago the English translation of a book by Dr. Carl G. Jung of Züruch, in which certain views based on the researches of psychoanalysis are applied to some mythological themes and the symbolism of some of the mystery-religions of antiquity'.[39] The impression given is that Mead did not know Jung personally[40] nor had significant familiarity with his work. Following this, however, psychoanalysis became a regular feature of *The Quest*, with Mead's gnostic articles largely drying up.[41] However, a letter from Mead to Jung in the Jung Archive at the University of Zurich, in which they discuss Gustav Meyrink (author of *Der Golem*) and Mead tries to get Jung to contribute to *The Quest*, demonstrates that the two were on friendly terms and had probably met in person during 1919.[42]

Jung was attracted to Gnosticism because he could fit it into his model of the history of the psyche. The history of the development of human consciousness, according to Jung, is a process of increasing awareness of the 'self' as object, separate from the rest of the world and from the unconscious of the subject from which it emerges. He divided this development into four stages, which also represent four psychological types: primitive, ancient, modern and contemporary. The conscious mind is not differentiated from the unconscious of the primitive, and thus, they do not differentiate their unconscious from the physical world. The unconscious is instead encountered as personalities at work within the world – gods – but as the primitive does not perceive any subjective 'self', they identify with both those projected gods and the other physical beings they encounter, like an infant or herd animal. Ancients have more sense of 'self', yet still project the unconsciousness onto the world in the form of gods. The difference is that they no longer identify with those gods. Ancient man means religious man (just like Eliade's *homo religiosus*) and includes the societies of the Greeks, Romans, Jews and Christians. Moderns possess a fully developed ego and reject the subconscious as non-rational. This type considers themselves entirely rational, rejects religion as pre-scientific and identifies solely with the ego, completely separate from the world. Finally, contemporaries also reject religion, yet are aware of their non-rational, unconscious side. Seeking the fulfilment that religion once provided, they seek non-projective expressions for the unconscious to replace the projective ones inherited from it.[43]

Jung considered most people of the twentieth century to be moderns, who, by repressing the non-rational, experience their unconscious as neurosis as it bursts into consciousness unannounced. A minority of contemporaries, however, accept the non-rational despite lacking ways to express it, and so experience not neuroses, but malaise.[44] Jung saw classical Gnostics as the counterparts of these present-day contemporaries, seeking to overcome their sense of alienation. Gnosticism, for Jung, becomes one version of the ubiquitous phenomenon of awareness of alienation from one's unconscious.[45]

Jung's influence here would appear to be Baur's 1835 *Die Christliche Gnosis*, in which Gnosticism spawned the Romantic tradition to which Jung was so indebted.[46] When he became interested in alchemy in the 1920s, Jung began to see it as linking analytical psychology with Gnosticism. Again influencing much modern insider discourse, he claimed that alchemy had both a physical aspect, the transmutation of metals, precursor to modern chemistry, and a psychic aspect – an opinion shared by Eliade.[47] This psychic aspect was in continuity with 'active imagination' activities founded by the Gnostics, Jung claimed, and perfected in his psychology. The Gnostics were 'apparently the first thinkers to concern themselves (after their fashion) with the contents of the collective conscience'.[48]

Theosophy, too, was part of the gnostic tradition. Although Jung was critical of Theosophy in *Psychological Types*, describing it as a distortion of the Mental Faculty,[49] he also owned both volumes of Blavatsky's *The Secret Doctrine* and two books by C. W. Leadbeater.[50] After noting (with apparent approval) the existence of gnostic churches in France and Germany, Jung himself claimed that 'Theosophy, together with its continental sister, Anthroposophy … are pure Gnosticism in Hindu dress. … The passionate interest in these movements undoubtedly arises from psychic energy which can no longer be invested in obsolete religious forms'.[51]

The problem is once more that there is no evidence of causal historical links. Hanegraaff traces the influence rather in German Romantic mesmerism and the work of Swedenborg, and goes on to identify a common theme of a competition between two powers – ancient Paganism and Christianity. This finds expression in Jung's repeated binaries: sun and moon, light and dark, reason and intuition, waking and dreams, conscious and unconscious, introvert and extrovert. Christianity was the light – reason, sun, extroverted consciousness – and Paganism, here identified by its transmission through Gnosticism, alchemy, Theosophy and now psychotherapy, was the dark – intuition, moon, introverted unconsciousness.[52] From this – and this may be a good deal of the story of Gnosticism – he extrapolated a psychological Theory of Everything.

The theme of the 1933 Eranos meeting was 'Yoga and Meditation, Eastern and Western', and Jung's presentation was entitled 'The Empirical Basis of the Individuation Process'.[53] Mead never would attend, as he died earlier that year; however, Quest Society members Robert Eisler and Caroline Rhys Davies would be regular attendees at Eranos through the 1930s.[54] With this more academic and less (openly) esoteric guestlist, the annual event became known as the Eranos meetings. Eranos – meaning in Greek a banquet in which each guest makes a contribution – was suggested to Fröbe-Kapteyn by Rudolf Otto.[55] Although Otto never attended, his theoretical influence on the participants ran deep, particularly his concept of *the numinous*, an ineffable quality specific to the realm of religion and arguably the clearest exposition of a sui generis theory of religion.[56]

Jung was already fifty-eight years old in 1933, but the early Eranos meetings coincided with a dramatic upswing in his international profile. He gave prestigious public lectures at Harvard in 1936 and Yale in 1937, American and British students sought his tutelage in Zurich and the circle around him took on a cultish tenor. As the Nazis continued to rise in Germany and eventually beyond, Jung increasingly stressed his Austrian nationality and deemphasized his völkische mystical leanings. Noll suggests that his increasing focus on alchemy 'helped to give the impression that there was still something Christian and monotheistic about his religious outlook', even though he retained a marked antipathy towards Christianity.[57] The same could be argued regarding his use of Gnosticism.

The meetings continued annually, in a much-reduced state between 1939 and 1945, reaching their heyday in the late 1940s and 1950s. As such, they were imbued with the sense of society in crisis and a hope for renewal or regeneration – Fröbe-Kapteyn wrote in 1934 that if the task of synthesizing the philosophies of the 'East and West' were achieved, Eranos would create 'the initial stages of a way to salvation for our time, which we especially need nowadays, in the general disorientation, in the quest for new considerations of old values'.[58] Jung attended every year until 1952,[59] and Fröbe-Kapteyn became increasingly reliant on him, to the point where she felt he was able to heal her with his touch.[60] Jung was in turn happy to accept her money to fund his travels in search of photographs of archetypal and alchemical images and, it appears, to send patients to her for mediumistic sessions. When, in 1936, he was inclined to accept an invitation to speak at Harvard over Eranos, she threatened to abandon the conference until he backed down.[61]

In fact, Jung had become the focal point of the meetings. Many of the attendees were members of Jung's circle or were otherwise influenced by his work, including Oskar Schmitz, Ingrid Strauß-Klöbe, Ellen Thayer, Toni Wolff, Erich Neumann, James Hillman, Laurens van der Post and Joseph Campbell, among many others. Paul Mellon, an heir to the Mellon Bank fortune and one of the richest people in the United States, attended the 1939 Eranos conference with his wife, Mary, after having previously dined with Jung in New York after attending his 'Dream Symbols and the Individuation Process' lectures in October 1937.[62] Mary Mellon was severely asthmatic and had been (unsuccessfully) seeking help from a Jungian analyst in New York, whom they believed to be fraudulent, yet they were both impressed by Jung himself. After Mary discovered that Fröbe-Kapteyn had almost bankrupted herself with the expenses and was looking to sell the Casa Gabrielle, the Mellons began to directly support the events financially.[63] Both Mellons were soon being treated by Jung himself (though Paul was notably less impressed than Mary), and they later established the Bollingen Press, named after their country estate, to publish his work, as well as the proceedings of the Eranos meetings.[64]

Testament to Jung's influence, several highly influential scholars of Gnosticism were regular attendees, although speaking about the subject was by no means limited to experts.[65] For Eranos participants, Gnosticism was essentially esotericism – the search for a secret, universal truth to religion, grounded in Otto's numinous.[66] Indeed, the Eranos circle was frequently described as gnostic – both by themselves and by their critics.[67] Indeed, many of the regular Eranos lecturers – including Jung and some of the most significant figures in the study of religion at that time, such as Mircea Eliade, Henry Corbin and Gershom Scholem – were both scholars and 'more or less explicitly, engaged and even passionate religious intellectuals'.[68] Eranos scholars saw themselves as the paragon of *homo religiosus*, with a firm stress on individual experience and a tendency to posit mysticism and esotericism as the pinnacle of religiosity.[69] Their Gnosticism, then, was Elite Knowledge in both senses of the term. And, like Jung and all of their generation, they were reacting to the trauma of the first half of the twentieth century. As Hanegraaff puts it, 'The religionists of Eranos were rebelling against the finality of history and time, change and impermanence'.[70]

This was certainly the case with Gershom Scholem, who was an Eranos regular for thirty years, beginning in 1949. Despite initial concerns that Jung had been a Nazi collaborator, the two shared a commitment to the idea that symbols, and myths, were not fixed signs, but rather powerful expressions of the irrational and ineffable.[71] However, while acknowledging Jung as the 'moving spirit' of Eranos, he retained some distance, particularly in avoiding using Jung's idea of archetypes. He wrote privately to Morton Smith in 1950, warning of

> the more extreme forms of psychoanalytical fantasies for which I cannot arouse much sympathy on my part. I feel that much of the amateurish character of psychological researches into the History of Religion, especially of both the Freudian and Jungian brand, is caused by the lack of a sound philological basis for their contentions.[72]

Figure 1: Jung and Corbin at Eranos in 1950. Reprinted with the permission of Association des amis de Henry et Stella Corbin (AAHSC), www.amiscorbin.com.

Biale suggests that the avoidance of Jungian terminology is driven not by a resistance to the idea of symbols expressing some transcendent reality, but rather by reducing the transcendent to the psyche.[73] Scholem was no strict empiricist in his personal life; he discussed with friends how he remained hopeful that the transcendent might reappear in mundane reality, that the eternal could appear within history, and admitted in a private 1937 letter that his interest in Kabbalah was driven by a desire to 'penetrate through the symbolic plain and through the wall of history'.[74] For Scholem, Kabbalah was key to the future of Judaism; his historiography served this end. Scholem recognized the paradox that his Zionist identity was predicated on the messianic expectation and was therefore historical, while considering Truth in a philosophical sense to be *outside* history. Scholem's religious identity and research were deeply connected, though he did a better job of keeping his spiritual leanings out of his academic work than some of his Eranos colleagues.[75]

The Islamist Henry Corbin took a much more radical, 'anti-historical' perspective, in which empirical *phenomena* have their origins and meaning in the immaterial realm. Corbin likewise 'discovered' (note the passive verb, implying something pre-existent) a gnostic tradition in medieval Ismaili Islam – though he admitted there was 'no trace' of historical evidence to connect them to the Gnostics of the heresiological sources.[76] However, in the absence of textual data, the historian can be aided by the phenomenologist, whose task is 'revealing the structural homologies and their meaning'.[77] Corbin identifies these homologies in the comparison between the perceived similarity between the Unknown God and the Redeemed Redeemer with certain figures from Ishmaili theology and the presence of gnosis – 'a teaching which does not aim at some pure theoretical knowledge, [and] a *mode* of understanding which is not a simple act of knowing'.[78]

While Corbin's Gnosticism seems to have been predominantly inspired by Heidegger via Hans Jonas, it was not pessimistic and, in his later years, he would call openly for religion of the future to be gnostic in character.[79] Echoing the spirit of renewal, he described Europe under fascism in mythic terms as 'the darkening of the world, the flight of the gods, the destruction of the earth, the transformation of man into a mass, the hatred and suspicion of everything free and creative'.[80] Only Gnosticism offered hope of salvation by transcending this fallen world. Corbin too was a religious intellectual as much as a scholar of religion, claiming that he was initiated by the eleventh-century Sufi master whose work he was reading.[81]

Figure 2: Corbin (right) and Scholem at Eranos, 1977. Reprinted with the permission of Association des amis de Henry et Stella Corbin (AAHSC), www.amiscorbin.com.

Henri-Charles Puech (1902–1986), a French philosopher and historian of Manichaeism, first attended in 1936. He was an important figure in the field, being secretary of the Section des Sciences religieuses of the Paris École Pratique des Hautes Études and editor of the *Revue de l'Histoire des Religions*, the oldest journal in the field.[82] In 1951, he presented on 'Gnosis and Time' (a striking echo of Heidegger's *Sein und Zeit*), in which he puts forth a gnostic model of time which 'shatters ... into bits' both the Christian and Hellenistic models of time. Puech opined that scholars had – again – 'discovered' that Gnosticism is 'a determinate genus, widely distributed in space and time, of which heretical Christian gnosis is only a particular species'.[83] And although this is reminiscent of Hans Jonas's gnostic religion, Puech is much more positive in his assessment; gnosis is 'an absolute knowledge which in itself saves'.[84] With staggering certainty, he writes:

> We shall be able to discern and understand the Gnostic attitude towards time only as a function of the total Gnostic vision of the world, the Gnostic *weltanschauung*. And since parts of this world view are inseparable, our enquiry must ultimately be directed towards Gnosis as a whole, considered in its essence, its structure, and its mechanisms. This and this alone will enable us to observe

that despite appearances, *despite the almost total absence of explicit testimony*, the problem of time lies at the very heart of Gnosis.[85]

No texts, no history.

Puech will have a significant role in transmitting Jungian ideas into the academic study of Gnosticism, often in collaboration with his younger Dutch colleague, Gilles Quispel (1916–2006). Quispel received his doctorate (on Tertullian's *Adversus Marcionem*) from Utrecht in 1943 and after the war sent copies of an article on Valentinism to Karl Barth, Aldous Huxley and Carl Jung. Although only Jung replied, Quispel's boldness paid off, and he was invited to speak on Gnosticism at the 1947 Eranos meeting. His paper, 'La Conception de l'Homme dans la Gnose Valentinienne', praised Jonas for introducing the phenomenological method and his description of alienation as the essential core of Gnosticism.[86] But he suggested that Jonas lacked a rigorous grounding in philology, which was why, given the paucity of sources at this point, he restricted his talk to Valentinus.

He was immediately struck by Jung personally, whose down-to-earth manner resonated with his own background. There were also practical benefits to the relationship – he immediately received a Bollingen research grant, and a Bollingen volume of his essays was planned, though never published.[87] Quispel became a regular attendee from then on.[88] It is often suggested that Jung's ideas of Gnosticism were inspired by his relationship with scholars like Quispel, but the reverse may be more true. Jung was already in his seventies when he met Quispel and had been reading scholarship on Gnosticism since at least the writing of his doctorate. Quispel, on the other hand, would be profoundly influenced by Jung's ideas, crediting him with having 'done more for the interpretation of religion than any other living person'.[89] Jung's great contribution to the study of Gnosticism was, Quispel explained in 1975, 'that this was not a sort of ideology, or a fancy of a madman, or a philosophy, but it was an authentic experience'.[90] So while Jung may have learned of new sources from these younger scholars, the perennial, sui generis interpretive framework came from Jung.

Like Scholem, Quispel was a fierce defender of the position that Gnosticism had a Jewish origin, but he also saw Gnosticism as a universal and trans-historical religious phenomenon. Despite the Jewish origin, however, Quispel's Gnosticism was not specific to Judaism, but was a perennial and universal tradition. For Quispel, gnosis was a third epistemological 'component' of European culture, distinct from both *faith* and *reason*.[91] As such, it extended beyond the ancient world to include the Cathars, Hermeticism, Hegel, William Blake, Rudolf

Steiner and – *naturlich* – Jung. And, as with Jung, his interest in Gnosticism was powered by an episode of depression followed by visions, during which he decided that 'the heretics were right ... there was a sort of crack in the universe.'[92]

The institutionalization of the Jungian movement was complete with the founding of the C. G. Jung Institute in Zurich, supported by the Mellons, in 1948. Popular publications in English translation of Jung's *Collected Works*, Eliade's *Shamanism*, Joseph Campbell's *The Hero with a Thousand Faces* and other works by Eranos scholars facilitated a 'remarkable transference' of a mythological, ahistorical, essentialist approach to the study of religion from Europe to the United States. In this way, the assumptions of the Eranos circle came to lay the theoretical agenda for much of late twentieth-century anglophone Religious Studies, particularly esoteric or occult subjects – not least Gnosticism. Eliade's professorship at Chicago sealed the deal – by the 1980s, it is said that half the professors in North America had studied under him or his close colleagues at the University of Chicago at some point.[93]

Jung and his interpreters are largely ignored in psychological and psychiatric literature today, with Jungian therapists training in privately run institutions, so the prominence of Jung's ideas in Religious Studies today should give us pause. Eranos is a perfect prototype of the 'religionist' History of Religions school, predicated upon the sui generis notion that religion is merely an aspect of human culture and society, but has a unique and irreducible essence – the encounter with the numinous. Wasserstrom writes of the Eranos scholars:

> Their form of 'pure' religiosity ... ironically expressed an ambivalent attitude to the monotheistic message. They rejected the Masters of suspicion, especially Marx, Freud, and Durkheim. Yet they themselves remained positioned in their own ironic posture, implying as they did a religious authority, but one esoterically occultated out of reach of ordinary believers.[94]

Two facts are important to recognize in what follows: first, the influence that Jungian scholars would have on the publication of and scholarly appraisal of the Nag Hammadi texts, and hence of post–Nag Hammadi 'Gnosticism' scholarship; and second, the influence the Eranos circle had on the development and apotheosis of a phenomenological History of Religions methodology in post-war Religious Studies.

5

No texts, no history: Nag Hammadi

'The concept of Gnosticism as a world religion was launched when the Nag Hammadi Codices came to light a generation ago', wrote James Robinson in his preface to Hans-Joachim Klimkeit's *Gnosis on the Silk Road*.[1] This may be so, but it was not as a result of their contents – Quispel and Jonas had made this claim without having read any of the texts, and it would be the 1970s before the contents were widely available. As we have seen, the concept of Gnosticism as a religious type was well established before their discovery in 1945 and, because of the three-decade delay in their publication, would largely remain unchallenged until the 1990s.

Jung's psychologized interpretation and Jonas's existential interpretation didn't gain much traction beyond their immediate circles until after the Second World War. By 1945, academic studies of Gnosticism were dominated by Rudolf Bultmann's take on the Bauer Thesis. Bauer's book did not have a large impact in Anglophone studies until the English translation, *Orthodox and Heresy*, was published in 1971, long after the discovery of Nag Hammadi, though before its general publication.[2] Before this, most Anglophone scholars knew it through its refutation by H. E. W. Turner in his *The Pattern of Christian Truth* (1954), with the exception of Helmut Koester's students at Harvard, who benefitted from his reading of the German original.

Inspired by Heidegger, Bultmann sought to reveal the existential truth of the biblical text for a modern context, using demythologization to separate the dubious historical and cosmological claims in biblical accounts from their ethical and existential truths. But Bultmann was also interested in the relationship between Gnosticism and early Christianity, and a proponent of using texts then generally identified as gnostic in New Testament exegesis. As Reitzenstein had, Bultmann's 1941 *Commentary* on the Gospel of John suggested that the 'redeemer Myth' was not only known to the Gospel writers (and John in particular) but in fact had also influenced them.³ As identified by Kurt Rudolph, its core elements of the Bultmann/Bauer Gnosticism were:

1. Gnosticism is an 'autonomous world' which arose before, or at least independently of, Christianity;
2. Its origins lie primarily in the East, that is, in Persian and late Babylonian sources;
3. It is a product of Hellenistic syncretism;
4. Despite its rejection as heresy, it nevertheless exerted a considerable influence on Christian theology;
5. It is therefore highly relevant to New Testament exegesis.⁴

Yet despite the geographical and temporal repositioning of Gnosticism, and the positing of formative relationship between Gnosticism and Christianity, Bultmann's project remains fundamentally normative: Gnosticism remained incomplete, primitive, inferior.⁵ What Bultmann had done was simply to redescribe the concerns of the polemicists using a comparative method. Moreover, the use of comparison allowed for theological evaluation through the discussion of *meaning*. Such a search for essences beneath the surface of texts would clearly not discourage the more speculative sui generis interpretations of Gnosticism – and the relationship with the New Testament also granted the subject a degree of respectability.

Nevertheless, Bultmann's theory proved rather controversial among more conservative scholars, who took this as a 'contamination' of the New Testament. They preferred the idea that Gnosticism post-dated the Gospels and early Christianity, and dismissed Bultmann as arguing from silence, proclaiming, 'No texts, no history!'⁶ This would change in 1947, two years after Hiroshima and the liberation of Auschwitz and two months after Quispel's debut at Eranos, when Puech received word from one of his doctoral students that papyri containing previously unknown gnostic texts were for sale in Cairo and that there might be more.

Officially, the texts now known as 'the Nag Hammadi Corpus' were discovered in December 1945 or possibly early 1946 by brothers Khalifah, Abu al-Majd and Muhammad 'Ali.⁷ Their father had been shot in retribution for killing an accused thief, on approximately 9 April 1945, and it is this event that the brothers date their discovery from. 'About six months later', they were digging for fertilizer in the Nile valley near the city of Nag Hammadi when they uncovered a jar buried at the base of a large, protruding rock. It was large, perhaps 60 centimetres tall and 30 centimetres in diameter, with four handles near the mouth, and was red, unlike the cream-coloured pottery common to the area. It was sealed with a matching bowl (which actually survives) and has been dated to the fourth to fifth centuries CE. Muhammad 'Ali claims he was initially concerned it might contain a jinn but then also realized that it might contain treasure.[8] In fact, the jar contained twelve leather-bound codices, plus eight loose sheets of papyrus and several fragments. Muhammad divided them up among the brothers and the other camel drivers present by physically splitting several codices, but the drivers would not take the proffered shares, and Muhammad took them all home. It is often claimed that 'Ali's wife had burnt two of the codices, but most concerned think this story is apocryphal, as the monetary value of papyrus is well known in Egypt. It is true, however, that Muhammad 'Ali and his family attempted to sell the codices singly to al-Qasr villagers for small amounts, mostly unsuccessfully.

A short while later, Khalifah, Muhammad and their five brothers took bloody vengeance upon the man who was suspected of killing their father. Muhammad asked a local Coptic priest to store one of the codices (Codex III) for him, as the police were regularly searching his home following the killing and had taken a number of the brothers in for questioning. The priest's brother-in-law, a history and English teacher named Raghib, saw it and, recognizing the potential import (or more likely, monetary value), asked for and was given it gratis. He then purchased a second codex (Codex I) from one of the brothers for a small amount.

By March 1946, the Cairo antiquities dealer Phokion Tanos had acquired two of the codices from unidentified sources, possibly via Fikri Jibra'il Khalil, who Mohammad 'Ali claims bought two for sugar and tea. Around this time, Tanos acquired a further two (II and VII) from a dealer named Bahij Ali for two hundred Egyptian pounds (*livre égyptienne*, or £É) each, after Jacques Schwartz of the Institute Français d'Archéologie Orientale du Caire failed to close a deal for them.[9] Tanos doubled down at this point and managed to purchase all remaining codices from one of the brothers, Bahij Ali, who had been on bad terms with Mohammad 'Ali ever since as a result. This left Tanos with eight complete codices (II, IV–IX, XI) and parts of three others (I, X, XII), for which he had paid close to £É2,000. These were finally seized by the Egyptian Department of Antiquities, then under the directorship of Togo Mina, in May 1952, and he was paid £É5,000.

Now realizing the potential value, the 'Ali brothers returned – armed – to Raghib to take back the two codices he had. The second was returned (Codex I), on pain of death, but the first (Codex III) had already been sent to Cairo to see if anyone there could tell anything about it. It was shown to the Coptic Pope

Joseph II, then resident in Cairo, as well as the curator of the Coptic Museum, and was mailed back to Raghib with some six pages missing. But Raghib had already been forced to settle with the brothers for £É15 or £É20. He took it to Cairo with him on his regular summer vacation there and showed it to a Coptic physician named Georgy Sobhy Bey, who told Raghib to return for it the following day. When he did, he found the director of the Coptic Museum, Togo Mina, and the director of the Department of Antiquities waiting for him. After being threatened with arrest, and a long period of bureaucratic obfuscation, he was paid £É250 for the manuscript.

In the meantime, Muhammad 'Ali sold the newly recovered Codex I to Nashid Bisidah, a grain merchant, for (probably) £É50. He in turn sold it in Cairo for £É350 to antiquities dealer Tawfiq, who in turn sold it to Albert Eid, a very respectable dealer with many academic contacts, who later acquired some further leaves from the same codex through unclear circumstances.[10] This codex would later find its way to Berlin.

Jean Doresse (1917–2007), a research assistant at the *Centre National de la Recherche Scientifique* and a doctoral candidate in Coptology was in Cairo carrying out research for the Institute Français d'Archéologie Oriental du Caire in 1947. His wife, Marianne, who accompanied him on all his expeditions to Egypt, had been a classmate of Togo Mina in Paris, and so they were invited to examine the codex that the Coptic Museum had purchased from Raghib (Codex III).[11] Although it was not known at the time, Mina had already shown the text to Henry Corbin and a young Egyptologist named François Daumas, the previous December. Corbin was 'delirious' and said, 'If it is Gnosticism, translate that immediately … it will be Gnostic mysticism. I do not guarantee the terms, but the meaning'.[12] They were sworn to secrecy, so as not to drive up the prices of the other codices in circulation, but Mina seemingly intended that he and Daumas would prepare the manuscript for publication.

After viewing the texts, Jean Doresse wrote to his doctoral supervisor Puech to inform him that the codex contained several previously unpublished texts which he thought (perhaps influenced by Mina and Corbin) were Sethian Gnostic and noted that the dealer Tanos had several more in his possession.[13] Puech urged him to find out all he could, and Doresse supplanted Daumas in Mina's publication plans.

The Doresses are major figures in this story, brokering both the major deals that put the great majority of the codices into the hands of the Coptic Museum in Cairo and providing the initial reports (written by Marianne) which provided the entirety of knowledge of the Nag Hammadi codices for the next ten years, until Martin Krause was given access to the collection at the Coptic Museum in 1959.¹⁴ Jean Doresse was tasked by Mina to oversee the publication of Codex III but would be cut out of the eventual programme of publication, for which the Doresses blamed Puech – with good reason, although Gilles Quispel was also responsible.¹⁵ Mina's sudden death in October 1949 meant that it was necessary to renegotiate the publication plans with his successor Pahor Labib, who had studied in Berlin and was not well disposed towards French scholars.¹⁶ There was a long legal battle over the sequestering of Tanos codices, and the Egyptian Revolution of July 1952 weakened the French scholars' position in Cairo, and ultimately it would be 1959 before another scholar was allowed to view the codices.¹⁷ Doresse's initial reports and the synopsis of the codex he hastily prepared from memory were used without acknowledgement in other scholars' publications as they raced to be first for publication.¹⁸

The find was announced in the press on 10 January 1948, and Puech presented a brief account of its provenance to the *Académie des Inscriptions et Belles-Lettres* on 20 February.¹⁹ The codices were named after the nearby city Nag Hammadi immediately, although Doresse in particular continued to refer to the discovery site as Chénoboskion, the Greek name of the modern hamlet al-Qasr. A connection was quickly made with the possible identification nearby of the ruins of a monastery, which Robinson suggested was encouraged by the discovery of the Dead Sea Scrolls near an apparent monastery in 1946/7.²⁰ Yet 'Ali's story changed considerably over the years; the best-known version (as recounted above) dates from the 1970s, but the version told to Jean Doresse in 1950 had the jar found in a cemetery in Qasr es-Sayyad.²¹ There was also equivocation over whether the codices were found in one or more jars, all of which suggests that the Nag Hammadi 'library' is likely ill-named – rather than a monastic collection, this was several collections belonging to a number of different private individuals.²² This explains a number of problematic features of the collection but also undermines some of the popular ideas about them. As Dillon suggests, however, the later popularity of the monastery origin story is likely due more to its fit with the popular idea of Gnosticism as a lost 'true' Christianity than any historical reasons.²³

The Nag Hammadi collection consists of eleven complete codices and fragments of two others, totalling more than a thousand pages and fifty-two more or less complete texts. These texts, most previously unknown, include gospels (*of Truth, Thomas* and *Philip*), doctrinal treatises (*Hypostasis of the Archons, On the Origin of the World*), liturgical texts (*The Prayer of Thanksgiving*) and an oddly translated section of Plato's *Republic*. They are written in Coptic, the local *lingua franca* of the day, transcribed using the Greek alphabet, and date from around four hundred CE, although in most cases the texts would have been composed much earlier. Two facts were assumed from the moment of the discovery in 1945 and continue to influence their interpretation today – the Nag Hammadi codices were a single collection, a 'corpus' or 'library', and they were the product of a group of Gnostics.

Most scholars today accept that the majority of the texts can be divided into two groups along doctrinal lines – Sethian and Valentinian – although there is some disagreement over which texts belong to which group.[24] Several of the texts are duplicated, and these facts together strengthen the thesis that the Nag Hammadi collection is not a single collection or library of a single group but was in fact made up of several smaller collections. However, the doctrinal distinctions don't match the paleographic evidence in any clear way, although significantly none of the groupings contain duplicate copies of the same text.[25] The cartonnage – scrap paper used in the construction of the bindings – tells us nothing that would help to clarify further but does give us a *terminus post quem* of the fourth century for the binding of the codices.[26]

Rejecting the idea of the texts as a collection explains these features – they are different because they belonged to different people, possibly at different periods. This is reinforced by the Egyptian context, as there was a long tradition of the burial of 'funerary texts'. The significance of this is that we need to look at the collection not as the product of a self-contained and possibly marginal group, but in a much broader context as texts owned by ordinary people alongside more conventional texts. It also means we can consider them together with the texts in the Bruce, Askew and Berlin codices as examples of the complexity and range of texts in use in the early Christian era.[27] The codices show the influence of Jewish, Hermetic, Platonic and even Zoroastrian ideas, and several texts are without any Christian imagery or language whatsoever. In fact, the codices seem to be evidence of a syncretic upsurge of religious fervor and innovation in the few centuries on either side of the birth of Jesus, an upsurge that may also have produced Christianity, Rabbinic Judaism and the Essenes and which took place in what Lim calls the 'common sectarian matrix' of prophecies and texts.[28]

Perhaps most significantly of all, none of these texts contained the self-designation *gnostikos*. Prior to the discovery, scholars could argue that the absence of self-designation was simply a lack of *any* evidence, but this was no longer the case.[29] The upshot of this was that socio-historical definitions were weakened as a rational for the category Gnosticism; typological definitions would thereafter become pre-eminent.

Yet this evidence took a long time before it began to challenge long-held preconceptions about the Gnostics and indeed is still resisted today by some biblical scholars and – far more vehemently – by some scholars of the History of Religions, who had co-opted Gnosticism long before Nag Hammadi was discovered and in fact made great efforts to keep control of the narrative surrounding the corpus – with some success, as we shall see. Moreover, many scholars continued to base their definitions in secondary sources (such as Irenaeus or the Manichaean texts), seeking support for these in the primary sources, rather than basing these definitions in the primary sources.

Quispel heard about the texts from Puech in the spring of 1948 and met Jean and Marianne Doresse in Paris later that year. They told him that Codex I, the single Nag Hammadi codex separated from the others, had been purchased by a Cairo antiquities dealer named Joseph Albert Eid, who had already offered it for sale, unsuccessfully, to the Boston Museum of Fine Arts and the Bibliotheque Nationale in Paris.[30] After discussions at the 1948 Eranos meeting between Quispel, Puech and John D. Barrett, editor of the Bollingen Series, the Mellons began discussions with the Doresses towards purchasing the 'Eid Codex'.[31] At the end of 1948, Eid exported the codex briefly to New York and then to Belgium – illegally, according to some, but certainly sub rosa.[32] While in New York, he offered the codex to the Mellon's Bollingen Foundation. The asking price of $12,000 was too high, however, and Eid died in 1950 before a deal could be reached, though Puech, Quispel and the Bollingen Foundation continued to negotiate with his estate.[33]

In early 1951, Quispel was invited to give a series of lectures at the C. G. Jung Institute in Zurich on the subject of the new finds, which were quickly published as *Gnosis als Weltreligion* (1951).[34] It argues that gnosis (and here he follows the European tradition of using 'Gnosis' to refer to the tradition) began in Alexandria and expanded to become a 'world religion' that spread throughout the Mediterranean during Late Antiquity, a proto–world religion, independent of and predating Christianity. In this regard, he echoes Jonas's work, although he disagreed on the centrality Jonas placed on a negative evaluation of the cosmos.[35]

But this historical account is underpinned by an essentialist narrative of which this *Weltreligion* was but one expression:

> A World Religion is newly discovered. So one might perhaps already now summarise the importance of the newly-found Gnostic manuscripts. Until now, a particular uncertainty and embarrassment has existed in the current assessment and classification of these strange things, as a result of the scantiness

of the materials and the difficulty of making the interpretation understandable. Now we see clearly, and the time is not far away when the entirety of Gnosis from its beginning to the outflowing, its phenomenological-physiognomical roots, can be worked out.[36]

Note that, despite the specific identification with Nag Hammadi, Quispel has not yet read any of those texts, instead working entirely from Jean Doresse's inventory, the errors of which he repeats and compounds by building further assumptions on top of them.[37] Despite this, Quispel was sure that the Nag Hammadi texts would prove his theory that Gnosticism had a Jewish origin *and also* the reality of Jung's theory of archetypes.[38] Although framed as a historical narrative – 'from its source to its outpouring' – Quispel nevertheless presents gnosis as a perennial essence, 'a basic structure of religious apprehension, a religious possibility among other ones, which emerges ever again from time to time'.[39] It is an experience of remembering our divine origin and nature.[40] Moreover, it is a 'secret knowledge of the concealed connectedness of the universe, an esoteric tradition of primordial wisdom, revealed to humanity by the gods; it is the revelation of the sense of our being in the world.'[41] Interestingly, he is not using Jungian terminology at this point, though this would become a central feature of his work in the future. The second edition of *Gnosis als Weltreligion,* for example, refers to gnosis as 'the mythical expression of the encounter with the self.'[42]

Jung, on Quispel's urging, wrote to the Bollingen Foundation in March 1951, putting further pressure on them to purchase Codex I. A plan was finally agreed at that year's Eranos meeting (which as fate would have it would be Jung's last year presenting) – the Bollingen Foundation would provide the money (although their involvement was to be kept secret), and the manuscript was to be returned to the Coptic Museum after publication.[43] In return, the C. G. Jung Institute would be provided with several further pages (usually referred to as 'the missing 40 pages') which were believed to be part of the Cairo collection. Puech kept Doresse in the dark during these negotiations. The Bollingen Foundation eventually pulled out, due to concerns over the legality of its exportation, which might impact their other activities in Egypt, but the C. G. Jung Institute stepped in and put up the money.[44] Quispel took possession of the manuscript on 9 May 1952, and the Eid Codex was immediately sent for conservation in Plexiglass and photographed.[45]

The codex consists of four compositions which were largely complete – the *Apocryphon of James*; the *Gospel of Truth,* which Quispel had decided was Valentinian and, indeed, the actual text of that name mentioned by Irenaeus,

Figure 3: Puech, Quispel and Michel Malinine examining the Jung Codex. Reprinted with the permission of Lemniscaat Publishing House, Rotterdam.

on the strength of a quick read of a single page;[46] the *Letter to Rheginos*; and the *Treatise on the Three Natures* – as well as the first leaf of a fifth, *Prayer of the Apostle Paul*, the remainder of which was assumed to be in the missing forty pages.[47] The codex had had a leather cover at one point, but by the purchase in 1952, this had disappeared. It later reappeared in the early 1970s; Robinson suspects that the Doresses possessed it all along.[48]

President of the Jung Institute Carl Meier's plan was to have a volume translating the complete codex ready for Jung's birthday in July 1953. This was unrealistically ambitious; eventually, an early draft of the French translation of just the *Gospel of Truth* was ready by 1953. Moreover, the translation team were unable to gain access to the missing forty pages, which included four pages from the *Gospel of Truth*. Nevertheless, Codex I – now renamed the 'Jung Codex' – was dedicated to Jung on 15 November 1953, in a lavish ceremony two days before his eightieth birthday, at which both Quispel and Puech gave presentations.[49] It was largely ceremonial; Jung would not take possession, and the arrangement was merely temporary.

A slim volume of essays, edited by Frank L. Cross, was published by Mowbray in 1955, and a critical edition of the *Gospel of Truth* by Quispel and Puech was published by Rascher Verlag in 1956. Neither included text from the missing forty pages. These early commentaries show that the texts were immediately interpreted according to the perennial, phenomenological, psychologized model established at Eranos. In his foreword to the 1955 edition, Puech describes gnosis as

> a psychological experience lived or imagined by him and which means for him the Advent to Knowledge, and, in a word, to Salvation? What, fundamentally, is Gnosis? An experience or a theory which has reference to some definite interior mental happening, destined to become an inamissible [sic] and inalienable state whereby in the course of an illumination, which is regeneration and divinization, man is re-established in himself, again remembers himself and becomes conscious of himself, of what he really is by nature and origin. In this way he knows or reknows himself in God, knows God and becomes conscious of himself as God.[50]

Yet he hopes that

> the collection will put our knowledge of Gnosticism on an entirely new footing. In place of the indirect accounts of the anti-heretical writers, which were more or less suspect of simplification or hostility, and of the small amount of Christian or Christianizing Gnostic literature, which had hitherto been preserved in Greek, we shall henceforth have at our disposal a large mass of documents. They come to us directly from the very circles that produced or possessed them and by their number, extent and quality infinitely surpass the few productions of an already decadent Gnosticism which we hitherto possessed in Coptic.[51]

Noble aims, to be sure, although as we will see, unsettling established categories are easier said than done. Here Puech begins with the category of Gnosticism intact, looks forward to reading gnostic texts and, like DeConick or Pagels, is sure that the heresiologists *misrepresented* them, not *invented* them. The texts were read, then as now, in that light.

Jung, too, was effusive about its contents:

> The discovery of authentic Gnostic texts is, especially for the direction our research is taking, of the greatest interest, all the more so in that it is not only of a theoretical but also of a practical nature. If we seek genuine psychological understanding of the human being of our own time, we must know the spiritual history absolutely. We cannot reduce him to mere biological data, since he is not by nature merely biological but is a product also of spiritual presuppositions.[52]

Like Puech, his hope for the collection is in no way modest – giving unprecedented knowledge of 'spiritual history' in order to gain 'genuine psychological understanding of modern humans'. He was less happy that the codex was being dedicated to him, however, and even threatened not to attend the presentation in a letter to Carl Meier:

> I do not want to come into the false light of a conceited person seeking recognition, which without fail threatens me. ... I hence ask you to be so kind as to leave out of account the participation of my person in every regard. I do not want to be the center of the celebration, nor do I want the Codex to be baptised in my name.[53]

We might speculate that at this point Quispel was attempting to co-opt Jung's fame to further his own career: he sought to dominate the editorial board, even to the detriment of the project[54], and sought to gain editorial control of the publication of all thirteen codices.[55] That said, it is clear that Jung and his interpretation of Gnosticism were a profound influence on Quispel and through him on all of the first generation of post–Nag Hammadi scholars. Quispel can legitimately be considered one of the driving forces in the decades-long efforts to make the codices available to scholars and the public. Quispel even enrolled the help of Queen Juliana of the Netherlands (1909–2004) to help broker a deal with the Egyptian government to regain the missing pages.[56] This was ultimately unsuccessful, but Quispel's work led directly to the formation of the International Committee of Gnosticism specifically to oversee the publication of the codices; it included both Puech and Quispel, Jean Doresse (who ultimately could not afford to attend), Meier of the C. G. Jung Institute and Pahor Labib of the Cairo Antiquities Museum, and met in Cairo from 29 September to 27 October 1956. Quispel also brokered the deal with Brill to publish a facsimile edition of the codices, although ultimately this never happened.[57] After protracted wrangling, the originals of the *Gospel of Truth* were returned to Cairo in October 1975.

Quispel and Puech were also among the editors of the first English translation of the *Gospel of Thomas*, published in 1959.[58] Yet the Nag Hammadi texts remained largely inaccessible, due to a squabble between French and German scholars. Only French scholars were granted access while the French Abbot Étienne Drioton was in charge of the Department of Antiquities in Egypt; after the French were expelled following the Second Arab-Israeli War in 1956, the assignments were given only to Germans by the new, Berlin-trained museum director, Pahor Labib. A move was made by the disgruntled French to pass control of the project over to UNESCO to publish photographic facsimiles and thus make the material available to international scholars, but this became mired in bureaucracy and inertia, and all but ground to a halt until the 1970s.[59]

For many of the scholars already fascinated by Gnosticism, Nag Hammadi provided an opportunity to support their presuppositions, often inherited from Theosophy, Jung or Heidegger. The result of the three-decade-delay in publication was that the Nag Hammadi texts were used to bolster the idea of Gnosticism, without being troubled by the broader categorical challenges its contents imply. The lack of publication did nothing to slow its popularity, and in fact only added to its mystery, while leaving it so pliable in the absence of data as to signify almost anything.

6

A revolt against history: Gnostic scholarship, after Nag Hammadi

Jonas gave his opinion of the Nag Hammadi texts in 1962 in the *Journal of Religion*, writing with foresight that 'if the picture becomes more blurred instead of more clear, this would be part of the truth of the matter'.[1] Yet this wasn't exactly what happened. Gnosticism, it seems, had now gained unstoppable momentum. More, Jonas was a large part of the reason – having given Gnosticism a centre by defining it essentially, he opened the door to an ever-widening gyre of essentialist models.

In particular, Gnosticism was adopted by a group of mostly German, mostly Jewish émigré scholars working in fields as diverse as philosophy, history, political science and literary criticism. Nevertheless, the assumptions and methodologies of the History of Religions school were their primary influences, as this chapter will show. The challenges of the Nag Hammadi corpus are routinely ignored; terminology from Jung and particularly Jonas is ubiquitous; the methodology remains predominantly phenomenological with a historical gloss.

A new motif became dominant, in which Gnosticism is used to critique modernity in general, perhaps even to diagnose modernity. Whereas before Gnosticism represented an existential malaise (for both Jung and Jonas), now it came to represent a critique of what had gone wrong in the twentieth century – and the Holocaust in particular. The scholars considered in this chapter each considered the divine to have retreated from the world, because of Nazism, or Communism, or technology, or secularization, and each drew the comparison with Gnosticism. Pre-war, most were interested in Gnosticism to establish the normative identity of Christianity; post-war, the main concern shifted to establishing the normative identity of modernity.[2] Just as Jonas saw Gnosticism as the cause of alienation, and Jung its cure, these historians were divided on whether Gnosticism was cause or symptom of the horrors of modernity. All agreed, however, that one way or another they were living in a Gnostic Age.

As early as 1924, Jung had written that the First World War had fundamentally challenged our relationship to the world:

> The revolution in our conscious outlook, brought about by the catastrophic results of the World War, shows itself in our inner life by the shattering of our faith in ourselves and our own worth. ... I realize only too well that my faith in the rational organization of the world – that old dream of the millennium when peace and harmony reign – has grown pale.³

After the Second World War, however, the problem of evil became a prime concern for him, evidenced by his *Answer to Job* (1952). The book was written quickly but was the culmination of many years of thought on the Book of Job and what it said about theodicy – which is to say, the problem of evil. It asks how an omnipotent, benevolent God can be reconciled with the treatment that Job receives from the Devil, with God's mandate. Part of the answer that Jung presents is that Jesus and Satan are brothers, both equally agents of God's will, an idea he claims to have drawn from Clement of Rome.⁴ More interesting, perhaps, is the conclusion that he draws from this – that God does not act consciously. The treatment meted out on Job and, indeed, the creation of the world, is 'the behaviour of an unconscious being who cannot be judged morally'.⁵ As such, however, God's actions are not *im*moral. Jung then argues that Job's refusal to lose faith *causes* the change we see between the wrathful God of the Old Testament and the God of love in the New. Because of Job, God incarnates as Jesus, and the answer to Job is the cry from the cross: my God, why hast thou forsaken me? At that moment, 'his human nature reaches divinity; God then discovers what it means to be a mortal man and drinks to the dregs the sufferings He imposed on His loyal servant Job.'⁶

Shortly after its publication, the German theologian Martin Buber published a piece in the journal *Merkur*, in which he argued that the subjectivity of the modern world was preventing connection to the transcendent.⁷ Buber had read *Septum Sermones ad Mortuos* and thought that by making the true self identical with God, Jung made the Old Testament God into a demiurge – something that Gershom Scholem seems to have considered true of Gnosticism more broadly.⁸ Buber accused Jung of being a Gnostic, but from Buber, this did not carry the rebellious charm it had among his Eranos colleagues. For Buber, gnosis – 'and not atheism, which annihilates God because it must reject the hitherto existing images of God – is the real antagonist of the reality of faith'.⁹ Wasserstrom suggests that the Jewish Buber was incensed that the German Jung seemed to be blaming the Hebrew God for the Holocaust, less than a decade after the fact.[10]

But Jung was still ruminating on Gnosticism and the problem of evil in one of the last writings of his life, the 'Late Thoughts' chapter of *Memories, Dreams, Reflections*. Jung states that in the twentieth century, 'evil has become a determinant reality'.[11] While Jung suggests that this 'violent eruption' was the Nazi regime – an 'outpouring of evil [that] revealed to what extent Christianity has been undermined in the twentieth century' – he adds that this 'naked evil has assumed apparently permanent form in the Russian nation'.[12] After again speculating on Job, he develops further the idea that God may not have been conscious while creating the world, now stating that God was conscious neither of himself nor of his creation, and had no plan.

On the whole, however, these gnostic critics of modernity – or sometimes critics of gnostic modernity, like Buber – were inspired less by Jung's model of Gnosticism than by Hans Jonas's. Perhaps this was in part because he shared with them the Jewish experience, and partly because he had outlined the contemporary parallels in *Gnosis und Spätantiker Geist* before the war. But I think most importantly it was because Jonas detached Gnosticism from history altogether.

After fighting in the 1948 Arab-Israeli War, Jonas left Israel, finally settling in Montreal in 1949. His research had by now moved on to the ethical issues around technology, a project which culminated in *The Imperative of Responsibility: In Search of an Ethics for the Technological Age* (1984). He now felt unable to return to complete the planned third volume of *Gnosis und Spätantiker Geist*, although Nag Hammadi, and the encouragement of the elderly Bultmann, provided the impetus to publish the second volume, written and typeset already by 1935, in 1954.[13] Instead of a third volume, he wrote *The Gnostic Religion* (1958), which was essentially a precis of the same argument, but was 'different in scope, in organisation, and in literary intention'.[14] More specifically, it was in English, much shorter, and aimed at a non-specialist audience. It sold very well, and even though scholars had been aware of his thesis since 1935, it was through *The Gnostic Religion* that a simplified, phenomenological version of Gnosticism entered popular discourse in English.

In the introduction, Jonas writes that his intention is to produce a philosophical *interpretation*, 'to grasp the spirit that spoke out of these voices, and ... to give a comprehensible unity back to the amazing diversity' and presenting this for 'our human understanding in general'.[15] This was an utterly phenomenological analysis, then, concerned with timeless essences and general types, and aimed at the spiritual benefit of humanity:

> That there was a gnostic spirit, and therefore *an essence of Gnosticism as a whole*, was the impression which struck me at my initial encounter with the evidence, and it deepened with increasing intimacy.[16]

Less obviously, there was a shift in Jonas's methodological approach – despite the philosophical terminology, *The Gnostic Religion* is actually based in the psychology of religion, rather than the existential analysis of *Gnosis und Spätantiker Geist*.[17] On close reading, we can find suggestions of a Jungian influence – for example, in his translation of 'pneuma' as 'inner self', as opposed to 'soul' or 'psyche'.[18] In fact, this version of Jonas's thesis is almost entirely stripped of Heideggerian terminology. He had by now broken with Heidegger, both personally and intellectually, and spoke publicly against his former *Doktorvater* in a speech before a group of theologians at Drew University in 1964.[19] The keynote – which Jonas was asked to give after Heidegger himself pulled out – castigated Heidegger for his Nazism and stressed the Paganism of his philosophy.[20]

In fact, it was clear from his 1952 paper 'Gnosticism and Modern Nihilism' that his position on the relationship of Gnosticism to existentialism had changed dramatically. The paper addressed the reconciliation of God with a post-Holocaust existence, and in it he argued that God was not absent, but was nevertheless powerless to intervene in human affairs. Jonas now saw Gnosticism as the root of the nihilism which was causing the crises facing the modern world.[21] Where before the war he had seen Gnosticism as anticipating Heideggerian philosophy, he now also saw Heidegger as a modern-day gnostic.[22]

Yet despite his firmly critical position on nihilism and existentialism, his attitude to Gnosticism was more complex. Some scholars have written of his later work as his 'overcoming' of Gnosticism,[23] though it is clear that he still feels the pull of its strange charm:

> Something in Gnosticism knocks at the door of our Being and of our twentieth-century Being in particular. Here is humanity in a crisis and in some of the radical possibilities of choices that man can make concerning his view of his position in the world, of his relation to himself, to the absolute and to his mortal Being. And there is certainly something in Gnosticism that helps one to understand humanity better than one would understand it if one had never known of Gnosticism.[24]

From later comments, it seems that Jonas came to associate the technological nihilism he perceived in modernity as associated with the archons (the demiurgic rulers of the physical world), rather than the Gnostics themselves, and in fact, he seems to pit himself with the Gnostics against Archontic nihilistic modernity.[25] Gnosticism now offers an answer to the problems of modernity – or at least, it is a metaphor that Jonas cannot help falling back into. Existentialism, on the other hand, offers only 'the absolute vacuum, the really bottomless pit'.[26]

Like his friend Gershom Scholem, Jonas now saw Gnosticism as fundamentally and theologically anti-Semitic – again perhaps encouraged by his break with Heidegger and the memory of the Holocaust.[27] For Jonas, Judaism was the paragon of legal observance and morality, which the Gnostics rejected.[28] The God of the Jews was good and created a good world, but the Gnostics inverted this by painting the Jewish God as the deranged and evil demiurge:

> The *Deus absconditus*, the hidden god (not to speak of the absurd God) is a profoundly un-Jewish conception ... a completely hidden God is not an acceptable concept by Jewish norms.[29]

This issue of the *Deus absconditus* gave new urgency to the question of Jewish origins: how could this gnostic modernity (or modern Gnosticism) give rise to the Holocaust if it was, in essence and origin, Jewish?

Nevertheless, Jonas and Scholem both remained committed to an early Jewish origin for Gnosticism and openly critical of scholarship which argued for an Eastern origin. Yet there was clearly an uncomfortable implication here – a Judaism which rejects the law and paints Yahweh as insane or evil must have been a profoundly alienated Judaism indeed. This was not an unusual view among scholars – Robert M. Grant, for example, placed the origins of Gnosticism in the failure or prophecy brought on by the destruction of the Temple and the failure of the Bar Kochba revolt in the first half of the second century CE.[30] Birger Pearson, too, wrote of Gnosticism as 'a movement of Jews away from their own traditions', a view shared by Kurt Rudolph.[31]

Quispel challenged Jonas on this issue of gnostic origins at the 1964 meeting of the Society of Biblical Literature in Nashville, Tennessee, which had the theme of 'The Bible in Modern Scholarship'. Although framed as though it will address the Nag Hammadi discovery directly, Quispel's paper, 'Gnosticism and the New Testament', instead argues that a doctrinal anti-Semitism does not mean that Gnosticism cannot still originate with Jews. He dismisses Geo Widengren and others' focus on the Redeemed Redeemer and therefore an Iranian origin as 'apodictic and uncritical', before suggesting – via a quote from Gershom

Scholem's *Jewish Gnosticism* – that this is due to an ignorance of Jewish sources.[32] Rather, he writes,

> Gnosticism is not a late chapter of the history of Greek philosophy and therefore a Christian heresy, an acute Hellenization of the Christian religions. Nor is it a fossilized survival of old Iranian or even Indian concepts, and certainly it is not derived from a supposed, consistent Iranian myth of the Saved Savior. It is rather a religion of its own, with its own phenomenological structure, characterized by the mythical expression of self-experience through the revelation of the 'Word', or, in other words, an awareness of a tragic split within the Deity itself. And as such, it owes not a little to Judaism.[33]

Jonas responded by arguing that while Gnosticism may certainly have been a reaction against Judaism, to argue that this was its sole origin and that this reaction was by Jews themselves took 'too narrow a view of Gnosticism [and] its autonomy as a spiritual cause'.[34] Again appealing to Scholem's *Jewish Gnosticism*, Jonas argues that there are no gnostic texts in Hebrew and no Jewish names.[35] Quoting Rudolf Otto, he concludes:

> I will keep an open mind but will not lower my price. A Gnosticism without a fallen god, without benighted creator and sinister creation, without alien soul, cosmic captivity and acosmic salvation, without the self-redeeming of the Deity – in short: a Gnosis without divine tragedy will not meet the specifications. … A Gnosis merely of the heavenly palaces, of the mystical ascent, the ecstatic vision of the Throne, of the awesome secrets of the divine majesty – in short: a *monotheistic* Gnosis of the *mysterium numinosum et tremendum*, important as it is in its own right, is a different matter altogether.[36]

Nag Hammadi was discovered just six months after the liberation of the Nazi concentration camps and the end of the Second World War. It is hard to overstate the impact of these events on the intellectual discourse of the day. Ginzburg refers to a wave of 'writings from Year Zero', written between 1940 and 1945 and emerging from the shared experience of the apparent imminent collapse of civilization. Ginzburg includes works by Walter Benjamin, Marc Bloch, Horkheimer and Adorno,[37] and we might well include Hannah Arendt in that list. Arendt insightfully set out the difference between the post–First World War and post–Second World War eras: the banality of Nazi evil showed that 'the problem of evil will be the fundamental question of postwar intellectual life in Europe – as death became the fundamental problem after the last war'.[38]

The fact is that for these Jewish scholars – many of whom had an interest in apocalyptic thinking – the Holocaust was, in Anson Rabinbach's apt phrase, 'the nonredemptive apocalypse'.[39] The question of *theodicy* runs like a leitmotif through the post–Nag Hammadi writings on Gnosticism. The term was introduced by Leibniz in his 1710 work, *Essais de Théodiceé*, to indicate reasoned defences as to why a universe created by an omnipotent, benevolent God includes evil and suffering. In other words, if God rewards the good, why do bad things happen to good people? For medieval scholastic theologians, like Thomas Aquinas and Augustine of Hippo, evil was simply the absence of good, the *privatio boni*, and so they blamed human free will for the existence of evil.[40] But Auschwitz, as Adorno would later write, made 'a mockery of the construction of immanence as endowed with a meaning'.[41] Consider Birger Pearson's interpretation of the Nag Hammadi text, *Testimony of Truth*:

> One can hear in this text echoes of existential despair arising in circles of the people of the Covenant faced *a crisis of history, with the apparent failure of the God of history*: 'What kind of God is this?' (48:1); 'These things he has said [and done, *failed to do*] to those who believe in him and serve him!' (48, 13ff.). Such expressions are not without parallels in our own generation of history 'after Auschwitz'.[42]

Jonas's answer (in 'The Problem of God after Auschwitz') was:

> Through the years that 'Auschwitz' raged God remained silent. The miracles that did occur came forth from man alone: the deeds of those solitary, mostly unknown 'just of the nations' who did not shrink from utter sacrifice in order to help, to save, to mitigate-even, when nothing else was left, unto sharing Israel's lot. Of them I shall speak again. But God was silent. And there I say, or my myth says, not because he chose not to, but because he could not intervene did he fail to intervene. For reasons decisively prompted by contemporary experience, I entertain the idea of a God who for a time – the time of the ongoing world process – has divested himself of any power to interfere with the physical course of things.'[43]

God had not abandoned the Jewish people, yet neither was He unable to control evil. In short, for Jonas, the Holocaust showed that God was not omnipotent. Here, Jonas seems a Jewish Gnostic in a world which is indeed evil, but it is the transcendent *Deus absconditis*, not the immanent demiurge, who is the God of the Jews.

For the scholars who adopted Jonas's model to critique post-Auschwitz modernity, Gnosticism and eschatology were interchangeable. Apocalypses and millennial dreams rely equally on the idea of some earthly and temporal evil from which one can be delivered, and for Jonas, Hans Blumenberg and Eric Voegelin, Gnosticism was simply the ultimate version of that, where temporal, earthly existence was inherently evil.[44] For them, any modern worldview that is pessimistic about secular modernity, yet yearns for redemption is therefore – metaphorically or literally – Gnosticism.

In part, this was because Jonas's ideas about the relationship between Gnosticism and modernity were incorporated into an ongoing debate about secularism.[45] Many German philosophers argued that the roots of secular modernity could paradoxically be found in theological thought and in particular that modernity's focus on progress and freedom was a secularized form of Christian eschatology. The debate had already begun between the wars in the demythologized eschatology of Rudolf Bultmann and the messianism of Gershom Scholem and Walter Benjamin, but it gained a new impetus after the Holocaust. Karl Löwith's definition of modernism as 'secularized eschatology' is the purest version of this thesis, published in 1949, although he had developed the argument in papers from the early 1940s.[46] The basic reasoning behind this equation has a simple logic:

> The eschatological notion of salvation is only conceivable assuming the existence of some form of worldly evil from which humanity has to be delivered. Thus eschatology implied deep pessimism about the present state of the world, which, according to these German thinkers, gave rise to Gnosticism's metaphysical rejection of all immanent reality as godless, fallen, and evil. Connecting modern thought to eschatology and Gnosticism essentially implied that secular modernity adheres to a deeply pessimistic worldview and to a theological concept of salvation.[47]

For Löwith – a student of Heidegger at Marburg with Jonas and Arendt – this meant that the Christian salvation of each believer in a spiritual sense is converted in modern thought into a collective salvation in a material sense. The transcendent perfect world is made immanent and historical. Löwith (who was Christian, despite Jewish descent) argued that this was a corruption of the Christian message, and he argued that this rejection of its transcendent message would lead ultimately to nihilism and purposelessness.[48] Jacob Taubes had argued essentially the same thing in 1947, using apocalypticism and Gnosticism for his more pessimistic take on modern secular eschatology.[49] Interestingly, both Jonas and Löwith considered Taubes to have plagiarized their work.[50] Nevertheless, his pithy phrase 'no spiritual investment in the world as it is' sums up the philosophers' diagnoses of the modern world, and perhaps their own moral plight too.[51]

But Taubes was receptive to the revolutionary potential of gnostic apocalypticism and indeed saw it as a legitimate and necessary aspect of modernity. It was not a corruption or degraded form of theology, but its next developmental stage.[52] We have already seen that Gershom Scholem, too, saw 'gnostic' heresy as a vital force in the history of Judaism. Their contemporary, the political historian Eric Voegelin (1901–1985), would argue precisely the opposite, however. Voegelin, a Catholic German national then teaching at the Louisana State University, had already argued in *Die Politischen Religionen* (1939) that mass political movements such as National Socialism and Marxism should be considered religious movements; in his major 1952 work, *The New Science of Politics*, he applied the term 'Gnosticism' to them. He defined 'political gnosis' as an attempt to replace this corrupt world (in the sense of human systems) with a new realm through revolutionary means, 'the pathological attempt to make a realm of transcendent perfection historically immanent'.[53]

Given that his thesis became highly influential in conservative circles in the United States, the identification of political gnosis as 'a pathological tumour'[54] is interesting, as it echoes Richard Hofstadter's pathologizing of dissent from the political centre as 'the Paranoid Style' in his famous 1964 *New Yorker* article. Thus, Voegelin's remarks can be seen as paralleling the internationalist, centrist consensus politics of the 1950s and early 1960s, which emphasized agreement on common values and downplayed the importance of struggle between different groups and classes in historical progress. Indeed, many of the things Voegelin identifies as Gnostic are simply the political movements of the left and the right from the 1930s to the 1960s – National Socialism, Communism, totalitarianism, progressivism. Totalitarianism is simply the most extreme version of this tendency within modernity, the 'journey's end of the gnostic search for a civil theology'.[55]

These arguments, however, all confuse Gnosticism with apocalyptic and millennial thought in general – an error which Voegelin himself seems to have realized in his later work.[56] In 1968's 'Science, Politics and Gnosticism', he defines gnosis as 'the experience of the world as an alien place into which man has strayed and from which he must find his way back home to the other world',[57] clearly inspired by Hans Jonas's existentialist reading, although as Hanegraaff notes, he seems to still hold to the old definition in practice, and this new one is perhaps intended to deflect criticism that he has misunderstood Gnosticism.[58] In fact, he continued to apply it more and more widely – for Voegelin, Marxism and positivism and psychoanalysis were all equally gnostic. Modernity was the Gnostic Age.[59]

For the philosopher and historian of ideas Hans Blumenberg, on the other hand, modernity was a reaction *against* the return of Gnosticism. In the historical outline the *Legitimacy of the Secular Age*, the history of Gnosticism is a history of theodicies.[60] Gnostic theodicy is simple and powerful – God isn't responsible for evil, a lesser god is – but its dualism and challenge to the Trinity made it unacceptable to early Christian theologians, as we saw in Chapter 2. Blumenberg argued that Gnosticism had been overcome when Augustine of Hippo's argument that human free will, and not God, produced evil was institutionalized in the scholastic school of philosophy/theology. But for Blumenberg, scholasticism had an inherent contradiction; it posited the immanent presence of God in the world, but at the same time insisted on God's transcendence and omnipotence. As a result of this 'failure', Gnosticism had returned again in the medieval period with Franciscan William of Ockham's nominalism, which denied that abstract concepts were ontological entities, and so reaffirmed the radical transcendence and absolute omnipotence of God. But modernity, ushered in by modern philosophy, and specifically Descartes, was the 'second overcoming of Gnosticism', as it returned the responsibility for salvation to humans, rather than a remote, inscrutable creator.[61] So in Blumenberg's reading, secular modernity does not mean that that world is therefore devoid of meaning, but rather that humanity is now free to address their finitude and embrace their potential within it.

As Bruce Lincoln writes, 'Struggles about the stories of the past may also be struggles over the proper shape of society in the present'.[62] Lincoln is writing about the interpretation of mythical narratives, but this applies just as well to the *study* of mythical narratives. And it is clear that post-war scholarship on Gnosticism reflects concerns about society in the post-war decades and the role of religion in it. In the more openly theological versions, we see a clear desire to reject modernity post-Auschwitz and post-Hiroshima, and return to a less technological and capitalist age. This also implies both a rejection (or at least limiting) of scientific materialism and a return to religion – renewed, reenchanted and removed from institutions.

More than simply a rejection of modernity, for many of these scholars, Gnosticism was a rejection of history itself. Taubes described it as 'an escape out of time and out of history' and thus the opposite of worldly, temporal politics.[63] Eliade (though he didn't use the term 'gnosis') called it 'the terror of history', the degrading temporality of the profane world, which could be escaped only through the cyclical renewal of and through myths and rituals, a drive to supplant rational, linear history with a mythic metahistory.[64] Wasserstrom puts it better than I can:

> The problem with a gnostic History of Religions is that it imposes patterns on the past that were never (demonstrably) there in order to draw lessons for a present that isn't (demonstrably) here. This ahistorical recycling, this eternal return of the same, suggest a gnosis arrogated to the historian by an a priori disgust with modernity, not by research into reality.[65]

Indeed, Ginzburg's 'writings from Year Zero' all, in one way or another, concern history. In their struggle to find a meaning in recent history, they were driven to ask, 'Does history have a meaning?'[66]

As such, Gnosticism may have had another appeal. For those in the religionist camp, gnosis was a perennial sui generis experience underlying all authentic religion and like Eliade's hierophanies – a term which Voegelin adopted – transcends human historical understanding. Gnostic revelation was, for Martin Buber, outside history – and indeed, this 'lack of a history is a mark of those higher experiences that cannot be communicated.'[67]

7

Tongues and misunderstandings: Messina 1966

Messina sits at the north-eastern point of Sicily, where the island is closest to mainland Italy, just three miles away across a narrow, shallow strait. The strait's most powerful current runs from the Ionian Sea in the south to the Tyrrhenian Sea in the north, but every six hours it switches to a smaller current running in the opposite direction. The powerful currents have long been regarded as treacherous to ships and may even have inspired Homer's Scylla and Charybdis.

Existential and Jungian currents came together at the 1966 Messina Congress of the International Association for the History of Religions (IAHR), where Gnosticism and gnosis were formally defined for the first time. It would be an obvious assumption to make that the congress was a response to the publication of the Nag Hammadi corpus, but in fact their publication was only just beginning in 1966, and the definitions produced simply codified pre–Nag Hammadi understandings. While these definitions have never been widely accepted and have all but disappeared from scholarly usage today, the split between a historically bounded religion called Gnosticism and an ahistorical gnostic essence continues to dominate discourse on Gnosticism, in academia and in the religious field. In the Messina definitions, we see the second stage of the category's essentialization – from a specific religion to a perennial religious type – ratified by the academy. This chapter considers this moment of competing narratives to consider the complex relationship between primary sources, academics and practitioners in category formation and how zombie categories can lumber on even when not supported by the data. In the chapters which follow, we will see that these definitions also continue to shape emic discourse to this day.

Seven irregular conferences were held under the name of the International Congress of the History of Religions between 1900 and 1950. At the last of these, in Amsterdam on 4–9 September 1950, the IAHR was formed, affiliated to UNESCO. The idea was first mooted in a letter from Mircea Eliade to

Raffaele Pettazzoni in April 1948, and they were the organizing force behind the formation.[1]

Gerardus van der Leeuw (1890–1950) became the inaugural president, with Raffaele Pettazzoni and Geo Widengren as vice-presidents, Claas Jouco Bleeker (1898–1983) as honorary secretary and W. A. Rijk as treasurer. The non-executive committee was completed with H. Frick, E. O. James, A. D. Nock and Henri-Charles Puech (who had also been involved in early discussions) chosen as representatives of the various countries then involved. Van der Leeuw held the presidency for only two months, as he died unexpectedly in November 1950, and was replaced by Raffaele Pettazzoni, because he was the eldest.[2] Puech took Pettazzoni's former position as second vice-president, a post he held until 1965.

At the initial meeting, Pettazzoni had proposed that Puech and Eliade should work together to establish an 'international review' to be the new organization's official journal. Puech, as we have seen, was heavily involved in the purchase and translation of the Jung Codex at this point, and when the first issue of *NUMEN* was published in 1954, it was with Pettazzoni as editor and Eliade as his assistant.[3]

Figure 4: The delegates of the VII International Congress of the History of Religions, 1950. Raffaele Pettazzoni is the short man near the centre of the front row, on the step; van der Leeuw is on his right; and Claas Jouco Bleeker is on his left. Reprinted with the permission of the International Association for the History of Religions.

It is striking how many of the founding committee members were also Eranos delegates. Inaugural president van der Leeuw attended each of the three meetings up to his death in 1950, and his successor Pettazzoni later recalled:

> I was in Ascona in 1950, I participated for three days in the ERANOS meetings, and I received a lasting impression. I do not know how much the natural beauty of the place, the serenity of the landscape that cheers the spirits and disposes them to recollection. But more than the frame and the background is the spiritual light that gives life to the picture, the current of sympathy that circulates among the defendants, lecturers and listeners, all gathered not to discuss and discuss, not to impose their own ideas, but in order to expose them and to propose them in all simplicity and frankness, in the sentiment of the common aspiration to understand and make understood the serious problems of the human spirit, of the human condition, of human life.[4]

Charles-Henri Puech, as we have seen, was a central figure in the post-war Eranos meetings, and increasingly so was Mircea Eliade. All four of these men attended the 1950 meeting. So, in the year that the discovery of the Nag Hammadi find was publicly announced, the first international society for the social-scientific study of religions was formed by men who also attended a private meeting named by Rudolf Otto, founded by Alice Bailey and centred on Carl Jung.

The IAHR was convened at a time when the various competing approaches to the study of religion – Dutch phenomenology, German *Kulturkreislehre*, Italian Historicism and so on – were beginning to coalesce institutionally under the name History of Religions. The need for the field to be better defined was keenly felt; if the History of Religions was now a discipline distinct from theology or classics, then it needed a non-confessional methodology. Article 1 of the statutes drawn up at that inaugural meeting of the IAHR states:

> The International Association for the Study of the History of Religions (I.A.S.H.R.)[5] ... is a world organisation whose aim is to promote the study of the history of religions through the international collaboration of all those whose scientific interests lie in this field.[6]

The juxtaposition here immediately suggests the methodological tension which continues in the IAHR – and indeed, the study of religion in general – until today: is the study of religion a matter of historical specifics, or timeless essences? One the one hand, we have the suggestion that the organization is based on a (social-)scientific approach; on the other, we have the History of

Religions in the title, which would increasingly become associated with a particular phenomenological approach.

We discussed the origins of phenomenology with Husserl and its adoption in the study of religion by Rudolf Otto and others in Chapter 4. However, phenomenology of religion has developed quite independently of philosophical phenomenology, despite their common ancestry, as this chapter will show. Moreover, even among phenomenologists of religion, there is considerable difference in the degree to which they understand the phenomenological method to be able to give access to the supposed sacred core of religious traditions – that is, to make ontological claims.

Chantepie de la Saussaye and Tiele, founders of the 'notorious' Dutch school of the phenomenology of religion, both sought to separate the History of Religion from theology, regarding the latter as being concerned entirely with Christianity.[7] Yet both, in their insistence on the sui generis common essence to religions, and their desire to classify in order to philosophically prove the existence of God, were clearly theological in the modern sense. Through Tiele's student William Brede Kristensen (1867–1953), who was professor of History of Religion at Leiden for thirty-six years, the Dutch school inherited an approach in which the essence of religion was to be sought through classification and phenomenological enquiry, through an empathetic phenomenological method in which 'there is no religious reality other than the faith of believers'.[8] As Jonathan Tuckett puts it:

> It is the substantive claims of this 'phenomenology' that the Sacred is part of the structure of man's consciousness: man, by his nature, directs himself towards the Sacred. The Sacred is a thing-in-itself and is therefore considered *sui generis* in the ontological (not subjective) sense.[9]

It is through van der Leeuw, Pettazzoni and Mircea Eliade that this approach to phenomenology came to dominate the History of Religions. In their work, we see a clear reflection of Protestant ideas in the construction of religion as based not in externals, but in direct experience of something inaccessible to reason alone. Here, scientific terms obscured that the phenomenological method was being employed (and adapted) in a search for theological Truth. Moreover, both scholars saw their task as being to combat the irreligious impulse which they saw – as did the German post-war philosophers of secular modernity – as part and parcel of post-Darwin science and industrialization.[10]

These various phenomenological approaches coalesced into a methodological norm known later as the phenomenology of religion, and the founding of the

IAHR enshrined phenomenology semi-officially as the de facto methodology of the History of Religions. The more scientifically minded scholars could remain unaware of the extent of Christian bias behind the original conceptions, while the more theological could pursue their metaphysical speculations under a 'scientific' banner and claim that they are discovering religion while clearly pursuing their own implicit understanding of what religion is. Despite some dissenting voices, the overall result was to lend institutional and disciplinary legitimacy to a sui generis essentialism.

Indeed, all of the original executive committee members of the IAHR (with the exception of W. A. Rijk, who was an accountant[11]) were committed phenomenologists. Pettazzoni's position was, as outlined in an article in that inaugural issue of *NUMEN*, was that history and phenomenology were 'two interdependent instruments of the same science, two forms of the science of religion, whose composite unity corresponds to that of its subject, that is to say of religion, in its two distinct components, interior experience and exterior manifestations.'[12] Pettazzoni was a supporter of phenomenology when tempered with the historical and with a domain limited to the interior of the individual. The History of Religions provided the facts of the exterior manifestations of religion, he argued, and phenomenology the meaning, but the two together must be unified in the Science of Religion. For Pettazzoni, phenomenology was the most significant innovation in the study of religion in the twentieth century – but I am with Weibe in viewing it not as its revitalization, but its subversion.[13]

Pettazzoni's presidential successor Geo Widengren was much more positivist, resisting anything claiming to be phenomenology that attempted to move away from the Husserlian 'things themselves'. In his encyclopedic *Religionsphänomenologie* (1969) – an expanded German edition of the Swedish *Religionensvärld* (1945) – he describes all speculations beyond the data as 'farfetched'. Widengren notes that, by viewing things not in themselves but as examples (or manifestations) of some larger theory or system, these essentializing phenomenologists are creating the very data they seek to describe. Phenomenology that was not absolutely empirical and based in solid historical and philological work meant 'a real danger ... that a phenomenological investigation may lead to highly superficial comparisons and therefore be absolutely misleading'.[14]

At the other end of the spectrum we find van der Leeuw and Bleeker. Both were students of William Brede Kristensen and through him inherited the Dutch phenomenological approach. Van der Leeuw's *Phanomenologie der Religion*, published in 1933, was described by Walter Capps as 'a phenomenological performance, not a discussion on phenomenology'.[15] Van der Leeuw argued that the *sine qua non* of religion was *power*, a terminology which obscures the direct influence of Otto's notion of the numinous.[16] Although van der Leeuw denied that the role of the scholar of religion was to establish the ontological reality of religions, many scholars have noted that his major concern was nevertheless integrating phenomenological comparative religion with Christian theology.[17] He famously understood phenomenology as clarifying the relationship between scholars, for whom religious power (typically, God) is the 'Object' of religion, and religious people, for whom God is the 'Subject'.[18] He argued that the subject–object distinction could be collapsed through his phenomenological method, which essentially meant the scholar understands (*versteht*) religious essence through intuition. This understanding is situated and fully involves the phenomenologist, and as a result is neither exclusively objective nor subjective (a theme we will return to when considering the work of Jeffrey Kripal in Chapter 12). It is something other, then, a third type of knowledge, not faith or objective science, but *understanding*. Or perhaps, gnosis? Indeed, van der Leeuw concludes that 'all comprehension, irrespective of whatever object it refers to, is ultimately religious; all significance sooner or later leads to ultimate significance'.[19] This, he claimed, was a 'change in direction of the history of religions'[20] – quite so: a U-turn.

Claas Jouco Bleeker (1898–1983) was actually professor of the Phenomenology of Religion at the University of Amsterdam and, like van der Leeuw, was a Dutch Reformed Church minister prior to taking up the post in 1946. He was greatly influenced by his peer van der Leeuw, more so even than their mutual *Doktorvater* Kristensen, particularly in his method of *epoché* (bracketing) and 'empathetic intuition'. Bleeker was more overtly essentialist even than van der Leeuw, however. While Bleeker stated that phenomenology could be a 'scientific method', the phenomenology he was interested in was an 'independent science' with the intent of identifying the *essence* of a given religion.[21] He sought to distance the phenomenology of religion from the philosophical phenomenology of Husserl and Heidegger, a distinction which continues among Religious Studies scholars even today.[22] He remained a staunch defender of the method, and his statement to this effect at the 1960 Marburg conference will crystalize the methodological debates in these early years of the IAHR – and the History of Religions more broadly.

These methodological debates were already well underway by the inaugural issue of *NUMEN*, where the question of what this 'phenomenology of religion' referred to was central. Bleeker writes that the 'confusion of tongues and misunderstandings' surrounding the term obscures that this is not 'the well-known philosophy of Husserl and his disciples, which bears the same name'. Rather, these phenomenologists were using *epoché* and the *eidetic vision* to establish the relationship between the 'object, namely the Holy or God' and 'the subject, i.e, man', and to establish the 'spiritual laws' upon which different religious traditions are built. He concludes by suggesting that sociology of religion illuminates the collective structures of religion and psychology of religion the individual motives of 'religious persons', but phenomenology of religion is necessary to transform 'the chaotic field of the study of the history of religions into a kind of harmonious panorama'.[23]

The debate flared up again at the 1958 Tokyo Congress, where Bleeker and Pettazzoni debated whether the IAHR should be historically oriented and non-normative, or pursue one or other religionist programme, with most placing phenomenology in the latter category. Pettazzoni died in 1959, with Geo Widengren assuming the presidency, and perhaps as a result of the new president's firmer stance on the limits of phenomenology of religion, the 1960 conference in Marburg – the alma mater of Jonas, Otto, Heidegger and Bultmann – became the site for a now-infamous statement by Bleeker. Entitled 'The Future Task of the History of Religions', it was presented to the General Assembly of international members on 17 September, the final day of the conference (although it had been circulated already). Bleeker's statement begins by expressing hope that the more truly international character of the 1958 Tokyo Congress would mean that scholars could learn from each other's approaches, but quickly moves to the *moral* imperative of the History of Religions:

> The student of the history of religions cannot fail to notice that at present a fierce struggle for the preservation of the moral and religious values of humanity is going on. It does not belong to his task as a scholar to take an attitude in this fight. However the question arises whether it is not part of his duty as a man of science and as a citizen to spread the light of his knowledge and of his insight because he is constantly occupied with the study of one of the highest human goods, namely religion. This is certainly what the ordinary man expects. Some people would even question the right of existence of the history of religions if it proves unable to provide this aid to society. All these deliberations form together a strong incitement to reconsider the fundamental principles of our discipline.[24]

He then states, apparently as a simple statement of common sense, 'The science of religion takes religious facts as part of the culture of society, that is as part of an immanent world which can be understood and clarified by human intelligence' – and lest you took that merely descriptively, he adds, 'the value of the religious truth can be understood only if we keep in mind that religion is ultimately a realisation of a transcendent truth'.[25]

This was not universally accepted by the delegates and indeed prompted a formal rebuttal in the form of a statement signed by many of the attendees, written by Raphael Zwi Werblowski – future editor of *NUMEN* (1978–91) and confirmed positivist. Yet undoubtedly, Bleeker's religionist, salvific phenomenology represented what many of the delegates believed.

Ironically, one of the signatories to Werblowski's rebuttal was Mircea Eliade. Although closely involved with the founding of the IAHR, Eliade was denied an executive role at first because he did not hold a position at an academic institution (although he would later become vice-president between 1970 and 1975).[26] During the founding of the IAHR, he was in self-imposed exile from his native Romania after the Communist regime had taken control in 1947 and was supporting himself with piecemeal writing and teaching jobs in Paris and elsewhere. By 1960, however, he had been appointed Joachim Wach's successor at the University of Chicago, where he would remain for the rest of his life, taking a professorial chair in 1964.

Eliade insisted that the scholar of religions needed to become the 'total man' and the History of Religions needed to become the 'total synthetic discipline' it ought to be.[27] Like Jung, Eliade's program was all-encompassing and not confined to his area of specialization. Indeed, Eliade's work is perhaps closer to Jung's than to his contemporaries in the IAHR. Their discursive objects are substantively the same – myth, symbol, image – and similarly leap from specific examples into flights of ahistorical comparison.[28] Eliade was a regular Eranos attendee between 1950 and 1963,[29] and while we don't know if he was in direct contact with Mead, he certainly frequented some Theosophists when he studied in India in the early 1920s (though he did not think too highly of their 'evolutionist' ideas).[30] Some of the similarity of their ideas is surely down to a similar intellectual environment (including various esoteric writings), but Eliade was clearly familiar with Jung's ideas by the 1940s. Eliade cited one of Jung's essays from a 1941 book co-written with Kerényi, *Einfürung in das Wesen der Mythologie*, in a 1943 essay, and also drew heavily on Kerényi's introductory essay.[31] We might also see Jung's influence in the title of *Archétypes et Répétitions*, the first section of Eliade's 1949 work, *Le mythe de l'éternal retour*.[32] While the oft-noted influence of far-right politics on Eliade's work is not particularly relevant here, the less-often-noted influence of various occult movements and esoteric traditions on his work certainly is.[33]

As with Jung, these influences were later downplayed; however, they were not the fleeting fascination of a peripatetic mind, but rather a formative influence which profoundly shaped the enquiry and conclusions of his later academic work.

Eliade's particular conception of the History of Religions began in the late 1920s, through his eclectic readings of classical scholars in the History of Religions, esotericists, theologians, Indian sources on yoga, Italian Renaissance philosophers, Romanian intellectuals and radical-right politicians.[34] Eliade's PhD thesis (published in 1936) was one of the first academic works on yogic techniques of ecstasy (including Tantra), for which he used the term 'gnose'.[35] For Eliade, the ultimate reality of religion – its essence – was the Sacred (the capital S underlining its ontological, not sociological, existence). The Sacred bursts into history in what Eliade called *hierophanies*, each of which is particular to its historical moment but nevertheless reveals this essence in its entirety:

> Man becomes aware of the sacred because it manifests itself, shows itself, as something wholly different from the profane. To designate the act of manifestation of the sacred, we have proposed the term hierophany. It is a fitting term, because it does not imply anything further; it expresses no more than is implicit in its etymological content, i.e., that something sacred shows itself to us. It could be said that the history of religions – from the most primitive to the most highly developed – is constituted by a great number of hierophanies, by manifestations of sacred realities.[36]

It was the task of the Historian of Religions to intuit the essence from these individual hierophanies. Therefore, the History of Religions (as Eliade termed his method) was intended to reveal ultimate *trans*-historical truth, not to detail historical facts. As he stated clearly in *Shamanism*,

> Although the historical conditions are extremely important in a religious phenomenon ... there is always a kernel that remains refractory to explanation, and this indefinable, irreducible element perhaps reveals the situation of man in the cosmos, a situation that, we shall never tire of repeating, is not solely 'historical'.[37]

As with van der Leeuw before him, *The Sacred and the Profane* (1957) drew directly on Otto; it was titled *Das Heilige und das Profane* in its original publication and quoted Otto's *Das Heilige* in its opening lines.[38] Eliade answered Otto's famous statement that those without religious sentiment could not study religion[39] with the counterclaim that *all* humans are at core religious, regardless of their own position on the matter; human beings are *homo religiosus*, with experience of the Sacred fundamental to their being. Otto and Eliade both posit a universal and invariant core to religion and claim that their methods can allow access to it.

Eliade's sacred and profane dialectic was not a sociological distinction, à la Durkheim, but rather an ontological one, à la Otto. Eliade's description of the Sacred bursting into history in the form of hierophanies is to be understood *literally*, as a description of an atemporal parallel realm, or as McCutcheon phrases it, 'an Autonomous Universe with its own Laws and Structures'.[40] As such, Eliade is making ontological, and indeed theological, claims. The hierophany is the *axis mundi* around which the world is organized, but is also a gateway between the domains, that takes a number of common forms (pillar, tree, ladder and so on). The experience of a hierophany is the foundational experience of religion, and without a hierophany there can be no religion. This theory was developed in *The Sacred and the Profane* (1957), applied cross-culturally in *Patterns of Comparative Religion* (1958) and presented in an extended case study in *Shamanism* (1951).

His writings on religion use a rhetorical, lyrical style which Dubuisson remarks dryly is 'averse neither to grandiloquence nor to a certain prophetic tone'[41]. It is designed to beguile and seduce, and Eliade's terminology remains entrenched in popular discourse on religion today. *The Sacred and the Profane* was widely employed at US universities as an introductory textbook and sold widely to the general public. Yet Eliade's mission was not only descriptive but also prescriptive – he saw the role of the Historian of Religions as being to

> try to grasp the centre of a religious belief, the meaning of it… in order to do justice to the religion itself and also to do justice to ourselves, to enrich ourselves with meanings that are new for us, rather than passing off all myth as superstition.[42]

To be clear, Eliade is not the originator of the sui generis approach to the study of religion, but rather its most eloquent representative; rather than imposing his views, he articulated something explicitly that was already assumed implicitly by most of those working in the field.[43] The Marburg Statement made this plain, and while the argument subsided, it was far from settled. Indeed, it remains an issue today, in debates about the involvement of groups like the American Academy of Religion (AAR) in the IAHR, something which warranted the addition of the line 'The IAHR is not a forum for confessional, apologetical, or other similar concerns' being added to the constitution at the 2010 Congress in Toronto. More recently, in 2017 the formation of the European Academy of Religion elicited an indignant response from the IAHR president Tim Jensen over their 'pursuit of normative theology and engagement in interreligious conversation'.[44] But interestingly, the next time this debate dominated an IAHR event, Gnosticism was the flashpoint – and indeed, Gnosticism had become a dog-whistle for the sui generis History of Religions approach.

The pattern of a congress every five years which continues until today was established with Marburg in 1960. Because of the longer gaps between congresses, a number of smaller Colloquia were organized.[45] These had a tighter thematic focus than the larger, quinquennial events; in Claremont, California in 1965, the theme was 'Initiation', and in Jerusalem in 1968, the question was on 'Types of Redemption'. The Messina Colloquium was held between 13 and 18 April 1966, in collaboration with la Societá Italiana di Storia della Religioni, with the declared aim of reaching 'a terminological and conceptual agreement' regarding 'The Origins of Gnosticism'.[46]

The unusually high level of specificity in the conference theme, and that this was held under the auspices of a general study of religion conference rather than a biblical studies organization, speaks to how seriously this question of where and when Gnosticism originated was taken at this time. History of Religions scholars continued to argue for an Eastern origin, but there was strong support for a Jewish origin, particularly from Eranos scholars. But this was effectively a synecdoche for the question of whether Gnosticism was a religion, or a religious *type* – a specific religion, with a specific place and time, or a timeless religious style with some sui generis essence at its core? Despite the title, then, the conference was as much about the nature of Gnosticism as it was about its origins. Moreover, the debate over gnostic origins was a microcosm of the broader methodological debates in the field – historical specifics or timeless essences?

The committee consisted of Ugo Bianchi (professor of the History of Religions at the University of Messina and later IAHR president between 1990 and 1995), Hans Jonas, Jean Daniélou, Carston Colpe and the standing president of the IAHR, Geo Widengren. Widengren's was not merely a ceremonial involvement, however. In *Religionensvärld*'s lengthy chapter devoted to Gnosticism,[47] as in his paper 'Les origines du gnosticisme et l'histoire des religions', which opened the conference, Widengren remained committed to an Iranian origin for Gnosticism, drawing particularly on Jonas's use of Manichaeism and Mandaeism.[48] However, his historical argument was subsumed by his systematic, comparative argument, which ranges freely through the New Testament, Islam, the Bhagavad Gita, the Rig Veda, the Saddharmapundarika Sutra and Zoroastrianism, and traces Gnosticism's influence through the Cathars and Bogomils, Freemasons, Rosicrucians and Romantic poets.[49] The narrative of the Redeemed Redeemer even appears, presented as a case study of a transformed pantheism in which the continuity between the deity and the cosmos is problematized by the idea that the world is illusory.[50]

But from the planning to editing the resulting book of conference proceedings, this was Bianchi's project. His keynote, 'Le probléme des origines du gnosticisme', sums up in terms now familiar to the reader who has persevered this far the state of the field:

> Since the beginning of this century, the historical-religious question of the origins of Gnosticism has thus been posed, especially in the circles of the *religionsgeschichtliche* school. At the same time, the studies of this school on the origins of Gnosticism (and its relation to Christianity) have been strongly influenced by the situation of the German cultural environment of the first three decades of this century; this is why it is of concern not to conflate these two things, historically linked but distinct – the problems of the *religionsgeschichtliche* theories of Bousset, Reitzenstein, Dieterich, Norden, Clemen, as laudable as they may turn out to be, and the simple historical-religious problem of the origins of Gnosticism, as it is posited by today's knowledge. It is true that the discussion sometimes continues to move in other directions as well – either one continues to search for the origins of Gnosis in the furrow of Jewish and Christian tradition, or we confine ourselves to an extreme historical hypothesis, reducing gnosis to 'syncretism'. But it should be noted that a 'Jewish' interpretation of gnosis, once it is sensitive to the problems posed by current knowledge of the Jewish environment, does not cease to be 'historico-religious' research (which is not equivalent to saying *religionsgeschichtliche* in the classical and historically conditioned sense of the word). The syncretistic solution, in turn, presents the danger of concealing and, in practice, denying the comparative problem – quite the opposite of a real historical-religious analysis. What is worse, it tends to unduly nullify the specific contents of the thought of the gnostic movement.[51]

Given the comments about Jewish Gnosticism and the historical context of Germany, it may not be surprising that Bianchi was also responsible for inviting Hans Jonas, who, as a result of the success of *The Gnostic Religion*, was by now regarded as the most widely read scholar on Gnosticism. He had no new research to share – his conference paper was a precis of his argument from *The Gnostic Religion*, itself summarizing his doctoral thesis from 1928.[52] Nevertheless, he made the most of the opportunity, as the Messina definitions would canonize his ideas for posterity. He later recalled

> the satisfaction I felt when, in Messina, at the first international conference on Gnosticism… I found that some of the vocabulary I had coined more than three decades before had become part of the lingua franca of the field and was used almost as a matter of course.[53]

The majority of the papers directly addressed the conference theme, many making their cases for particular points of origin; Bleeker for Egypt, Kurt Rudolph for Mesopotamia, Quispel for Judaism, and others for Manichaeism, Christianity, Iran and Greece.[54] Edward Conze (1904–1979), the German-born scholar of Prajñāpāramitā literature and a former Theosophist, argued for the similarity of Buddhism and gnosis (drawing from Jonas and Puech), showing that Blavatsky's ideas still had some currency.[55] A few papers talked directly about the Nag Hammadi discoveries, and Martin Krause's 'Situation of the release of the Nag Hammadi Texts' updated the delegates on the ongoing delays. When it became clear to the delegates that UNESCO had not made available archival photographs of the codices, as promised in 1956, the IAHR issued a statement 'concerning the urgency of the definitive publication of all the texts of Nag Hammadi', which were 'of quite fundamental significance for the study of Gnosticism, which is itself of considerable importance for understanding the context of ideas out of which our modern world emerged', signed by Bianchi and Widengren.[56] Yet UNESCO did not act, partly because of the breakout of the Six-Day War in June the following year, and ten more years were to pass before publication commenced.

On the final day, Monday, 18 April, draft definitions (in French) were proposed, debated and amended at a three-hour session. Significantly, these were written in advance by the committee, so rather than the congress being where the definitions were produced, it was merely where they were revealed and authorized. They were published in Italian, French, German and English in the conference proceedings, although they are best known today in their English translations by James M. Robinson.[57] Robinson was then a coptologist working at the American School of Oriental Research in Jerusalem but would later become the organizer behind the codices' eventual publication. He had had some contact with the Coptic Museum and was one of the few native English speakers there, so he was roped in to help with the translation, although he did not consider himself sufficiently expert to contribute to the debate or even to pose for the official photograph.[58]

Figure 5: Delegates of the Messina Congress, 1966. Reprinted with the permission of the International Association for the History of Religions.

The proposal begins,

> In order to avoid an undifferentiated use of the terms *gnosis* and Gnosticism, it seems advisable to identify, by the combined use of the historical and the typological methods, a concrete fact, 'Gnosticism', beginning methodologically with a certain group of systems of the Second Century A.D. which everyone agrees are to be designated with this term. ... The Gnosticism of the Second Century sects involves a coherent series of characteristics that can be summarized in the idea of a divine spark in man, deriving from the divine realm, fallen into this world of fate, birth and death, and needing to be awakened by the divine counterpart of the self in order to be finally reintegrated.[59]

The influences of Jonas and Jung crash together in this definition and will remain entangled going forward. Jonas's influence is clear in the line referring to the divine spark having 'fallen into this world of fate, birth and death', drawing from Heidegger's *verfallen*.[60] As a committee member, Jonas presumably wrote this line himself. The influence of Jung is also clear – that 'pneuma' means 'the divine substance of one's transcendent self', not 'soul' or 'spirit' or 'atman', is an act of classification, not disinterested recognition.[61] Indeed, this whole definition is more typical of Eranos presentations than any text from Nag Hammadi.

Gnosis, on the other hand, was defined as 'knowledge of the divine mysteries reserved for an elite' (though adding that 'not every *gnosis* is Gnosticism').[62] Here we find echoes of Reitzenstein's definition: 'Immediate knowledge of God's mysteries received from direct intercourse with the deity – mysteries which must remain hidden from the natural man'.[63] Indeed, this definition is strikingly similar to Quispel's review of Scholem's *Jewish Gnosticism, Merkabah Mysticism and Talmudic Tradition* (1960), in which he writes:

> If by Gnosticism we understand a religious movement that proclaimed a mystical esotericism for the elect based on illumination and the acquisition of a higher knowledge of things heavenly and divine, then Judaism has certainly produced its own shade of Gnosis.[64]

The result then was to define Gnosticism as a historically bounded religious tradition, with features drawn from Jonas's existentialist reading and Jung's psychological gloss, with gnosis defined as a kind of special 'higher' or 'elite' knowledge. Gnosis and Gnosticism had long been used interchangeably, particularly outside of Anglophone scholarship, but as a result of the ongoing processes of essentialization, and the popularity and influence of Jonas's and Jung's ideas, a clear disjunction was emerging in Anglophone scholarship, where Gnosticism was increasingly reserved for the historically bounded religious tradition (whatever its origin), and gnosis was used to indicate its ahistorical *essence*. In other words, the terms were already being used to indicate different ways of thinking about Gnosticism, but Messina codified that distinction.

Predictably though, the congress failed to settle the question of gnostic origins. Instead, they coined two further categories: 'Pre-Gnosticism' and 'Proto-Gnosticism'. Pre-Gnosticism was described as 'the pre-existence of different themes and motifs constituting a "pre" but not yet involving Gnosticism' (though the specific difference is left unspecified), specifically in Jewish apocalypticism.[65] Proto-Gnosticism, on the other hand, involved 'the *essence* of Gnosticism already in the centuries preceding the Second Century AD, as well as outside the Christian Gnosticism of the Second Century', including Iran, India and the Greek world.[66] In other words, there was no conceptual agreement, only a terminological codification of the different approaches already in play.

Neither Pre- nor Proto-Gnosticism became widely used. Nevertheless, as we will see in the next chapter, the Messina definitions were important for the several new gnostic religions which formed during this period. In popular discourse, too, the Messina definitions were widely accepted, if not always explicitly. *The Nag Hammadi Library in English* was published in 1977, making the texts freely available for the first time, more than thirty years after their discovery, and James Robinson's editorial introduction stays close to the Messina definition (which, after all, he had helped to translate). He appeals to Jonas with the observation that Gnostics have been 'duped and lured into the trap of trying to be content in an impossible world, alienated from their true home', although his comment that 'the merger into the All which is the destiny of one's spark of the divine' pointedly avoids Jungian language.[67]

As analytical categories, however, the Messina definitions were failures. Already in 1969, Bleeker and Widengren's *Historia Religionum: Handbook for the History of Religions* dismisses the Messina definitions (in a chapter on Gnosticism written by Jean Doresse) because claims to gnosis were not exclusive to so-called Gnostics, instead opting to define it as a worldview where the cosmos is the flawed creation of an evil creator – foreshadowing Williams' biblical demiurgic traditions by some thirty years.[68]

But the less-noted effect was that it coded a putative 'special knowledge' in the academy, giving the IAHR rubber-stamp to a putative type of experience. As such, the Messina Congress and the definitions it proposed reproduced in microcosm the broader debates of the IAHR and the academic study of religion more broadly – historical or phenomenological? Texts or essences? The Oriental construction of Gnosticism favoured by the Religionsgeschichtliche Schule fell away as the Nag Hammadi texts were gradually published, and gnosis and Gnosticism in Religious Studies became increasingly associated with ideas of special knowledge – which is to say, elite access to a transformational and salvific sacred essence. As such, after Messina, Gnosticism and the phenomenological History of Religion become increasingly indistinguishable.

8

Takes a Gnostic to find a Gnostic: Contemporary gnostic groups

The tendency for scholars to describe contemporary self-identifying gnostic groups as 'neo-Gnostic'[1] underlines that they are viewed as somehow illegitimate. The reason, surely, is that without a direct historical lineage, they should not be understood as 'really' gnostic. Historical transmission is of course a very common strategy of legitimization used by new religions themselves, and Gnostics are no exception. But Bentley Layton has argued that the best practice historiographically is to use the name that a group uses for itself, and moreover only in that sense, 'because ambivalent usage would introduce disorderliness into historical discourse'.[2] If this were true, then it is possible that today's self-identifying gnostic religions are the only ones there have ever been.

On the other hand, by using an essentialist understanding of Gnosticism, many scholars can and do identify many contemporary religions as gnostic, regardless of historical lineage or self-identification. 2019's encyclopedic *The Gnostic World*, for example, includes chapters on G. I. Gurdjieff, the Nation of Islam, Sri Aurobindo, Babiism and Scientology, as well as many of the figures and groups we have already encountered. To its credit, the book also includes a chapter on the Gnostic Movement of Samael Aun Weor,[3] but this is outnumbered by chapters on gnostic themes in popular fiction. Indeed, many volumes with material on contemporary Gnostics do not make mention of the various groups identifying as Gnostics today at all. DeConick's *The Gnostic New Age*, for example, makes no mention of the Aun Weor groups, despite their explicit identification of Aun Weor as the avatar of the New Age.[4]

The reason for this is the essential features of this sui generis gnostic current does not match the features of these actual Gnostics. The data doesn't fit how these scholars wish to construct Gnosticism. So, scholars are forced to simply pretend that they do not exist in order to avoid having to contradict their own definitions or explain why scholars, and not Gnostics, are deciding what gnosis *really* is. This fact alone exposes that the essentialized category of Gnosticism used by contemporary Religious Studies scholars is an invention which refers to no existent group, ancient or modern – when the data challenges the category, pretend the data doesn't exist.

This chapter concerns the three major self-identifying gnostic religions operating today – Ecclesia Gnostica, the Apostolic Johannite Church (hereafter AJC) and Samael Aun Weor's Gnostic Movement.[5] The descriptions will of necessity be brief, though I intend to follow this book with one focused entirely on these groups. I am not concerned here with either historical legitimization or essential features. Rather, this chapter will focus on how these groups construct their Gnosticism and the strategies they use to establish legitimizing connections to the past. This past is the past imagined by scholars, by Theosophical antiquarians, Eranos delegates and exiled philosophers, rather than historical actuality. We will see how they draw from the same process of essentialization which we saw in preceding chapters, and see that these groups engage actively with scholarship, though in almost every case this is with the History of Religions school, rather than more recent critical or historical scholarship. But this is not to imply that I see these contemporary groups as 'appropriating' this scholarship. As Styfhals writes in his study of Gnosticism in post-war German philosophy, it can be 'difficult to make a clear methodological separation between modern Gnosticism scholarship, the modern revivals of Gnosticism, and the philosophical studies that used the concept of Gnosticism to define or criticize modernity.'[6] That scholars create the categories we study is a well-rehearsed argument by now; less often recognized is that these categories become the options that people draw from in the construction of their religious identities. Like Shamanism, Paganism, even Hinduism, Gnosticism escapes its etic context to become an emic self-identifier.

Most importantly, all these contemporary groups present Gnosticism as a tradition based on a set of suppressed texts from biblical times and also part of a broader, perennial current based in appeals to gnosis. In each case, these groups present themselves as Christian bodies, and although they differ in their adherence to mainstream Christian dogma, all model their ecclesiastical structure and ritual practices on Roman Catholicism and claim legitimate apostolic succession. All the groups mentioned in this chapter have bishops, perform Mass and call themselves a church (*eclessia, igreja*). They conceive of gnosis as direct religious experience, and the personal quest for said experience as being the true form of Christianity, long since suppressed by the Roman Catholic Church. So, they share the critique that mainstream Christianity has become over-reliant upon 'faith' and the institutional validation thereof with the earliest scholarship on Gnosticism. Karen King argued that Gnosticism was invented to police the boundaries of normative Christianity in the early modern period;[7] it is clear in the case of contemporary gnostic groups that it still does. However, in some groups there is considerable tension between this rejection of normative Christianity and an appeal to authority through apostolic succession to 'wandering bishops' of various lineages (see Chapter 2). Their close links with esoteric groups, either the Theosophical Society or the OTO, is often somewhat downplayed, though close investigation shows these groups more resemble initiatory organizations than the Catholic Church.

There is also a subtle but profound shift in theodicy, wherein *cosmos* is interpreted as 'systems', rather than 'nature' – the human world, rather than the natural world. In other words, matter and nature are not evil, but in fact inherently good, and the evil of the world is in fact the systems of the world. It is not the universe that is at fault, but rather human systems. For example, Stephan Hoeller, presiding bishop of the Ecclesia Gnostica, argues that the Greek κόσμος is better translated as 'systems', as opposed to to γῆ (Gē, Gaia), which signified planet Earth and which the Gnostics regarded as 'neutral, if not outright good'.[8] Jordan Stratford of the AJC explains:

> The system is not the world; the daily waking reality of economics and politics and bureaucracy, of cruelty and injustice, was not created by the Divine, but by the forces of ignorance and greed. We don't reject rocks and trees and flowers and sex, we reject an unjust system imposed upon these things. This system forces us to feel separated from God, when the reality is that this separation is just an illusion. The system doesn't like to be understood in this way; it thinks it should be in charge, and our divinity and our humanity should take a back seat to 'the way of the world'. In this way the system is adversarial to the Gnostic. We see others 'worshipping' this system, as though it were the true God.[9]

The importance of this shift is that it allows for the identification of Gnosticism with the post-war boom of new religions, and in particular the New Age movement, wherein a sacralization of nature is combined with a holistic theodicy in which 'evil' is not a separate antagonistic force, but rather the negative counterpart of the positive in a system which ultimately balances itself out. This 'procosmic' version of gnostic cosmology derives ultimately from the post-war scholars who saw Gnosticism as the forerunner of later esoteric traditions, something we will return to in the next chapter.

The longest-running contemporary gnostic religion is the Ecclesia Gnostica, formed in 1976.[10] Its founder, Bishop Stephan Hoeller, still oversees the activities of the Los Angeles parish and a few smaller parishes and satellite groups around the United States. Its liturgy and orders are modelled on Roman Catholicism, except that the offices are open to both men and women. As they require no initiation or formal membership, it is difficult to ascertain how many adherents the Ecclesia Gnostica can claim or how long or how deeply they are involved for. My own fieldwork in 2019 suggests a small core of committed members, many of whom have been involved for decades, and a larger cohort who more or less regularly attend services. However, Hoeller himself has a high public profile, and his ideas reach a wider audience than just his parishioners – his book *Gnosticism: New Light on the Ancient Tradition of Inner Knowing* (2002) has consistently sat near the top of the search term 'Gnosticism' on Amazon.com for over a decade.[11]

For many years, the Ecclesia Gnostica was based in a low-ceilinged room behind a storefront on Hollywood Boulevard, but following a fire in 2004, they moved to the Besant Theosophical Lodge on Glendale Boulevard, a remarkable 1930s converted cinema beneath the Hollywood sign (see Figure 6). Hoeller

Figure 6: The Besant Lodge, Los Angeles, in April 2019. Photo by the author.

was 86 when I met him in 2019, still presiding over Mass most Sundays, and giving frequent lectures on subjects such as depth psychology, alchemy, mysticism and the occult. The bulk of the Ecclesia Gnostica's sacramental activity consists of the Gnostic Mass, which in the Los Angeles parish is performed twice weekly, on Sunday by Hoeller and on Thursday by other clergy, with a third, smaller Mass on a Tuesday in the chapel to the rear of the Besant Lodge, officiated by Hoeller, and by invitation only. The Mass is modelled closely on the Roman Catholic Mass, replete with incense, candles and vestments, but the text is adapted to suit Hoeller's particular conception of Gnosticism. Congregations are not large, perhaps twenty or thirty on a good day, and slowly but steadily declining, although younger new congregants continue to appear.

Hoeller was born in 1931 in Budapest, Hungary. The Nazis arrived when he was ten, and in 1946 the Red Army took control of the government. His father was shot and his uncle killed while Hoeller was a Cistercian seminarian. Perhaps unsurprisingly, he left Hungary upon reaching adulthood, going first to Belgium, where he came into contact with the Eglisé Gnostique, and then to Austria, where he pursued a doctorate in psychology.[12] He describes his first encounter with Jung's *Septum Sermones ad Mortuos* as a life-changing moment:

> Life was not, could not be the same after that magical moment. ... Like a volume of sacred scripture or a codex of transformative formulae of power, the transcribed words of the mysterious little book changed a life. The safe harbour of orthodoxy lost all its attractiveness, and with it the establishments of time-honoured belief and tradition.[13]

He eventually relocated to the United States in 1952. In Los Angeles, he joined the Gnostic Society, a discussion group founded by Theosophist James Morgan Pryse in 1928, and mixed with Liberal Catholics, from whom he received the priesthood in 1958.[14] He also had a long collaboration and friendship with Freemason and Rosicrucian Manly P. Hall (1901–1990), the author of *The Secret Teachings of All Ages* (1928) and founder of the Philosophical Research Society in Los Angeles (a nonprofit organization maintaining a lecture hall and research library), where Hoeller continues to lecture regularly.

Hoeller's own account of the origins of the Ecclesia Gnostica attempts to establish him as the authoritative voice of contemporary Gnosticism, primarily by appeal to apostolic succession.[15] This is interesting, as Irenaeus argued that lines of apostolic succession *support* orthodoxy, yet it is exactly these genealogies that modern-day gnostic churches make appeals to for their authority. His account makes a number of attempts to establish the position of the Ecclesia

Gnostica as the gathering together of these lines of succession through the *episcopi vagantes*. First, he attempts to connect the Ecclesia Gnostica to the French gnostic churches of the nineteenth century, although in reality there is no direct historical connection.[16] Hoeller's apostolic succession comes through Richard Jean Chretien, Duc de Palatine, an Australian wandering bishop who founded the Order of the Pleroma in the 1950s. Hoeller was himself consecrated a bishop in 1967, and in 1970, de Palatine moved to Los Angeles, where he founded the Pre-Nicene Gnostic Catholic Church.[17] A possible reason that Hoeller glosses over the details of this line of transmission is the bitter feud between him and de Palatine, which lasted until de Palatine's death in 1977.[18] A stronger reason, however, is that de Palatine's apostolic credentials are dubious in the extreme. Hoeller and most of the members of the Pre-Nicene Church split with de Palatine in 1970, forming the Ecclesia Gnostica.

Although Hoeller aligns himself with a Christian conception of Gnosticism, his conception of a 'new Gnosis' interprets the 'esoteric' conception as exemplified by Theosophy through Jung's psychological conception, and Hoeller has far stronger connections to the Theosophical Society than to the Catholic Church.[19] The wording of the Gnostic Mass used by the Ecclesia Gnostica draws from Mead's *Fragments of a Faith Forgotten*, and Hoeller describes the Theosophical Society as the end point of the 'pansophic tradition', the purported line of transmission of Gnosticism through 'esoteric' teachings.[20] Blavatsky wrote in *Isis Unveiled* that 'the dogma of apostolic succession must fall to the ground',[21] nevertheless, for Hoeller, Jung and Blavatsky are the two 'modern reviver[s] of the Gnosticism of the first centuries of the Christian era'.[22] These two approaches are, he argues,

> both the expression at their particular levels of existential reality of a Gnosis, a knowledge of the heart directed towards the inmost core of the human psyche and having as its objective the essential transformation of the psyche.[23]

Yet Hoeller writes that while 'existentialist and phenomenologist philosophers came to recognize the common ground that they shared with Gnosticism', it is an oversimplification to describe Gnostics as anticosmic.[24] To achieve gnosis, he writes, 'we must disentangle ourselves from the false cosmos created by our conditioned minds'.[25] 'What the Gnostic struggles against is not so much the cosmos as the alienation of consciousness from the ultimate reality underlying the cosmos, which in monotheistic language is called "God"'.[26]

Hoeller is working in a post-Auschwitz moral framework, but unlike Jonas and Scholem, he presents Gnosticism as our hope of salvation. The rediscovery of Gnosticism amid the 'upheaval of two world wars and the accompanying psychological wreckage' was no mere coincidence,[27]

> synchronistically converging with their mysterious connection of meaning; The exploding of the first nuclear weapon at Hiroshima, the discovery of the *Gnostic collection of scriptures* at Nag Hammadi, and the unearthing of the Essene scrolls in the cave at Qumran.[28]

Note the reinforcement of the two problematic assumptions here – they are Gnostic, and they are a single collection. Further, they are referred to as 'scriptures', echoing the tendency to talk of 'Gnostic Gospels' in popular works and sometimes scholarship, a strategy which reinforces the perception of them as the corpus of a discrete religion. Indeed, Hoeller presents the Ecclesia Gnostica as not only legitimately Catholic, but in fact the custodians of the original and most pure form of Catholic Christianity:

> Why should occult or gnostic persons … practice the sacraments of the Roman Catholic Church? The answer is not difficult. Gnostic movements of various kinds that survived secretly in Europe were all originally part of the Roman Catholic Church. Although they differed with their relative and were frequently persecuted by her, they still regarded her as the model of ecclesiastical life. They may have considered the content of their religion as quite at variance with the teachings of Rome, but the form of their worship was still the one that ancient and universal Christendom had always practiced.[29]

Roman Catholicism, he charges, cannot adequately provide the individual with direct religious experience and has actively suppressed women doctrinally and ecclesiastically. The priesthood of the Ecclesia Gnostica is open equally to women and men (and indeed Rosamonde Miller, the most prominent female gnostic Bishop, was consecrated by Hoeller), and Ecclesia Gnostica liturgy frequently appeals to Sophia as the feminine aspect of god, with Mary Magdalene similarly prominent in the church's liturgical calendar.[30] His interpretation of Sophia is drawn entirely from Jung, and the complexities and contradictions in the various accounts in the Nag Hammadi texts are completely ignored.[31] However, Hoeller draws on Pagels's *The Gnostic Gospels* to portray Gnosticism as a legitimate early form of Christianity that was actively suppressed by what would become Roman Catholic orthodoxy.[32] Yet Pagels's larger argument that Gnosticism was a polemical construction in order to legitimize the Catholic apostolic lineage and demonize other lineages is ignored – unsurprisingly, given the high degree of importance the Ecclesia Gnostica places on its own claims to apostolic succession. While sacramentalism may provide a parallel with some classical 'gnostic' groups in terms of practices – Valentinus and his followers were among the earliest Christians to create a sacramental system, and the *Gospel of Philip* from Nag Hammadi mentions sacraments – the idea of these taking place within a valid apostolic succession does not. Indeed, apostolic succession was likely institutionalized by the early church specifically to *combat* heresies like Gnosticism.[33] As Tertullian wrote in *The Prescription against Heretics*, the 'original sources of the faith must be reckoned for truth, as undoubtedly containing that which the (said) churches received from the apostles, the apostles from Christ, Christ from God. Whereas all doctrine must be prejudged as false which savours of contrariety to the truth of the churches and apostles of Christ and God'.[34]

Hoeller is keen to portray the Ecclesia Gnostica as central to a wider 'gnostic revival' movement[35] (and indeed his wide-ranging narrative of the origins of the Ecclesia Gnostica is in part an attempt to create this impression), but in practice, there is a good deal of competition going on between the groups, and he is not always willing to accept other groups as being legitimately gnostic. One group he has been willing to work with, however, is the AJC.

The AJC[36] was founded in 2000 by James Foster, a former member of the Temple of Set.[37] Foster, who took the patriarchal name Tau Johannes III, claimed that the AJC was a continuation of *l'Église Johannites des Chretiens Primitif*, founded by the French priest Bernard-Raymond Fabré-Palaprat in 1804. I haven't been able to establish this link. It appears that Foster was consecrated on 20 January 2000 by James Graeb, a bishop of the Ecclesia Gnostica Catholica.[38] Despite claims to the contrary dating from the 1980s, these successions gain their authority ultimately from Crowley, so cannot be considered legitimate Catholic successions.

Nevertheless, the AJC has worked to build relationships with other gnostic groups to create a unified presence for the 'Apostolic Gnostic movement'.[39] They were the architects behind the formation of the North American College of Gnostic Bishops (between 2000 and 2002), a body which sent representatives to the 2009 Parliament of World Religions. It still exists, although it has been inactive since around 2010.[40] Interestingly, this included Stephan Hoeller and several Thelemite Bishops, despite Hoeller's earlier public denunciation of Thelemite gnostic churches as illegitimate due to a lack of apostolic succession:

> That they might call themselves some other names which would more truthfully describe their orientation, such as Kabbalists, Magicians and so forth and leave the name Gnostic to those whose teaching and practice *resembles the original*

model more closely. Meanwhile we feel dutybound to uphold our own Gnostic traditions and as far as we may be able to do so to prevent them being confounded with what they are not.'[41]

The AJC also produced the 'All Saints Accord' in 2002, a statement of common principles for apostolic gnostic churches, to which twelve bishops were signatories, including three from the AJC and several Thelemites, although this time Hoeller was not a signatory:

1. The right to open participation and veneration of the Sacred and divine in its traditional and contemporary forms irrespective of social status, organizational affiliation, gender, sexual orientation and creed.
2. The common bond shared by all active apostolic gnostic churches in liturgical ministry through the agency of the one apostolic succession and thereby the validity and value of the Sacramental and Liturgical ministry maintained by those same active apostolic gnostic churches when conducted in an ethical and upright manner.
3. The invitation to all members of the gnostic church, and indeed all spiritually minded people, to partake of our communities, free of all obligation but Respect and Charity.[42]

The other prominent influence on the AJC is Freemasonry. While it isn't a requirement for membership, so far as I can tell, most members are also Freemasons, and particularly the clergy – which is also the case with the Ecclesia Gnostica. So, the AJC is essentially an initiatory esoteric Christian order, although the Christian aspect is most stressed in the organization's public-facing materials. This is true also of the Ecclesia Gnostica, where on Tuesday nights a distinct variety of ceremonial magic is taught which combines Golden Dawn–style ritual with gnostic terminology and Catholic liturgical elements including the censer and holy water.

The AJC grew quickly through the 2000s; they are highly organized, have a professional Web presence and had a charismatic and active spokesperson in Jordan Stratford. Indeed, his success as a writer, particularly of children's fantasy fiction, has meant that he has stepped back from this role in recent years (though he remains archpriest and prefect with responsibility for ecumenical relations and rector of the Victoria Parish in British Columbia).[43] His 2007 book, *Living Gnosticism: An Ancient Way of Knowing*, remains a popular work for those exploring contemporary Gnosticism. It is an invaluable source for how the apostolic Johannites wish to present their version of Gnosticism;

problems with apostolic lineage are again glossed over, Freemasonry and initiations are minimized (though not ignored) and the idea of the Gnostics as groovy spiritual rebels – 'angelheaded hipsters' – fighting the evil Catholic Church is foregrounded.[44] Overall, the presentation is designed to draw the curious spiritual seeker in, rather than addressing matters of historical fact or ecumenical discussions.

The book demonstrates a high level of engagement with contemporary scholarship, however – of course, which scholarship is supported and which is challenged is of interest here. What it shows is again the influence of an essentialist conception drawn from the History of Religions. Stratford defines Gnosticism as a 'knowledge of the heart'[45] – he may here be quoting from Bishop Hoeller,[46] or from Quispel,[47] but given that Hoeller and Quispel both use the term in the 1980s, it seems likely that the term comes ultimately from Jung. Indeed, Stratford described himself as a Jungian in an email to me, adding that he doesn't take the mythology literally.[48] Rather, the demiurge and the archons are not physically real, but rather are representations of psychological realities.[49] The material world is an emanation of God, and is therefore intrinsically good; however, humans worship human systems *as though* they were a god.

The church draws on a range of 'gnostic' sources, including the familiar Nag Hammadi texts, Fabré-Palaprat's *Lévitikon*[50] and Clement of Alexandria's *Excerpta ex Theodoto*. The latter's exhortation that 'what makes us free is the gnosis of who we were, of what we have become; of where we were, of wherein we have been cast; of whereto we speed, of wherefrom we are redeemed; of what birth truly is, and of what rebirth truly is' is presented without the preceding lines about the need for baptism, of course.[51] Nevertheless, this was also a favourite passage of Jonas, due to his translating 'ἐνεβλήθημεν' as 'verfallen', which fitted his existential reading.

The AJC has actively nurtured a relationship with scholars of Gnosticism, and Birger Pearson (2011),[52] Zlatko Pleše (2014)[53] and even Karen King (2016)[54] have presented at their annual conclave (though, of course, none have presented arguments which challenge the AJC's historical claims). My own conversations with Stratford began when he contacted me a few months after I put my MSc thesis on contemporary gnostic groups up on Academia.edu in late 2010. He was polite but firm on a number of issues, particularly defending apostolic succession, and the centrality of gnosis to anything claiming to be Gnosticism, something he repeatedly stressed was not present in Thelemite or Aun Weor groups. Thelemite Gnostics *do* in fact stress just this – 'We are Gnostic because we accept the emanationist cosmogony of the Gnostics ... and their doctrine of individual redemption/illumination through Gnosis.'[55] Stratford told me, 'The Weor people [are] not looking for the "individuation" aspect. ... They're simply willing to accept what Rodriguez claimed was *his* gnosis. And obviously that's unrelated to ... the gnosis of Gnostic literature.'[56] Weor's commentary on *Pistis Sophia* makes it clear that Weor Gnostics see theirs as exactly the gnosis of gnostic literature. On the other hand, Stratford suggested that other gnoses are legitimate, providing they have a salvific quality. Clearly, these have no connection to the 'Gnostic literature' either; ultimately, experience is the arbiter. Ultimately, we are back to having to trust Stratford's judgement. It takes a gnostic to know a gnostic, it seems.

The internal response to critical scholarship has not been so friendly, however, as shown by the 2010 argument between Stratford and Jesse Folks, a Biblical Studies graduate student and then member of the AJC, on palmtreegarden.org, a discussion group for disgruntled contemporary Gnostics (now defunct). Interestingly, Palm Tree Garden was founded by Jeremy Puma, a former member of the Ecclesia Gnostica, whose encounters with Williams's work led him to break with the apostolic Gnostics and promote his own version of post-deconstruction contemporary Gnosticism.[57] The blurb for *This Way: Gnosis without 'Gnosticism'* (2011) states that Puma

> embraces the most recent scholarship which concludes that there was no ancient 'Gnosticism'. Consequently, modern organizations which refer to themselves as 'Gnosticism' are in no way related to ancient heretical sects in historical reality, but are, instead, entirely modern creations. As a response, 'This Way: Gnosis Without "Gnosticism"' presents an applied spirituality based on the writings found in the Nag Hammadi Library and Zen Buddhism, for people interested in a simple, mature approach to gnosis that doesn't rely on unprovable claims of apostolic succession or New Age neo-Templar silliness, but instead acknowledges the limitations of the material.

When, on Palm Tree Garden, Jesse Folks similarly challenged the AJC's historical account of their gnostic transmission, and the degree to which their holistic interpretation was to be found in the Nag Hammadi texts, Stratford went on the defensive, accusing Folks of being a 'neo-heresiological anti-Gnostic who wishes to erase our history in hopes of erasing our presence'. Similarly, Stratford argues that Williams wants 'to insist that that there's no such thing *as us*'.[58] This latter claim suggests that there is truth in Dillon's claim that the appeal of contemporary Gnosticism is largely to do with identity.[59]

This is remarkably similar to the debates among Wiccan pagans following the publication of Ronald Hutton's *Triumph of the Moon* in 1999, which convincingly demonstrated that Gerald Gardner's claims of continuity back to pre-Christian Dianic worship was a beguiling fiction. Many pagans saw this as an attack, yet many simply adapted to it. If experience was the final arbitrator in the validity of Paganism, then what did history matter? Moreover, even as an invented tradition, Paganism was still part of a lineage of Romanticism and joyous nature worship going back to at least the Enlightenment. Indeed, Puma's work makes these very arguments.

These internal debates and internecine tussles notwithstanding, all the apostolic gnostic churches are united in decrying the Gnostic Movement, an archipelago of groups which promulgate the teachings of Samael Aun Weor throughout South America, Latin American communities in the United States and worldwide.[60] Stratford has accused unnamed 'South American sex-cultists' of 'abusing the term' Gnostic,[61] whereas Hoeller told me in 2019 that he regarded them as less worthy of serious attention than even the Thelemite churches. Yet in terms of numbers and global reach, the Gnostic Movement is the largest contemporary gnostic religion, even if it is little known in the Anglophone world and has received little academic attention.[62]

Samael Aun Weor was born Victor Manuel Gómez Rodríguez in Santa Fé de Bogotá, Colombia, on 6 March 1917. As a young man, Rodríguez was very much a 'seeker', involved to some degree with a range of alternative religious practices, including Freemasonry, the Theosophical Society, spiritualist groups and the teachings of Armenian-Greek 'guru' George Ivanovich Gurdjieff (1866–1949).[63] At the age of eighteen, Rodriguez joined the Fraternidad de Rosacruz Antiqua, a group led by the German Arnoldo Krumm-Heller, also known as Frater Huiracocha.[64] Krumm-Heller was 'Délégué Genéral pour le Chili, Perou et Bolivie' of the Martinist Order (appointed by Papus personally); grand representative general for Mexico, Chile, Peru and Bolivia of the OTO; and a bishop of Bricaud's Église Gnostique Universelle.[65] Weor talks of Krumm-Heller as a mentor,[66] though Krumm-Heller's successors deny that, and some deny that they ever even met in person.[67] But directly or indirectly, Krumm-Heller certainly influenced Weor's later teachings, in two significant ways: OTO sex magical techniques that would form the core of the gnosis, and the gnostic terminology which came from Krumm-Heller's reprinted material from the Église Gnostique. As Zoccatelli puts it, 'We might say that in Weor's system Gurdjieff provided the theory and Krumm-Heller the practice'.[68]

Weor recounts that, following Krumm-Heller's death in 1949, he was contacted by the 'Venerable White Lodge' and underwent a series of mystical experiences which culminated in 1954 with his final initiation in an underground temple in Santa Marta, Colombia. Here he was charged with a sacred, threefold mission: 'forming a new culture', 'forging a new civilization' and 'creating the Gnostic Movement'.[69] He took the name Venerable Master of the Bodhisattva Samael Aun Weor and began to promote a system he called 'The Gnostic Philosophy' or simply 'The Gnosis', described as 'the Synthesis of all Religions, Schools and Sects'.[70] Despite the primacy of Christian terminology, Weor's bricolage is exhaustive:

> The teachings of the Zend Avesta are in accordance with the doctrinal principles contained in the Egyptian book of the dead, and contain the Christ-principle. The Illiad of Homer, the Hebrew Bible, the Germanic Edda and the Sibylline Books of the Romans contain the same Christ-principle. All these are sufficient in order to demonstrate that Christ is anterior to Jesus of Nazareth. Christ is not one individual alone. Christ is a cosmic principle that we must assimilate within our own physical, psychic, somatic and spiritual nature through Sexual Magic. Among the Persians, Christ is Ormuz, Ahura Mazda, terrible enemy of Ahriman (Satan), which we carry within us. Amongst the Hindus, Krishna is Christ; thus, the gospel of Krishna is very similar to that of Jesus of Nazareth. Among the Egyptians, Christ is Osiris and whosoever incarnated him was in fact an Osirified One. Amongst the Chinese, the Cosmic Christ is Fu Hi, who composed the I-Ching (The Book of Laws) and who nominated Dragon Ministers. Among the Greeks, Christ is called Zeus, Jupiter, the Father of the Gods. Among the Aztecs, Christ is Quetzalcoatl, the Mexican Christ. In the Germanic Edda, Baldur is the Christ who was assassinated by Hodur, God of War, with an arrow made from a twig of mistletoe, etc. In like manner, we can cite the Cosmic Christ within thousands of ancient texts and old traditions which hail from millions of years before Jesus. The whole of this invites us to embrace that Christ is a cosmic principle contained within the essential principles of all religions.[71]

The Gnosis was not successful initially, however, and was for a short time incarcerated in Columbia on charges of 'quackery'.[72] His system was first presented in *El Matrimonio Perfecto* in 1950 (revised in 1963) which remained his most popular book despite publishing more than sixty others. He had already attracted a few followers by the time he moved to Mexico in 1956, where his public life was mostly based. He proclaimed the commencement of the Age of Aquarius on 4 February 1962 and declared himself the avatar of the Christ spirit for the New Age.⁷³ He legally established the Movimiento Gnóstica Christiano Universal (MGCU) in 1976, shortly before his death on 24 December 1977.

The MGCU originally had five branches or arms, not all of which are still in existence; these included the Iglesia Gnóstica Christiana Universal (IGCU), the ecclesiastical wing; the Gnostic Association of Scientific, Cultural and Anthropological Studies (AGEACAC), the academic wing; a branch devoted to socially beneficial works, and POSCLA, the Latin American Christian Workers' Party, the political wing. Following Weor's death in 1977, there was a long battle to determine his successor, and today dozens of different groups exist, official or unofficial, and often with confusingly similar names. The largest today are those founded by Joaquin Amortegui Valbuena (1926–2000; generally called the Venerable Master Rabolú), based in Colombia with a more millennarian reading of Weor's teachings⁷⁴; the Gnostic Christian Universal Church, founded in Uruguay by Teofilo Bustos (1936–2005); known as the Venerable Master Lakshmi)⁷⁵; and the Igreja Gnóstica do Brazil (IGB), actually an independent entity, which gained legal status as a religious organization in April 1994.⁷⁶ The IGB is the most ecclesiastic version of Weor's teachings, with its officials regularly carrying out the Gnostic Mass in full vestments, although they also offer online courses in Weor's teachings.

In every case, however, the gnosis is presented on three levels. I underwent the 'exoteric' First Chamber with the Gnostic Cultural Association (a group in the Lakshmi lineage) in Edinburgh in 2017–18.⁷⁷ The main teaching was the Three Factors of the Revolution of the Consciousness – death (death of the Egos, here conceived of as parasitic entities gained through previous incarnations, rather similar to the Scientological idea of Thetans), birth (specifically the birth of subtle bodies, through sexual alchemy) and sacrifice (working to pass on The Gnosis).⁷⁸ We were taught a number of exercises, beginning with the division of the attention (an exercise clearly drawn from Gurdjieff), the Rune FA (a combination of movements, vocalizations and visualizations) and the SOL Key (an act of conscious self-remembering). Later we were taught some aspects of Weor's cosmology, and while no secret was made of the sexual aspects of the gnosis, they didn't go into any detail.

With the 'mesoteric' Second Chamber, students move from theory to practice and are introduced to specific rituals such as the Gnostic Mass, taken from the French gnostic churches, adapted from the Eglise Gnostique.⁷⁹ However, students are required to undergo initiation to begin this level, including an oath of secrecy, and so I was not permitted to proceed. The central teaching of The Gnosis is put into practice only in the 'esoteric' Third Chamber: 'He who wants to become a God, should not ejaculate the semen'.[80] By retaining the semen, Weor claims that the energies it possesses are made available to drive the spiritual development of the (male) individual.[81] This he claims is the essential truth transmitted by all initiatory groups and their symbolism, and leads to an introspective experience of unity with the divine in which the individual ego is dissolved.[82] While the former point about the energies contained in bodily fluids was fairly widespread in the Victorian and pre-Second World War period, the latter point would seem to be drawn from Tantrism. However, no tradition of seminal retention leading to the establishment of astral bodies in Tantra can be established. The crystallization of substances within the body to construct higher being-bodies is, however, a central Gurdjieffian teaching.

As with the apostolics, Weorites appeal to 'gnostic' sources often and (the constant use of Christian language notwithstanding) make a wider range of appeals to other 'world religions' than the apostolics do. Indeed, as Weor's gnosis is 'the synthesis of all religions', so is more overtly perennial. Weor also presents his teachings as a restoration of pre–Roman Christian doctrine[83] and makes reference to a lineage of gnostics – which he dubs the 'Primitive Catholic Christian Gnostic Church' – including Simon Magus (naturally), Valentinus and, more surprisingly, Clement of Alexandria and even Irenaeus, the arch heresiologist.[84] The inclusion of Irenaeus shows that Weor had little knowledge of academic scholarship on Gnosticism. The only Nag Hammadi text he engages with is the *Pistis Sophia*, which was of course available long before, as part of the Askew Codex. His interest in it seems to have come through Krumm-Heller, who described it as the 'highest book of the doctrines of the gnostics', and was to the gnostic church what the Koran is for Muslims and the Bible is for Christians.[85] But he adds that the deeper meaning is available only to initiates – that contrary to the Catholic Church's teachings on celibacy, spiritual enlightenment was to be reached through control of the sexual impulses and fluids.[86] Weor's commentary, the posthumous and unfinished *El Pistis Sophia Develado* (1983), is based on a Spanish translation of Mead's version of the text and Krumm-Heller's interpretation. Weor's commentary presents a psychological interpretation of the text, which, naturally, is a mythological/metaphorical rendering of his own system, with a particular concern to identify sexual teachings, even though these are rather strained.[87] There is a long history of connecting the gnostics of the second to fourth centuries CE with sexual impropriety; an 'Aryan' origin for Gnosticism was common before the discovery of the Nag Hammadi texts, so it is not a great leap for Krumm-Heller or Weor to connect the two and present Tantric practices as gnostic.

Whereas the apostolic groups have had little success outside of North America, the Aun Weor groups have. In part this is due to an active outreach programme to offer courses in many major cities, which is one option for members to fulfil the 'Sacrifice' portion of the Three Factors. Presenting Weor's teachings in a language drawn from Roman Catholicism has allowed them to receive legal recognition as religious organizations and to operate in historically Catholic countries (most successfully in Brazil), as was the case with the French gnostic churches of the nineteenth century. Yet in Europe, they have had more success with courses which avoid Catholic language, hierarchical initiatory material and – more problematically – sex magic, instead presenting the gnosis as part of the broader decentralized spirituality of the New Age milieu.[88]

Claims of apostolic succession and the use of sexual magic are at the root of internecine struggles for authority between these contemporary Gnosticisms. Takes a gnostic to find a gnostic. And yet there are some striking similarities nevertheless – the claim to authentic, original Christianity; the adoption of a psychologized interpretation of Gnosticism, most often drawn from Jung; and the concomitant rejection of anticosmism for a less existential, holistic cosmology. As Dillon argues, a large part of the appeal of these groups is that people who were raised in mainstream Christianity, but experienced some estrangement from their upbringing, could reconnect with Christianity through the counter-memory of a suppressed spiritual, egalitarian alternative Christianity which the Nag Hammadi codices enabled.[89] These 'religiously 'homeless'' individuals

> found a way to reinterpret the symbols of Christianity with the modern American context. They found a feminist icon in Mary Magdalene. They found in the historical Gnostics a form of Christian practice that did not just tolerate, but embraced religious and cultural diversity. They found a Jesus who was not a 'king' to whom they had to be 'subjects,' but a democratic leader encouraging each individual to find their own personal divinity. And they found early Christians who were suspicious of the political power implicit in canon formation that legitimized their efforts to open Christian ecclesiology and the canon to radical new formulations.[90]

In each case, however, the approach to the texts and the strategic use of scholarship is basically identical to the History of Religions approach – different traditions can have a common essence, despite surface differences, which is fundamentally timeless and can be understood by interpreting ancient texts through contemporary frameworks. Experience is the core, whether interpreted psychologically or metaphysically, and the ultimate arbitrators of truth-claims are those with access to this higher knowledge, be they prophet or scholar. Moreover, this higher knowledge – this gnosis – has a salvific quality, for the gnostic individual, and the world at large.

9

The third way: Gnosticism in Western esotericism

'Influence', writes J. Gregory Given, 'is a messy thing to chart. But it is worth being attentive to the subtle genealogies that quietly emerge from the webs of citations – and the real human relationships that played out beyond them.'[1] This chapter, and the two following, look at three recent examples of appeals to gnostic traditions in contemporary Religious Studies, one European and two North American, to show how they are all part of the lineage(s) established in the previous chapters, albeit in different ways. I will show how the methods and theories of the History of Religions continue to dominate scholarship on Gnosticism in the early twenty-first century. In some cases, Gnosticism is used almost as a codeword for this approach, and the strange charm of Gnosticism demonstrates that such an approach is alive and well in Religious Studies.

In each of these chapters, we find gnosis being defined in essentialized form – not tied to a historically and geographically bound movement (i.e. Gnosticism), but a religious style, type or essence which is found in both the ancient world and the modern. An ahistorical current, rather than a specific tradition with a historical transmission, established through perceived philosophical or psychological affinities, although these are frequently built upon to posit similarities of social context or spiritual need. In the first of these chapters, this legacy of the History of Religions has become something of an albatross around the neck of scholars of Western esotericism, as they strive to establish the legitimacy of their area of study. In the second, Gnosticism is at the heart of a normative and confessional subtext to work on the New Age movement. In the third, gnosis is the key to transforming the study of religion and, through it, saving the world.

In defining gnosis as elite knowledge of the mysteries, the Messina Congress had legitimized the academic use of 'gnosis' for any form of occult or esoteric knowledge. Various religious groups continued to use gnostic motifs in various kinds of esoteric Christianity, as we saw in the previous chapter. In academia, however, the perceived link between esotericism and National Socialism predicated 'a sharp and definitive caesura' in the academic study of esoteric material after 1945, particularly in the German-speaking world, although established scholars like Scholem and Corbin continued to publish esoteric traditions in Islam and Judaism.[2] There was strong 'Christian backlash' in the study of religions after 1945; there was a fiercely anti-Christian bias in the Nazi-controlled states, and the swing against this was shored up by the Allies, who saw the churches as being a stabilizing influence.[3]

Fittingly, the first known usage of the term *l'esotérisme* came from Jaques Matter's *History Critique du Gnosticisme* (1828), possibly from where Eliphas Levi adopted it in his publications beginning some fifty years later.[4] The first modern study of esotericism in a Western European context only begins again with the publication of Frances Yates's *Giordano Bruno and the Hermetic Tradition* in 1964, however. Yates, a cultural historian at the Warburg Institute of the University of London, argued that modern science emerged from occult writings on Neoplatonism during the seventeenth century. Yates's work was roundly criticized for a careless and perhaps even polemical use of sources and for being too vague in what Hermeticism referred to.[5] Yates was not a religionist, but her work did propose a narrative of a distinct countercultural and underground Hermetic tradition which appealed to the religionist scholars and esotericists alike.[6] Shortly thereafter, the Scottish historian James Webb published *The Flight from Reason* (1971), the first in an influential series of books exploring what he referred to as 'Rejected knowledge', the idea of esotericism as a form of epistemological marginalization. This is a theme that will be picked up again later by Hanegraaff and others in the Amsterdam circle.

The specific term '*Western* esotericism', however, comes from Antoine Faivre, professor of History of Esoteric and Mystical Currents in Modern and Contemporary Europe at the École Pratique des Hautes Études at the Sorbonne – the only chair in the world on these subjects at the time. As previously noted, the *laïcité* enshrined in the French Republic meant that such heretical and heterodox religious traditions flourished in the nineteenth century, so it is perhaps unsurprising that the first chair on Western esotericism should be founded there. It was established in 1964 – the same year as the publication of Yates's book – as 'History of Christian Esotericism' on the suggestion of Henry Corbin, but renamed on the retirement of the previous incumbent, the aptly named François Secret, in 1979.[7] Faivre was a regular attendee of the Eranos conferences, which he began attending in 1973, and a disciple of Henry Corbin.[8]

In 1974, Corbin formed the Centre International du Recherche Spirituelle Comparée (also known as the 'Université Saint-Jean de Jérusalem'), made up of about thirty scholars who wished to 'rebel' against the academy's fixation on 'historicism' and 'scientism', apparently modelled on Eranos; both Faivre and Eliade were members.[9]

In a model first presented in 1991, and most influentially published in the monograph *L'ésotérisme* in 1992, Faivre defined esotericism as a 'pattern of thought', consisting of four essential elements and two additional contingent factors. These are:

1. The belief that a vast complex of correspondences underpins reality;
2. The belief that all life constitutes a single organism;
3. The belief that the imagination can access extra-mundane levels of being through ritual, meditation or symbolism;
4. The belief that individuals, as well as nature as a whole, can undergo ontological transformations, which Faivre, drawing from Corbin, terms gnosis.[10]

The additional factors are that of (5) *concordance*, that the various teachings share some common fundament, and (6) tradition, that is transmitted or initiated through masters.

Points (1) and (2) conceive of esotericism as possessing of a holistic view of the cosmos, in which networks of correspondences link all existence into one great being. This positive view of the material world is a ubiquitous feature of those traditions identified as part of Western esotericism – Hanegraaff writes that 'esotericism is a product of the "discovery of nature," and has, from the very beginning, displayed a strong interest in understanding the secrets of the natural world',[11] and van den Broek states, 'Nowhere in the Hermetic texts do we find the idea that the cosmos is bad, or that it had been created by an evil demiurge. On the contrary, the cosmos is God's beautiful creation'.[12] Clearly, this is a tension between the Western esoteric use of gnosis, and all of the academic conceptions of Gnosticism we have encountered thus far, in which alienation (whether philosophical or psychological) is seen as the defining feature.

To get around this, Faivre explicitly differentiates between Gnosticism as a 'religious system' of Late Antiquity, which he associates with anticosmic dualism, and 'gnosis in general' which is a 'spiritual and intellectual attitude' typifying esotericism more broadly.[13] In this, he is repeating the Messina categorization, itself developing from Quispel and Jonas. Yet this is to take the actual historical evidence – that is, the texts and contemporary accounts – and extrapolate from

Figure 7: Gilbert Durand (another Centre International du Recherche Spirituelle Comparée member), Henry Corbin and Antoine Faivre at Eranos in the 1970s. Reprinted with the permission of Association des amis de Henry et Stella Corbin (AAHSC), www.amiscorbin.com.

them a 'spiritual attitude' that is at odds with the evidence, despite generating them and then finding this throughout history.

Faivre defines this gnosis-in-general as 'a spiritual and intellectual activity that can accede to a special mode of knowledge' with a soteriological function.[14] His use of 'accede' could be read as meaning that a person with such an attitude is likely to assert such a special mode of knowledge, but Faivre's elaborations make it clear that he means it more substantively than this and that he himself is acceding to its existence. Gnosis, he writes, 'aims at integrating the self and the relationship of the subject to the self, as well as to that of the entire external world, in a unitary vision of reality'.[15] The Jungian influence is apparent here, remembering that nowhere before Jung does 'the self' appear in primary or secondary sources. But here Faivre is not using Quispel's model of gnosis as a third epistemological tradition; rather, his model of gnosis integrates scientific knowledge and 'abolishes the distinction between faith and knowledge'.[16] Gnosis is, then, 'an integrating knowledge, a grasp of fundamental relations including the least apparent that exist among the various levels of reality, e.g., among God, humanity and the universe'. Nevertheless, his model reflects the phenomenological essentialism of Eranos – Henry Corbin, Mircea Eliade and French Traditionalist René Guénon (whose pseudohistorical works had a significant impact on Eliade and other scholars of religions) are the only twentieth-century intellectuals and scholars cited in the section defining gnosis, alongside Husserl, Sri Aurobindo, St Paul and a couple of nineteenth-century 'theosophers'.[17]

Eliade's own writings on Gnosticism from the time similarly lean into the Eranos definitions, distinguishing between Gnosticism proper and various forms of gnosis, which he identifies with esotericism – 'the initiatory transmission of doctrines and practices restricted to a limited number of adepts'.[18] Eliade's student (and 1977 Eranos delegate) Ioan Culianu's work on Gnosticism also deserves a mention here.[19] Culianu's *The Tree of Gnosis* (published in 1992) builds on his historical-cognitive project to plot the cultural evolution of all religious ideas in an everlasting efflorescence or growth of mental bifurcations (or digital options), to show Gnosticism as the primary and most baroque example of this.[20] His taxonomy of religious dualism(s) is organized according to two criteria – (1) the degree to which the universe can be considered good, or intelligent, and (2) the degree of commensurability between the universe and human beings.[21] Christianity, Judaism and Platonism confirm both criteria, he argues, and Manichaeism affirms the first but denies the second, but Gnosticism denies both – in other words, gnostic dualism is inherently anticosmic.[22] Culianu's murder in May 1991 meant that his argument remained a sketch and something of a methodological cul-de-sac. Yet it is important to the broader arguments of this book as it places gnosis at the centre of an attempt to re-establish the History of Religions along cognitive lines.

At a 1992 conference in Lyon, where Faivre was presenting his recently published definition of Western esotericism, Wouter Hanegraaff presented him with a draft paper based on Quispel's epistemological definition of gnosis. Hanegraaff was then a doctoral student at Utrecht, under Roelof van den Broek, professor of Hellenistic Religious History and a former student of Quispel. Two years later, after submitting his PhD thesis, Hanegraaff began a postdoctoral fellowship which included a year working in Paris with Faivre.[23] Hanegraaff's thesis, quickly published as *New Age Religion and Western Culture: Esotericism in the Mirror of Secular Thought* (1996), argues that New Age religion/s are a popularized, secularized and commodified version of Western esotericism, typified by gnosis:

The traditions based on gnosis can be seen as a sort of traditional western counter-culture, and this goes a long way to explaining why New Age religion expresses its own criticism of dominant western culture by formulating alternatives derived from esotericism. Like the New Age movement, western esotericism has from the beginning been characterized by an ambiguous position 'in between' official religion and science. Like the New Age movement, it is critical of dualism and reductionism (even if not all its alternatives are equally successful in avoiding it), and strives for a 'higher synthesis' most congenial to the epistemological attitude of gnosis. The fundamental complaints of New Age religion about modern western culture are similar to those of western esotericism generally; in fact, all the elements of New Age culture criticism listed above would be quite acceptable to western esotericists in earlier periods. There is, however, one fundamental distinction: traditional esoteric alternatives to dominant cultural and religious trends were formulated in the context of an 'enchanted' worldview, while the New Age movement has adopted that worldview in a thoroughly secularized fashion.[24]

Theoretically, *New Age Religion* combines Faivre's definition of Western esotericism – which he notes, apparently with approval, was an attempt to 're-mythologize' the 'disenchanted modern world'[25] – with Quispel's epistemic tripartite model of gnosis. Indeed, it opens with a preface in which Hanegraaff tells the reader that his first experience of Gnosticism was as a boy, where he felt a 'vague feeling of fascination' towards a book by Hans Jonas – that 'strange charm' again – and then years later by a book which presented gnosis as a 'third pillar' of knowledge alongside reason and faith.[26] The book is not explicitly named, but is clearly Quispel's *Gnosis: De derde component van de Europese cultuurtraditie* (1988).[27] Quispel was the only academic known for writing about esoteric themes in the Netherlands at that time, presenting himself to the public as a 'Wise Old Man', as Jung had. The impetus for Hanegraaff's subsequent development of Quispel's model came through his supervisor (and Quispel's former student), van den Broek.

Van den Broek's account of 'Gnostic religion' clearly shows the influence of the Eranos group's sui generis essentialism and Jung's psychologization. Gnosis is

> an esoteric, that is partly secret, spiritual knowledge of God and of the divine origin and destination of the essential core of the human being which is based on revelation and inner enlightenment, the possession of which involves a liberation from the material world which holds humans captive.[28]

As such, van den Broek considers gnosis and gnostic to be equally applicable to 'all ideas and currents, from Antiquity to the present day, that stress the necessity of esoteric knowledge'.[29] So, typically, van den Broek rejects Gnosticism as an abstract, second-order category, but is happy to use gnosis as a second-order category, describing many traditions as gnostic that do not identify themselves as such. Surprisingly, van den Broek marshals Williams's critical deconstruction of the category from *Rethinking 'Gnosticism'* to *support* the historical-Gnosticism/ahistorical-gnosis dialectic – because we can't talk about a specific historical religion called Gnosticism, van den Broak argues, we should instead talk about a 'religious current characterized by a strong emphasis on esoteric knowledge (Gnosis)'.[30]

The tradition is transmitted through masters. Hanegraaff's model, presented in *New Age Religion*, clearly develops out of van den Broek's historical model, Faivre's equation of esotericism and gnosis, and Quispel's reason–faith–gnosis tripartite. However, he attempts to develop clearer epistemological justification for this division:

> *Reason:* Truth through rational and sensory faculties of humans. Accessible by all, and open to verification and/or falsification.
>
> *Faith:* Truth revealed from transcendental sphere. Accessible, but not falsifiable. Ultimate authority lies with a God, mediated through institutions.
>
> *Gnosis:* Truth through inner personal revelation. Not generally accessible, nor falsifiable. Ultimate authority lies with inner experience.[31]

Interestingly, Hanegraaff notes that the 'experience' which differentiates gnosis from reason and faith is of 'God and the Self', indicating some Jungian influence.[32] Indeed, while Hanegraaff does acknowledge that Jung was influenced by esoteric traditions, he downplays Jung's influence on Quispel by noting that Quispel came into contact with Jung when he was already an old man and critiqued his interpretation of Gnosticism.[33] But the issue is not that Quispel influenced Jung, so this is not very relevant – Jung's influence on Quispel's model of Gnosticism was considerable, and it was through Quispel (and others) that Jung's ideas were transmitted into mainstream academia. Although Hanegraaff is right to point out that Jung's conclusions are ultimately derived from religious revelation and *völkische* ideas rather than empirical evidence, he avoids the implications of this for his own work in utilizing Quispel's methodology.[34]

To be clear, Hanegraaff stresses that he is employing the tripartite epistemic categorization analytically, not as a historical reality, and as such, differently from Quispel. As early as *New Age Religion*, he takes care to present his approach as empirical and distinct from 'religionist approaches', and I do not want to argue here that he fully essentializes the category (i.e. in a sui generis way, although some others in the Western esotericism field have, including van den Broek and Versluis).[35] While Western esotericism draws on the lineage of Eranos and the History of Religions school, the influence is of a different order than the latter two examples I present here.

That said, Hanegraaff's attempt to establish this faith–reason–gnosis tripartite systematically raises a number of questions. Are *all* claims which are neither communicable nor verifiable gnosis, or are there subdivisions or further nuances which one might identify, such as salvific quality or union with the godhead?[36] How have 'communicability' and 'verifiability' been selected as the epistemic characteristics? There are numerous descriptions of gnosis – on what grounds is Hanegraaff, therefore, identifying it as not communicable, but Christian faith as communicable? Importantly, given that other terms are available, why does Hanegraaff use gnosis, rather than a more neutral term? It does not seem that Hanegraaff has started with an analysis of knowledge claims to which he has adopted 'gnosis' to identify one; rather, he has started with the Quispellian model and sought an epistemic justification post hoc – which is to say, starting with the category and looking for data to support it. Moreover, the examples furnished to support the category do not themselves use the term 'gnosis', so they do not prove the category, merely present examples of how Hanegraaff has used the category.

His 1998 'On the Construction of Esoteric Tradition' – a lengthy article which marks this move towards a more discursive and historical methodology – addresses this explicitly: such a 'nominalistic and non-historical perspective' might be 'theoretically valid as a heuristic tool' but is problematic in establishing an academic field of study because as an etic theoretic construct, it 'cannot possibly have a social or a historical-developmental dimension'.[37] Gershom Scholem is raised as a possible exemplar of a more historical approach, or rather 'counter-historical', in which a neglected aspect of history must be brought to light to enable a more complete historical reconstruction (although we might recall Scholem's religious and political motivations also).[38] He concludes that 'although *a priori* typologies [*nota bene*] such as developed by myself may validly be applied to the field of "esotericism," they should not themselves be the foundation for construing that field'.[39] Rather, the *intuitive* [again, *nota bene*] notion of a triad 'faith-reason-gnosis' can be given a precise historical meaning: 'gnosis' is not just equivalent to a vague notion of higher, absolute or perfect knowledge, but stands much more specifically for the possibility of direct and unmediated, supra-rational, salvational access to the supreme spiritual level of reality.[40]

In this later presentation then, Western esotericism as a field is construed as *a tradition of discourse regarding the possibility of gnosis*, rather than a tradition of gnostic experiences per se.[41] Still, by combining Faivre's typology with Quispel's epistemological definition of gnosis, Hanegraaff is effectively creating a historical heuristic out of sui generis essentialist cloth. As such, Hanegraaff has helped to perpetuate the aspects of the Eranos circle, as well as the gnosis–substantive/Gnosticism–historical distinction of the Messina definitions.

So, if as he says, the Quispel epistemological tripartite is not historical reality, but an analytic heuristic, of what analytical function is it and for whom is it useful? Why the need to establish a category for analysis with such a narrow focus on a particular set of marginalized knowledge and only in 'the West'? It is hard not to conclude that access to such non-rational knowledge is a real concern for Hanegraaff. But in part, at least, the aim is to legitimize a field of study called Western esotericism. Like Nicholas Goodrick-Clarke's chair in Western esotericism at the University of Exeter, which was supported financially by the Blavatsky Trust,[42] Hanegraaff's Amsterdam chair is privately funded. While this does not in itself suggest a normative agenda, it does imply that there is a symbiotic relationship between scholars and practitioners of Western esotericism – though this is by no means unusual in the modern academy, given the considerable influence of the John Templeton Foundation. Yet we might pause to consider that we have categories deriving from Eranos and the History of Religions – that were first-order categories even then and remain so now – being mobilized again as theoretical support in the establishment of a new subfield in Religious Studies.

In July 1997, Rosalie Basten, a wealthy Dutch businesswoman, and her lawyer approached van den Broek to help her in founding a chair in Hermetic philosophy at a Belgian or Dutch university. She had previously been frustrated during her studies in philosophy during the 1980s but was fascinated by Yates's book and had come across van den Broek's name in his translation of the *Corpus Hermeticism* with Quispel (1990).[43] The *Bibliotheca Philosophica Hermetica* (also called the Ritman Library) was under threat, which was gaining attention in the press, so their proposal was timely. In

August 1997, they approached the Board of Governors of the University of Amsterdam, who liked the idea and proposed an 'ordinary professorship' (i.e. one which falls under the full jurisdiction and standards of the university, although externally funded). The 'Foundation Chair of History of Hermetic Philosophy and Related Currents' was established on 20 February 1998, with van den Broek, Basten and her lawyer Willem Koudjis as Board of Governors, although it would take until November for the financial details to be worked out. Finally, it was established as a 'chair group' at the Department of Theology and Religious Studies, in the Faculty of Humanities. While this was happening, they held a small conference in Beaulieu in January 1998, with Antoine Faivre an invited speaker.[44]

Since then, the foundation has funded the professorial chair, two assistant professorships, two doctoral candidates and a secretary, although the hiring committee was assigned by the university. Wouter Hanegraaff was appointed as the chair in July 1999, and Jean-Pierré Brach and Olav Hammer were both appointed as assistant professors the following year.[45] Jean-Pierre Brach became Faivre's successor at the Sorbonne in 2002 and was replaced at Amsterdam by Kocku von Stuckrad; Hammer moved to the University of Southern Denmark, Odense, in 2004, and was replaced by Marco Pasi. This team remained for five years, until von Stuckrad became professor at Groningen and was replaced by Peter Forshaw in 2009. On top of the two PhD candidates, the group has maintained an annual intake of around twenty, mostly international, Masters students.[46]

In the first ten years, the group produced a remarkable output of research, including ten monographs, eleven other books and around two hundred journal articles. The books included the massive *Dictionary of Gnosis and Western Esotericism* for Brill, which Hanegraaff edited with assistance from Faivre, van den Broek and Brach, and which was eventually published in 2005. The volume was originally proposed by van den Broek as the *Dictionary of Gnosticism and Western Esotericism*. Faivre insisted that Western esotericism could only be considered to begin in the Renaissance, so this schema would exclude non-gnostic esoterica from Antiquity and the Middle Ages. Hanegraaff proposed using 'gnosis' rather than 'Gnosticism' as a solution. So while pragmatically, rather than programmatically, motivated, this certainly reinforced the impression that gnosis was the sine qua non of the category Western esotericism. Moreover, the distinction between the historical Gnosticism and the ahistorical gnosis reproduces the Messina definitions, and both titles assume continuity (historical or phenomenological) between the Gnosticism of Late Antiquity and the esotericism of the Renaissance.[47]

Hanegraaff was also co-editor of *Aries: Journal for the Study of Western Esotericism* from its reestablishment in 2001 until 2010.[48] He was also president of the European Society for the Study of Western Esotericism (ESSWE, now affiliated with the IAHR) from its foundation in 2005 until 2013. Rosalie Basten and Faivre both served on the board of the ESSWE until 2010. What is clear then is that, although not the instigator of Western esotericism as an academic field, Hanegraaff has been its driving force. We might also note that while the chair is in Hermetic Philosophy and Related Currents, it is under the term Western esotericism that the larger subfield has coalesced. Yet through the influence of Quispel (through the tripartite epistemological model), Corbin (the use of gnosis as the essence of esotericism) and Jung (the historical narrative of gnosis's passage through Antiquity to the Middle Ages and modernity), Western esotericism is a direct descendent of the History of Religions approach to Gnosticism. However, this is by no means its only forebear, and historians of natural philosophy and Renaissance and early modern thought were just as influential, indeed perhaps more so. Which is to say, many of these scholars were not trained in Religious Studies, so perhaps some naiveté is understandable – but the reception they have received from the field is rather harder to justify, albeit predictable given the argument presented in this book thus far.

Hanegraaff's work gradually abandoned the Quispellian terminology and had moved to a more strictly historical model of esotericism by the 1998's *On the Construction of Esoteric Traditions*. Since then, Hanegraaff's students and colleagues have had a strong influence on the shape of the field – Brach, Hammer and von Stuckrad are each full professor in their own right, and Pasi was general secretary of the European Association for the Study of Religions (EASR) from 2014 to 2019. The group has not been without disagreement, however, and methodological and theoretical issues have been at the forefront from the beginning.[49] Perhaps the most significant of these debates has been over the introduction of a discursive approach by von Stuckrad, in a series of articles beginning in 2003[50] and culminating with the monograph *Locations of Knowledge in Medieval and Early Modern Europe* in 2010, in which esoteric discourses are identified as those in which '*claims* to "real" or absolute knowledge and the means of making this knowledge available' are made.[51] For von Stuckrad then, the importance of esotericism for the study of religion is not as a marginalized current or tradition, but rather as a significant site of contestation in the discourse on the legitimization of different forms of knowledge, and in particular the (shifting, putative) boundary between religion and science in the medieval and early modern periods. He argues that this would address what von Stuckrad sees as the two major 'challenges' in the field. The first is methodological – Faivre's definition is not consistently used and often a common-sense understanding relating to secrecy and concealment is used instead; there is a lack of clarity over the time period in which esotericism may be found, and the West is neither a clearly defined geographical area nor one disconnected from outside influences.[52] The second challenge is that, strategically, Western esotericism may be more of a hindrance than a help, in terms of careers and the acceptance of the material's import. He states that 'the common presentation of esotericism as being linked to rejected, oppressed, fringe, or countercultural knowledge … has repeatedly reinforced the narratives that this critique addresses and unintentionally confirms the fringe status of esotericism research'. He goes on to suggest that it is time to leave the category Western esotericism behind.[53]

Hanegraaff responded to this at some length in *Esotericism and the Academy*.[54] Among several critiques, his primary concern seems to be that the details of these marginalized historical texts will cease to be of importance and may even disappear from academic sight once again.[55] Here Hanegraaff reveals that, while not religionist, there is nevertheless *something* in these texts that he seems himself as custodian of, or even advocate for – as suggested by his stress that, despite his second-order heuristic, his work is nevertheless 'empirical', not discursive. Hanegraaff is concerned that, with a shift from historical textual analysis to analysis of power relations, we also move from a concern with what the texts were telling *their* readers, to 'only what his discourse may be telling *us*'.[56] It's hard to escape the impression that it is telling us something about access to special knowledge, even if the term 'gnosis' is not being used.

Hanegraaff continues: in making 'history subservient to theory', discourse analysis becomes 'exclusivist and reductionist' and implies that all other methods are covertly '"religionist," "essentialist," or "phenomenological"'.[57] Well, he's not wrong – discourse analysis, like all critical methodologies, inevitably exposes implicit assumptions, and in Religious Studies these are more often than not religionist to some degree. Historicism which doesn't adequately separate first-order and second-order categories – something that has dogged the study of Gnosticism since day one – cannot help but reproduce the episteme in which the texts were produced. Nevertheless, it's an interesting point; does discourse analysis impose modern frames of understanding onto historical materials, much as the History of Religions did onto non-Western cultures? Perhaps so – though I would argue that the difference is that it doesn't then ascribe those understandings to the writers and audiences of those texts, and so keeps the separation between first-order and second-order categories. Moreover, while von Stuckrad's analysis is concerned with the European history of religion, there is no reason why such an analysis could not be used in a finer grain analysis of specific texts. However, Hanegraaff's apparent belief that somehow theory could be subservient to history – as though history were simply 'out there', pristine and accessible to the historian without theoretical mediation – suggests an affinity with the Historicism of Scholem and the History of Religions. And indeed, in the 2019 newsletter of the ESSWE, Hanegraaff makes it clear that he does seek to restore these esoteric histories to their rightful place, to restore, renew and perhaps re-enchant the West:

> In my opinion, now that we have deconstructed those old triumphalist narratives, I think it is time to start building again. That is to say, we need to start reconstructing 'Western culture' on new and better foundations that 'reject the previous rejection of rejected knowledge.' In other words, I'm convinced that we need a new grand narrative of 'Western culture' that includes and accepts all those dimensions that used to be 'othered', discredited and rejected, and integrates them as legitimate and vital parts of what 'the West' is really all about.[58]

It is unclear to what degree such theoretical debates motivated von Stuckrad's move away from Hanegraaff, but it is certainly the case that his work since has abandoned the terms 'Western esotericism' and 'gnosis'. Interestingly, Hanegraaff himself has moved away from these terms, and *Esotericism and the Academy* has only a single, slightly dismissive, mention of the Quispel tripartite. A new expansion of the *Dictionary of Gnosis and Western Esotericism*, currently in production, edited by Egil Asprem, is renamed the *Dictionary of Contemporary Esotericism*, and the 'official' book series renamed the *Brill Esotericism Reference Library*. The 'Western' qualifier has also been dropped, as the field continues to reassess its methodological heritage.[59]

The introduction to a volume marking the twentieth anniversary of the Amsterdam chair, co-written by Hanegraaff, announces that it is now 'safe to conclude that the battle for academic legitimacy has been won, or at the very least that the Rubicon has been crossed'.[60] Hanegraaff and the other scholars associated with the Amsterdam Western esotericism school have been instrumental in the continuing influence of the gnosis–essentialist/Gnosticism–historicist split introduced by Jonas and Quispel and codified by the Messina Congress. Heuristic or otherwise, this connection with exclusive, countercultural or at least special, knowledge may in fact be part of the appeal for students and scholars, and scholars may still occasionally make appeals to elite knowledge.

10

Knowledge of the heart: The gnostic New Age

That there is a gnostic character to the many new religious movements that emerged in the quarter century following the Second World War is hardly a new claim. As we have seen, many Theosophists and esotericists thought that the Gnostics were their forerunners in the nineteenth century, and several French heterodox churches were specifically identifying themselves as gnostic. Many of Rudolf Steiner's works used the term 'Lucifer-Gnosis' to identify his philosophy.[1] Several post-war new religions identified themselves as gnostic – Samael Aun Weor even declared himself the avatar of the New Age. While the Nag Hammadi texts were mostly yet to be published for a general audience, Gnosticism was one among the many countercultural ideas circulating in the alternative communities (such as Findhorn in the north-east of Scotland) and wider networks that came to be known as the New Age movement by the mid-1960s.[2] Between 1985 and 1999, *Gnosis* magazine was a leading publication in what they termed 'the esoteric spiritual traditions of the West' (New Age having fallen out of favour as an emic identifier by then) and featured interviews with such familiar figures as Gilles Quispel, Joscelyn Godwin and Stephan Hoeller.[3] Terms and cosmological ideas drawn from Jungian and Theosophical interpretations of Gnosticism can be readily identified in the work of David Icke beginning in 1992, continuing through his development of a more pessimistic and conspiratorial worldview in the wake of the perceived failure of the prophesied New Age to transform the world for the better.[4] I found that the abductees at Whitley Streiber's 'Dreamland' event in Nashville in 2012 often used gnosis to describe their extraterrestrial and paranormal experiences.[5]

Ingvild Gilhus suggests that this gnostic narrative in New Age discourse represents a resistance against the decentering of the self in the contemporary world. She writes:

These myths represent countermoves against routinization and bureaucratization, which reduce human beings to numbers in statistics and to anonymity. As countermoves, they offer strategies for making the self whole, potent and free – on a spiritual level. In these myths, imaginative spaces are created, confined spheres, within which human beings are set free from the control of society.[6]

Her presentation here resembles Blumenberg's interpretation – Gnosticism is not a nihilistic threat, but an opportunity for humans to take charge of their own salvation. Most post-war writers saw Gnosticism as something negative, however, and many saw the New Age as evidence of that.

Like Voegelin and Taubes, the political theologian Carl Raschke saw Gnosticism as intrinsically anti-modern. In *The Interruption of Eternity: Modern Gnosticism and the Origins of the New Religious Consciousness* (1980), he identifies as gnostic a chain of thought from German Romantics, Jung, the Nazis to New Religious Movements, in which disaffected intellectuals reject the modern world and retreat into imaginary utopias. This 'gnostic consciousness' which emerged in the nineteenth century is a rejection of history over knowledge of the self, Raschke argues, and a dangerous flight from contemporary realities. The failure of the revolution of the 1960s led not to the establishment of new paradigms for social organization, but to a retreat into the individual consciousness.[7] Drawing from Puech and Eliade, he described the Gnostics as in 'revolt' against any materiality and, particularly, time: 'The Gnostic complains that time in any form cannot satisfy man's most authentic desires. … The Gnostic admits no past or future; he lives solely in a coruscating present of his own desperate musings.'[8] Raschke's modern Gnostic shares with his classical forebears a preference for esoteric illumination over rational enquiry; self-salvation over collective redemption (*contra* Voegelin); a tendency to look to the past for inspiration; and an obsession with the evils of the present order. Negative evaluation notwithstanding, I suspect that many contemporary Gnostics and New Agers would agree with him. Nevertheless, while Raschke later became a somewhat respected political theologian, his early work (including *The Interruption of Eternity*) is pure evangelical polemic, and his later *Painted Black* (1992) is widely regarded as hysterical, with Arthur Versluis describing it as 'breathless sensationalism'.[9]

Harold Bloom, Yale professor of English, read Jonas's *The Gnostic Religion* during a bout of depression in 1965, triggering a 'kind of "religious" conversion' which 'rescued' him from his depression.[10] He came to realize that the transcendent stranger God or alien God of Gnosticism, being beyond our cosmos, is no longer an effective force; God exists, but is so hidden that he has become a nihilistic conception, in himself. He is not responsible for our world ... he is so estranged and exiled that he is powerless.[11]

He began to refer to himself as a 'Jewish Gnostic', in terms which would have been quite understandable to Jonas, Scholem and the others:

> I am nothing if not Jewish. ... I really am a product of Yiddish culture. But I can't understand a Yahweh, or a God, who could be all-powerful and all knowing and would allow the Nazi death camps and schizophrenia.[12]

It inspired his first and only novel, *The Flight to Lucifer* (1979), in which Valentinus is transferred to the twentieth-century United States, and years later he published a commentary on the Gospel of Thomas.[13] His primary focus remained literary criticism, however, where he developed an idiosyncratic but influential model of gnosis as a form of poetic knowledge – knowledge of the timeless, divine *pneuma* (as opposed to the temporal, mundane self), experienced through deep engagement with poetry, even union with the poem.[14] More than this, in challenging the authority of the biblical texts and their author(s), Bloom argues that Gnosticism is 'the truly first Modernism'.[15]

When he moves into writing about contemporary popular religion in *The American Religion* (1992) and *Omens of the Millennium* (1996), Bloom shifts to a more normative evaluation, distinguishing the 'pure' gnosis of the Valentinians – 'a knowledge of something in the self that cannot die, because it was never born'[16] – with what he considered the commercialized and trivial versions of the New Age milieu. Yet other forms of contemporary American religion – Mormons, Jehovah's Witnesses, even Pentecostals – are, for Bloom, gnostic in a more positive sense; a revival of an experiential, salvific, pure Christianity.[17]

Bloom is a brilliant, polemical writer, with endless bitter *bon motes*, which helps to cover the generalizations and leaps of creative comparison which increasingly came to typify his work. But like Voegelin and Raschke, it's hard to escape the impression of someone who is so shocked that some dislike the social order which suits him so well that he finds it necessary to pathologize them.

Bloom's condemnation of the New Age was echoed in a number of polemical works by Christian scholars – which, perhaps unsurprisingly, often equated it with Gnosticism. These include Cyril O'Regan's *Gnostic Return in Modernity*

(2001), Catherine Tumber's *American Feminism and the Birth of New Age Spirituality* (2002) and Peter Jones's *The Gnostic Empire Strikes Back* (1992), which asks, 'What if the New Age is actually a more potent form of ancient pagan Gnosticism, whose Satanic dimensions and spiritual bankruptcy led so many astray in the past before it was exposed and denounced by the early church?'[18] Jones warns:

> History, albeit diabolical history, is repeating it before our very eyes. We can therefore begin to understand the changes taking place in our contemporary culture. The Earth Summit, homosexuality, feminism, mandated cultural and ethnic diversity, etc., are not unrelated phenomena ... they are deeply related aspects of a coherent religious agenda whose goal is the creation of a new humanity made in the image of the god of this world. This bottom line should convince you to take the New Age with utmost seriousness.[19]

Most of the early scholarly works on the New Age movement, however, presented it as something merely trivial and capricious, if commercialized and rather vulgar.[20] A few, notably Paul Heelas and Michael York, presented a much more sympathetic perspective, though often reproducing emic discourse rather uncritically.[21] A 'second wave' of scholarship on the history of the New Age movement began in the 1990s, in which the broad, comparative surveys of the earliest scholarship are developed with contextualized historical and ethnographic studies and more fully developed theoretical models.[22] Here, I am using New Age entirely as an etic sense, in the way it has become established in Religious Studies to refer to the loosely structured milieu of noninstitutionalized metaphysical beliefs and practices. This is not entirely satisfactory – (When does it start, and end? What is included? How does it relate to the discourse on 'spirituality?) – but I stick with it here for shorthand and because this is the term used by a number of first- and second-wave scholars who have also used Gnosticism as a model to understand this milieu.[23]

We have already encountered Hanegraaff's *New Age Religion*, which argued that the New Age movement was a secularized manifestation of Western esotericism, defined by claims of gnosis. In hindsight it is clear that Hanegraaff is really more concerned with conceptualizing Western esotericism than with New Age – his definition of New Age is vague and circular, though his historicization of the movement into *sensu strictu* to indicate the millenarian, post-Theosophical groups of the 1950s and 1960s, and *sensu lato* for the later free market 'self-spirituality' remains a useful and important contribution.[24] A more recent and forceful argument comes from April DeConick's *The Gnostic New Age* (2016), and this will be the central case study of this chapter.

But for scholars to present the New Age as a contemporary expression of Gnosticism, or perhaps more accurately of 'gnostic spirituality', is I argue to make the tail wag the dog. The proto-New Age Theosophical teachings influenced later academic understanding of Gnosticism, not the other way around. In other words, it is no historical discovery that New Age and Gnosticism have parallels – the categories emerged at the same time, from the same context and many of the same people, and show the concerns of their day, both academic and personal – the critique of traditional religious institutions and the social mores they upheld, the emphasis on experience and individual growth, and of a common perennial spirituality.

For example, DeConick writes that the discovery of the Nag Hammadi texts triggered a 'Gnostic awakening' that 'inspired an unprecedented renaissance of Gnostic [i.e. New Age] spirituality in America'.[25] Yet the roots of New Age far predate the 1946 discovery, developing out of late Theosophical ideas in alternative communities in the interwar years.[26] It took until the 1970s for popular editions of Nag Hammadi texts to be widely available, and any ideas that were in circulation about Gnosticism before then were drawn from Jung, Jonas and the like. As we saw in Chapter 2, the heresiological legend of the Gnostics was already part of the cultic milieu through the Theosophical Society by the beginning of the twentieth century, and these texts, along with their perennialist interpretation, circulated freely in the proto-New Age communities. After the Second World War, both New Age and Gnosticism increasingly incorporated Jung's psychological interpretations, which would have further encouraged comparison between them. From the 1960s, the baby boomers began to abandon the traditional churches in search of authenticity and expressive individualism, reproducing the unregulated free market social order of the post-war West. The New Age and Gnosticism were a perfect fit, and as we saw in Chapter 9, a number of New Age groups appealed to the Gnostics for legitimacy. Yet none of the scholars who want to connect the New Age to Gnosticism seem to have any interest in these self-identifying modern gnostic religions and indeed barely acknowledge their existence.

If it is true that the sui generis, essentialist, psychologized, experiential spirit of post-war phenomenology of religion lives on in the New Age movement, as Wasserstrom claims,[27] then the motif that the New Age movement is gnostic in character, as Hanegraaff, DeConick and others suggest, is particularly telling.

Although the comparisons are substantively different, DeConick and Hanegraaff share the idea that the Gnosticism of Late Antiquity is just one flowering of a perennial tradition called gnosis, which re-emerged in Catharism, esotericism, existentialism and/or the New Age movement – an idea directly inherited from Jung, Quispel, Mead and Blavatsky.[28] The History of Religions and the New Age movement were mutually supportive, for example through the mass publication of Eliade's books (in some cases, by the Jungian Bollingen Press).[29] The proto–New Age Theosophical teachings influenced later academic understandings of Gnosticism, *not the other way around*.

This may explain why there is often a normative or confessional aspect to work that connects Gnosticism and the New Age – not only is Gnosticism something accessible today; it is *a good thing*. It is a bulwark against stagnant religious institutions, a chance of renewal in a disenchanted world – just as it was in Late Antiquity, if many of these scholars are to be believed. In his introduction to Widengren's *The Gnostic Attitude*, Birger Pearson writes – in words that might well describe the History of Religions as much as the New Age movement – of

> a widespread current of feeling in the Western World ... that is quite comparable to that 'spirit of late antiquity' ... from which the various gnostic sects of the early centuries of our era were nourished: a feeling of world-weariness, of powerlessness in the face of dark and impersonal forces at loose in the social and political arena, a fascination with the occult and with esoteric lore, a quest for meaning in the face of meaninglessness, and a search for ego identity.[30]

DeConick's work is embedded in post–Nag Hammadi Biblical Studies, however. During this time, a number of scholars wrote works aimed at a more general audience, especially after the success of *The Nag Hammadi Library in English* in 1977.[31] Elaine Pagels's *The Gnostic Gospels* (1979) is perhaps the most influential of these and argued that the heresiological construction of Gnosticism was due to issues of authority and leadership, rather than theological disputes. Reversing the standard approach, she asks what social function is derived from gnostic theology. She suggests that the 'Gnostic modification of monotheism' was primarily understood as an attack upon apostolic authority.[32] In her interpretation, Irenaeus's problem with gnosis is that it 'offers nothing less than a theological justification for refusing to obey the bishops and priests'.[33] This provides her with a commonality in the Nag Hammadi texts, which is not theological, but doctrinal nonetheless – the rejection of episcopal authority.

Pagels began working on the as-yet-unpublished Nag Hammadi texts as a postgraduate under Helmut Koester (a staunch defender of the Bauer Thesis) and George MacRae at Harvard in the late 1960s and early 1970s.[34] She would go on to write introductions for four of the texts in *The Nag Hammadi Library in English* in 1977.[35] Random House then published *The Gnostic Gospels*, a reworking of some previously published papers into a readable narrative aimed at a popular audience. In this, it was undeniably successful, selling in huge numbers for a work of biblical scholarship and winning both the National Book Award and the National Book Critics Circle Award. Public interest in Gnosticism and 'lost Gospels' remained high after the discovery of Nag Hammadi and the Dead Sea Scrolls, which certainly created a market for such a book. Others tried the same formula, though rarely as successfully, such as Philip Jenkins's *Hidden Gospels* (2001) or the journalist John Dart's *The Jesus of Heresy and History* (1988).

Perhaps as importantly, the book also draws parallels between Gnosticism and New Age, which in 1979 was arguably reaching its apex: an interest in the sacred feminine, and its absence from mainstream Christianity; a focus on religion's allegedly therapeutic psychological function, which can be uncovered in its mythological writings; and a particular attention towards experience as the fundament of spirituality – to whit, 'true' religion. As the introduction to her recent festschrift puts it:

> In a period when many Americans had become dissatisfied with traditional Christianity, viewing its institutions as patriarchal, its sexual mores as repressive, its reliance on creeds and clergy stifling, and its association with establishment power alienating, the story of these lost gospels offered an alternative vision – not a different set of creeds or authorities to follow, but rather an understanding that Christianity could be *other than it is*. While many children of the 1950s and '60s were turning away from Christianity to explore Buddhism, Hinduism, and 'New Age' mysticism, Pagels delved back into the depths of the Christian past to discover alternative spiritual paths, and in doing so, she brought many people along with her. Ironically, despite the vitriol sometimes aimed at her by conservative Christians, Pagels has no doubt 'saved' Christianity for many people, giving them a way to reclaim it for themselves.[36]

Several earlier papers showed that Pagels was already interested in the place of women in the early church and early Christian theology.[37] The *Gnostic Gospels* devotes considerable space to demonstrating the feminine aspects of gnostic theology, particularly the figure of Sophia and how her presence again challenges the authority of orthodox Christianity.[38] However, it lends itself in places to a simplistic reading which would support the thesis of the Gnostics as spiritual rebels, cruelly suppressed by 'organized religion':

> For nearly 2,000 years, Christian tradition has preserved and revered orthodox writings that denounce the gnostics, while suppressing – and virtually destroying – the gnostic writings themselves.[39]

She also appeals to the Jungian narrative that Gnosticism is essentially psychological in nature, presumably via Quispel. The knowledge which gnostics seek – gnosis – is self-knowledge, she writes, awareness of the self.[40] Again, the phenomenological core of this individual quest is *experience* – 'the source and testing ground of all religious ideas'.[41] This too would appeal to the New Age milieu of the late 1970s, as would the narrative of individuality:

> For Gnostics, exploring the *psyche* became explicitly what it is for many people today implicitly – a religious quest. Some who seek their own interior direction, like the radical gnostics, reject religious institutions as a hindrance to their progress. (emphasis in original)

Pagel's recent work, including *Beyond Belief: The Secret Gospel of Thomas* (2003) and particularly *Why Religion?* (2018), is open about her attraction to the historical material being driven by her personal religious explorations. Whether you find this 'refreshing' or 'alarming', I at least prefer my confessional scholarship to be open, rather than tacit – then a conversation is possible. Significantly, Pagels also frames her religiosity in terms of transcending mere faith and a hope for transformation:

> What is faith? Certainly not simple assent to the set of beliefs that worshippers in that church recited every week … traditional statements that sounded strange to me, like barely intelligible signals from the surface, heard at the bottom of the sea. Such statements seemed to me then to have little to do with whatever transactions we were making with one another, with ourselves, and – so it was said – with invisible beings. I was acutely aware that we met there driven by need and desire; yet sometimes I dared hope that such communion has the potential to transform us.[42]

None of this necessarily invalidates Pagel's work, of course, and it is notable that Williams and King both contributed to her festschrift. Another contributor is DeConick, whose career shows similar concerns and a similar trajectory to Pagels's, particularly the quest for a more 'authentic' and egalitarian original Christianity which prioritizes experience. One of the examiners for her PhD thesis – submitted to the University of Michigan in 1994 – was Gilles Quispel, who she considers her '*Großdoktorvater*', as she later wrote in the foreword to his festschrift.[43] Quispel's model of Gnosticism runs through her work, and like

Quispel, when she extends her analysis into a broader comparative register, the normative phenomenological legacy of the History of Religions becomes clear. According to Gregory Given,

> in Quispel and DeConick's work the script is flipped – an Orientalist polemical category such as Gnosticism is no longer deployed to stake out the Other against which normative Christianity can define itself. Here, instead, a lost expression of authentic Christian religious experience is found preserved in the rigorously ascetic traditions of the East; the scholar's task is to retrieve this archaic vestige and present it to the West as the core of the Christianity it never knew it was missing.[44]

When Jeffrey Kripal became chair of the Department of Religion at Rice University, Houston, Texas, in 2004, he began to actively push to attract DeConick to the department.[45] She joined in 2007, and together they developed the *Gnosticism, Esotericism, Mysticism* (GEM) program, the largest centre for scholarship into Gnosticism in Religious Studies today. Despite their very different specialisms and approaches, there are some similarities between their work – not least that both have engaged actively with essentialized Gnosticism, albeit to somewhat different ends.

The program uses teaching staff from across the department, with courses including the Bible and the Brain, Divine Sex, Advanced Tibetan Language and Culture, American Metaphysical Religion, Islam's Mystical and Esoteric Tradition and – interestingly for this volume – the History of Religions School. The focus on the experiential and heretical is clear in the official description of the GEM programme:

> Traditionally the study of religion has privileged the authoritative voices of the religious experts and the scriptural texts that uphold orthodox faith traditions. ... For too long, scholars have been reluctant to consider this 'other' material central or vital to academic discussions of religion. ... It is our opinion that such an approach has failed to consider fully the process of the construction of orthodoxy and heresy out of a plurality of competing religious voices. This failure creates and sustains political narratives of religion that serve to protect orthodoxies from criticism and promote their biases as historically sound. ... GEM takes into account the plurality of religious voices and expressions, including the neglected currents, in order to reconceive religion. This approach also engages the psychology and the phenomenology of religious experience, rather than relying exclusively on the authorial framings taught by the faith traditions and transmitted in their scriptural texts, interpretations and rituals.

While we recognize that the comparative categories of gnosticism, esotericism and mysticism are modern constructs, each provides us with different nuances that can assist in asking the sort of dialectical questions that will result in a more honest assessment and thick description of religion and the religious traditions we study.[46]

Progressive stuff – though we might just detect some push and pull between positively engaging with 'the psychology and the phenomenology of religious experience' and recognizing these as 'modern constructs'. We will return to this later.

In addition to its teaching program, GEM has hosted two conferences, beginning with Gnostic Countercultures in March 2015. Focusing on the supposedly transgressive qualities of Gnosticism, the conference moved from the early Christian period to the medieval, to the modern, with the entirety of the third day taken up by papers on gnostic themes in contemporary fiction. The second, Gnostic America, was held on 28–31 March 2018. Here the focus was firmly on Gnosticism in the contemporary world, with panels on Gnosticism in fiction and in the movies, in Theosophy and the New Age. There was a clear normative impulse to several papers, including at least one contribution from an insider (Miguel Conner, host of the Aeon Byte podcast). But tellingly, the 'Gnostic New Religions' panel did not have papers on any of the self-identifying gnostic traditions in the world today, such as the Aun Weor groups, Ecclesia Gnostica or the Apostolic Johannite Church – in fact, neither conference had one presentation on either of these groups (although there were papers on two of their forerunners, namely the OTO and Bishop Richard, Duc de Palatine). Rather, papers sought to identify gnostic tendencies in religions which do *not* identify as gnostic, specifically 'African American Religion', Heaven's Gate and Scientology.

DeConick was instrumental in the founding of a new journal with Brill in 2016, entitled *Gnosis: Journal of Gnostic Studies*, of which she remains executive editor, along with Lautaro Roig-Lanzillotta of the University of Groningen. Here, the essentialized, ahistorical, experiential construction of Gnosticism is unambiguous:

The study of Gnostic religious currents from the ancient world to the modern, where 'Gnostic' is broadly conceived as a reference to special direct knowledge of the divine, which either transcends or transgresses conventional religious knowledge. It aims to publish academic papers on: the emergence of the Gnostic, in its many different historical and local cultural contexts; the Gnostic strands that persisted in the middle ages; and modern interpretations of Gnosticism – with the goal of establishing cross-cultural and trans-historical conversations, together with more localized historical analyses.[47]

Here, 'Gnostic religious currents' and 'modern interpretations of Gnosticism' reflect the Messina definitions, with Gnosticism indicating a historically bounded movement and gnosis indicating 'special direct knowledge of the divine'. Despite the two executive editors being trained in Biblical Studies, the journal is by no means concerned only with the period of early Christianity – the description clearly indicates that they accept the Jungian thesis of a continuation of Gnosticism in the medieval period and in 2018 published a special issue on Hermes Trismegistus. There have been papers too on Theosophy and New Age, and a number that follow the cultural studies template of 'Gnostic Themes in [insert novel or sci-fi film]'.

This is in line with a broader thesis that has been developing in her work since around 2010 – that while there was no such religion as Gnosticism in Antiquity, there were gnostics whose beliefs and practices represented a particular 'metaphysical orientation or spirituality'.[48] This culminated in *The Gnostic New Age: How a Countercultural Spirituality Revolutionized Religion from Antiquity to Today* (2016), the first volume in a projected 'Gnostic Spirituality' trilogy.[49] It argues that Gnosticism is (note the use of present tense) a 'countercultural orientation towards a transcendent God and the divine power of the human' which emerged in Antiquity but is re-emerging today in the New Age milieu.[50] It is a 'paradigm shift in our understanding of religion', according to Birger Pearson's back cover blurb – but in fact, it is a continuation of the essentialized phenomenological approach to Gnosticism, the history of which this book has traced. Gnosticism is presented sui generis, 'its own unique form of spirituality', 'a therapy that restored them to spiritual and psychological wholeness'[51]. She writes that 'Gnostic initiatory rites are an early form of religious psychotherapy', and when 'the true self has individuated, it is ready for the final step in the Gnostic process of self-actualisation'.[52]

Despite the title *The Gnostic New Age*, New Age is addressed directly only in the final ten pages. There New Age remains undefined, beyond being an 'aggressively countercultural' and transgressive 'form of spirituality' (itself an untheorized emic term), and recent research isn't drawn upon.[53] This is perhaps because her use of it is somewhat at odds with most recent scholarship and seems to include what most would regard as New Religious Movements rather than New Age. Even so, the comparison with Gnosticism is forced. The usual anticosmic understanding of Gnosticism is hardly consonant with the ecological holism of the New Age milieu, but DeConick dispenses with this in a single, short paragraph:

> The Gnostic spirituality of the Hermetics is quite tempered when it comes to our universe. ... It is this tempered form of Gnosticism, not the forms that framed our world as a dark, demonic place, that became the undercurrent of Western spirituality.[54]

Throughout, DeConick's analysis tends towards the ahistorical, with difference downplayed and a common core being stressed. In his review, Philip Tite addresses a number of examples of this in her use of early Christian sources, where first-century writings are interpreted through the lens of later theological and ecclesiastical events in order to fit her model of gnostic religion.[55] This is because she sees Gnosticism as rooted in a particular religious experience, and she is happy to label such an experience 'gnosis' if it fits her argument, whether there is a demonstrable historical connection or not. She writes:

> The spirituality of a people, their orientation toward the existential, transcendent, and sacred, that generates an organised religion in which the people can come together in community. The religion serves as the institutional platform, reinforcing the spirituality that originally generated the religion.[56]

It is hard to see this as anything else than a normative statement, clearly echoing the discourse of insiders like Hoeller and Weor. None of these terms are properly theorized, and the historical sweep clearly echoes the theories of Eliade or Otto – the transcendent and the Sacred are pre-existing, sui generis realities, and experiences of them 'generate' religious traditions.

The logic is circular, however. What makes it gnosis is that it is claimed by Gnostics, but what makes them Gnostics is that gnostic experience. More than this, the scholar is deciding the data set, so it is not the Gnostic claiming the gnostic experience, but the scholar identifying the Gnostics in the first place – as we saw in the preceding chapter, Gnostics have incompatible conceptions of gnostic experience anyway, and that is to assume that the scholar's data set includes all and only those who claim to have gnostic experiences, which is never the case. This would also render comparison with the Gnostics of Late Antiquity off the table.

In a number of reviews of DeConick's work[57] (and that of others[58]), positive comment is made of the renewed focus on experience in the study of Gnosticism. It is perhaps her biggest takeaway from Pagels but is not the first attempt – Dan

Merkur's *Gnosis* (published as part of the SUNY Studies in Western Esotericism series in 1993) sought to locate gnosis within a typology of mystical experiences. Merkur, a Jungian therapist, posits a scale running from secular, 'intrapsychic' visions (such as daydreams or drug-induced hallucinations), where the visionary is aware that what they are seeing is no more than the contents of their imagination, through to the visions of shamans or Christian mystics which, in so much as they refer to a collective symbolic language, are taken as possessing some kind of objective reality. At the far end of this scale are unitive experiences, where the visionary experiences identification with the vision, which is therefore understood as transcendent reality.[59] In some of these experiences, the individual experiences bonding with the divine without loss of individual identity. This, Merkur (drawing from Gershom Scholem and Henry Corbin) proposes, is gnosis.[60]

Several critiques might easily be raised here. First, the very notion of experience is nebulous. While there have been recent attempts to rehabilitate the idea of religious experience (the work of Ann Taves being perhaps the leading example), it is nevertheless tied to a phenomenological tradition which prioritizes insider accounts, typically ignores the social discursive context and claims analytical access to inner states.[61] Most importantly though, if no *specifically* gnostic experience can be identified, then we are again putting the theoretical cart ahead of the empirical horse. Isn't this just phenomenology again – the scholar's job being to intuit an experiential essence from a few scattered writings?

More recently, DeConick has suggested that we view gnosis in terms of the sociology of knowledge. She states that her aim is not phenomenological, but rather 'to understand how gnosis, *which was understood by Gnostics* to be the direct apprehension of a transcendent deity' led to the foundation of gnostic spirituality in Antiquity, and again in 'modern America'.[62] But rather than an examination of *claims* of gnosis, as this description might suggest, we find normative and frankly phenomenological descriptions of gnosis: 'when we are dealing with gnostic spirituality, we are not dealing with ordinary knowledge'.[63] In fact,

> Gnosis is non-ordinary knowledge. When mobilized socially, it impacts the person, religion, and society, by exposing Dionysian ways of knowing through tears in the fabric of Apollonian knowledge.[64]

Perhaps this Nietzschean need to express Dionysian ways of knowing through the Apollonian strictures of academia is at the root of the apparent contradictions in DeConick's work. She wants gnosis, and she wants society to experience it too. Like Pagels (and Quispel, Jung, Scholem, Corbin, et al.), DeConick's scholarship is in the service of a personal quest. She says as much in the introduction; her role, she makes clear, is to *advocate* for the Gnostics and explain why these writings which 'captivated' and 'electrified' her became 'forbidden'.[65] *The Gnostic Awakening* will, according to the description on her website, 'explor[e] how gnostic spirituality emerges in dislocated spaces, in the margins of religions, among people who are dissatisfied with traditional faith' and 'investigat[e] what happens when experiences of the transcendent God engage religious seekers to question reality as it is normally perceived and to expand the self into suprahuman dimensions'.[66]

Like the Eranos scholars, then, DeConick speaks to *homo religiosus*, with a firm stress on individual experience as the pinnacle of religiosity.[67] Thus, we should not be surprised when the closing pages turn to open advocacy for how Gnosticism can reform contemporary society for the better:

> Gone is the God of damnation. Gone is the focus on sin and retribution. In its place is the God of Love that the Gnostics claimed to know. Separation from God and reunification with the sacred has become the story of salvation. Behind it all is the individual as the divine human agent empowered to do great things. The demand is for therapy, for religion that is useful. To be successful, religion today must promote personal well-being, health, and spiritual wholeness. It must be attuned to a raising of consciousness, to global awareness, to life that is linked with the transpersonal or transcendent.[68]

This phenomenological Gnosticism imposes onto the past the concerns of present-day scholars. The strange charm of a gnostic New Age is fundamentally a religious impulse – an alienation from modernity and striving for an experience which transcends it, revealing that there is more to the world than mere matter.

11

The greatest heresy: Jeffrey Kripal's gnostic scholarship

'The greatest taboo among serious intellectuals of the century just behind us', writes Victoria Nelson in *The Secret Life of Puppets*, 'in fact, proved to be none of the "transgressions" itemized by postmodern thinkers: it was, rather, the heresy of challenging a materialist worldview'.[1] This is certainly what we have seen with the gnostic scholars of the History of Religions school and, in the most extreme forms, not merely relativizing materialism or pointing out its rightful purview, but advocating for a return to an enchanted, even mystical *weltanschauung*. So great a heresy was this, in fact, that it became equated with the archetypal heresy, Gnosticism itself.

Styfhals suggests that for the German post-war scholars, Gnosticism appealed because they perceived not only that they lacked concepts with which to understand the modern world but also the failure of conceptual thought in toto. By 'transcending the world and human reason, Gnosticism could inject the "iron cage" of modern rationality with theological, esoteric, heretic and apocalyptic inspiration'.[2] This may help to explain DeConick's treatment of critical work on Gnosticism, which she dismisses through polemical arguments which reveal her personal umbrage at the challenges to the category. As van der Leeuw had in 1938,[3] DeConick shows her disgust for the 'trendy' academic work which threatens to dismantle the category upon which she has placed so much professionally – and possibly personally.[4] But she also suggests her disgust with modern society – or at least what she sees as religion's conservative role in it.

Philip Tite sees DeConick's *The Gnostic New Age* as a case study of the developing 'post-theoretical shift' in the study of Gnosticism and the study of religion more broadly.[5] Here, he is drawing from McCutcheon, who describes such scholars as believing that they can somehow get behind or beyond theory, to the so-called empirics of the matter ... to the so-called first order data on the ground, thereby acquiring some sort of impeded access to the world.[6]

I would take this further to argue that Gnosticism has *always* been a dog-whistle for an essentialist phenomenological approach which claims unimpeded access to the empirics of religious experience. This is perhaps clearest in the case of DeConick's Rice University colleague, Jeffrey Kripal. As Ambasciano notes, Kripal's popularity in Religious Studies – and the almost-total silence from his peers on the problems of his work – is 'a symptom of something more visceral going on: an antimodernist resistance to science'.[7]

Despite his protests to the contrary,[8] in arguing for the ontological reality of paranormal events and the transformative potential of religious scholarship, Kripal repeats the Eliadian notion of the historian of religions as *homo religiosus*, and Gnosticism is again presented as elite knowledge. Kripal is not so much a scholar of Gnosticism as a gnostic scholar, for whom Gnosticism indicates

> a kind of visionary exceptionalism that could be taken seriously even while remaining respectably inside the academy. These 'phenomenologists of religion' – under a Neitschzian influence diffused through a Jungian prism – thus glorified a heroism of private insight. They claimed to find 'structures of consciousness' and 'modes of being' and 'heirophanies' and 'religious realities' and 'archetypes' *out there in history but also in here available to the needy reader.*[9]

In his work, gnosis is not only a matter of self-transformation but also a complete revolution in the study of religion itself. Kripal – who has quoted Nelson's above words with approval more than once[10] – advocates a 'gnostic scholarship' in which scholars 'do not so much "interpret" religious "data" as they unite with sacred realities'.[11] More than this, Kripal's gnostic Religious Studies seeks to save the academy from the limitations of science itself:

> I have sought to challenge the epistemological structures (basically dualist and Kantian) and ontology (basically materialist) of the humanities as they are commonly practiced today. I have argued that the study of religion as a contemporary discipline, as a structure of thought, as a field of possibility, could well function as a most potent and healthy challenge to these assumptions.[12]

Kripal grew up in Nebraska in the 1970s, in a Catholic working-class family. He had been an athletic child but as a teenager suffered from anorexia nervosa. Upon graduating high school, he enrolled in a monastic seminary, where he also began psychoanalysis and gradually began to recover.[13] He started his undergraduate degree (religion, with a focus on structural anthropology) at the University of Chicago in 1985; Wendy Doniger was then Eliade's successor as department chair, though Eliade was still around (he would die the following year). His time living in this monastic community, and an experience in which he was flooded with energy in Calcutta during Kali Puja,[14] inspired his doctoral research and then his first two books – *Kali's Child* (1995), on sublimated male (hetero)sexuality in the work of Ramakrishna, and *Roads of Excess, Palaces of Wisdom* (2001), which reads mysticism psychoanalytically and psychoanalysis mystically. His interest in mysticism has continued but has moved steadily Westward and towards contemporary popular religion – first with his exhaustive history of the *Esalen* community at Big Sur, California (2007); then with his two-part meditation on supernatural experience and twentieth-century popular culture, *Authors of the Impossible* (2010) and *Mutants and Mystics* (2011), followed by *The Super Natural* (2016; co-written with American novelist and abductee Whitley Strieber).

But a new theme emerges in *The Serpent's Gift* (2006), in which Kripal uses the biblical narrative of Adam and Eve – told from the point of view of the snake – to critique the restrictions of the academy and of science itself. With this book, Kripal made it public that he had eaten the Tree of Knowledge and was leaving the garden of strict empiricism. 'Gnostic' takes on a complex role in a broader and more complex argument, which he continues to develop up to his 2017 autobiographical work, *Secret Body*. The argument seems to be spiritual, institutional and epistemological at the same time:

> I take the ancient gnostic myth as a powerful and ultimately positive parable for all of us who would wish to 'grow up', leave the garden of our sexual and religious innocences (and the two, I will argue, are almost always connected), and venture forth into larger, if admittedly more ambiguous, visions of the world, ourselves and the divine.[15]

Kripal's gnostic scholarship is in part a drive to prioritize experience, inherited from his studies in Chicago, which he shares with DeConick. But it is also a call to make space for a broader range of anomalous experiences and phenomena in the study of religion – something I agree with (and indeed, Kripal and I share some research interests, particularly the work of Whitley Strieber). But it is also a call to allow the confessional. I certainly agree that many supposedly impartial works 'are often catalyzed by the mystical or anomalous experiences of the intellectuals themselves … camouflaged in their texts and secreted in their theories of religion' and that we should be more open about this, but my response would be that this would allow us to become more aware of, and thereby ultimately avoid or at least mitigate, such crypto-theological theorizing, rather than embrace it.[16] But perhaps I am one of those scholars with a 'chip on their shoulder' which Kripal describes, 'out to prove religion wrong, to reduce it to psychological, social or economic forces'.[17] Like DeConick, Kripal sees the non-confessional academic study of religion as a problem to be overcome, though he restates his commitment 'both to the most robust rational-critical methods and to the metaphysical reality that is the object (really, I suspect, the subject) of religious experience and expression'.[18]

Kripal makes it clear that his use of the term is idiosyncratic, not 'big-G Gnosticism ... with all of the dualisms and unbelievable mythologies that those ancient systems often carried'[19] but rather 'employing the trope of Gnosticism in rhetorical and essentially theological ways to advance my own intellectual agendas'.[20] Yet we might then ask (as we did with Hanegraaff), why use this term, with all its baggage and historical associations and entanglements, if it has nothing to do with the group after which it were named? In fact, I did ask him, and some of his responses were paraphrased in the opening of this book.

Kripal's gnostic scholarship anticipates a '(post)modern consciousness',

> not a pure, untroubled reason that refuses to think a thought that cannot be quantified, falsified, and reproduced in a controlled laboratory (there is little controlled or even controllable about religious experience). Neither, however, is it antireason, even if it sees the limitations of any strictly conceived rationality ... the form of gnosis I am arguing for here claims to know things that other forms of knowledge and experience (like traditional faith or pure reason) do not and probably cannot know.[21]

Here Kripal glosses Quispel's tripartite faith/reason/gnosis distinction, which he later refers to simply as 'three major strands of Western culture', adding that gnosis is 'traditionally in order to acquire some form of liberation or salvation from a world seen as corrupt or fallen'.[22] The Gnosticism upon which Kripal is drawing then is unambiguously that of the Eranos circle. Indeed, in his own essay on the History of Religions school (published in 2017, but written in 1999), he describes a scholarship in which 'academic method and personal experience' unite to transcend objectivity to produce 'an interpersonal communion with the object of their study'.[23] Kripal's gnostic scholarship would transcend both faith and reason:

> The study of religion possesses both Enlightenment and Romantic roots. Both together can form gnostic epistemologies that employ robust rational models to

'reduce' the religious back to the human only to 'reverse' or 'flip' the reduction back towards theological or mystical ends. These are what we might call reflexive rereadings of religion.[24]

This special way of knowing, this 'academic gnosticism', is moreover 'transformative, and sometimes salvitic'.[25] Knowledge of the mysteries, reserved for an elite.

In *Roads to Excess*, he states, apparently with approval, that 'historians of religions … are often closet mystics',[26] and more recently, he cites Gershom Scholem's wish for philology to have a 'genuine mystical function'. 2016's *The Super Natural* proposed 'an updating and re-visioning of Eliade's "*heirophany*"', which does not propose a strict ontological distinction between sacred and profane, but rather sees the sacred as utterly a part of the human world, while also 'Other or More'.[27] It would seem that in fact Kripal's gnostic scholarship is indeed identical to the History of Religions phenomenology of the Eranos circle, despite his protestations.[28] This book has shown that the roots of the History of Religions are indeed entangled in mystical literature – yet I reach quite different conclusions, summarized in the concluding chapter, about the ramifications of this for contemporary Religious Studies.

For one, I am committed to keeping a strict separation between the etic and emic, between description and theory, whereas Kripal is committed to *not* doing so.[29] In his conclusion to *The Serpent's Kiss*, Kripal mounts a defence of Otto and his famous dictum that a scholar could not understand religion unless they had had a religious experience themselves, giving the example of someone writing about sexuality who had never had an orgasm.[30] Yet this assumes that the work of a scholar of religion is *explaining* religious experiences, but this need not be the case. Many scholars from sociological, anthropological or historical approaches would attest instead to studying how people claim and mobilize such experiences rather than attesting to their truth one way or another. It may be telling that it is such an approach that Kripal and DeConick are critical of. Nor is it the case, as Kripal writes, that all contemporary scholarship posits 'no nonhuman and transhuman agents ("spirits" and "gods") are active in human history'[31] – rather, the assumption is that scientific empiricism cannot say anything about their existence one way or the other.

There are some obvious points of comparison between Kripal and Jung: an autobiographical impulse with a heavy mythological style; an anomalous 'experience' which goes on to inspire new lines of thinking[32]; the aim of integrating the rational and irrational aspects of the human mind in a new paradigm. And, as with Jung, he uses Gnosticism to indicate this new paradigm of knowledge and human potential. However, the most common point of comparison is with Eliade.[33] In particular, Kripal's model of history as an 'almost entirely invisible, mostly unconscious, probably hyperdimensional super-reality' seems identical with Eliade's notion of a transcendental Sacred which manifests in the world and at the same time transcends it.[34] But we do not need to look for clues and implications; Kripal quotes Eliade often,[35] and even uses his work as a source,[36] adding (perhaps as a point of comparison with himself) that he 'has been more interested in the history of religions for what these literatures and practices can tell us about *what a human being might yet become*'.[37]

Perhaps Hanegraaff puts it best: 'Kripal's "gnostic study of religion" is not so much a methodology for studying religion(s), but rather a religious and normative (meta)discourse about the nature of religion'.[38] Indeed. And here it is – 'Consciousness as such is the New Sacred', which means that he desires to write 'a history of consciousness as such, which is to say *a new history of religions*'.[39]

12

Elite knowledge: Gnosticism and the study of religion

And so, like a snake eating its own tail, we come back to the beginning.

At this point, it is worth recalling Culianu's witty – and undoubtedly true – recollection:

> Once I believed that Gnosticism was a well-defined phenomenon belonging to the religious history of late antiquity. … I was to learn soon, however, that I was naïf indeed. Not only Gnosis was gnostic, but the catholic authors were gnostic, the neo-platonic too, Reformation was gnostic, Communism was gnostic, Nazism was gnostic, liberalism, existentialism, and psychoanalysis were gnostic too, modern biology was gnostic, Blake, Yeats, Kafka, Rilke, Proust, Joyce, Musil, Hesse and Thomas Mann were Gnostic. From very authoritative interpreters, I learned further that science is gnostic and superstition is gnostic; power, counter-power and lack of power are gnostic; left is gnostic and right is gnostic; all things and their opposite are equally gnostic.[1]

And yet, in all these contradictory constructions, always same ideas that informed the Messina definitions continue: the phenomenological gnosis and the historical Gnosticism; Quispel's tripartite epistemological division; Jung's psychologization, particularly the association of the divine spark with 'the self'; Jonas's existentialism, and 'thrownness'; special knowledge with a salvific quality; a quest for pure experience and pure knowledge; purportedly anti-establishment and against the suffocating orthodox elites; still always elite knowledge, the possession of scholars of religion – and religious scholars. Available for the needy reader and scholars who desire a return to the phenomenological comparison of the History of Religions school.

More, we see throughout that the strange charm of Gnosticism – for contemporary Gnostics and gnostic scholars – is to create revitalized forms of (Christian) religion, distinct from what they perceive as intellectual strictures and staid institutions. While Christian institutions, and especially their connection to outmoded moral and social norms, are rejected, the Christian symbolic world is not, and so they do not turn to new religious movements or atheism, but to radical (though supposedly original and authentic) forms of Christianity.[2] As DeConick puts it: 'The God of goodness and providence that I knew from my personal religious life did not seem to be present in any of the traditional Christian churches I attended. … It wasn't until I read the Gospel of Thomas that I felt aligned with Christianity'.[3] In doing so, they renew Christianity, spirituality and the world from which they are alienated.

For many scholars, though, there is another appeal. To put it in a nutshell – gnosis *is* the sui generis essence of religion. Whether using religion to inform a new form of scholarship, or scholarship in service of a new form of religion, each of our case studies argued for a third way, neither faith nor reason, but somehow transcending the two. This is why we find such ardent rejection of naturalistic and critical approaches in contemporary scholarship on Gnosticism.[4]

The call for the *necessity* of a distinct discipline of Religious Studies is frequently connected to the positing of a sui generis religious phenomenon. Indeed, it was for this reason that the History of Religions school was so strongly invested in the phenomenological method. This circular logic creates a kind of 'feedback loop' – the phenomenological method assumes an ahistorical sui generis essence; the existence of such an essence necessitates the phenomenological method.[5] The scholars of the History of Religions were drawn to Gnosticism because gnosis is a sui generis reality, a kind of experience common to various esotericisms, and perhaps all 'genuine' religion. An event outside history. There will continue to be a place in Religious Studies for confessional and sui generis work so long as there are scholars who want it to be that way.

It is incumbent on scholars of religion to understand the field historically and its concepts as products of their time. Despite the progress of the critical project on exposing the colonial and theological assumptions of the categories of our field, grand essentializing theories continue to be used – as we have seen in our case studies here. Those who say they aren't interested in theory and just want to study religion 'out there' are consciously or unconsciously defending and reinforcing the religionist leanings of the field. These claims often come with a rejection of explicit theorizing – indeed, it often seemed like for such scholars, theory was a problem, something to be 'got around'. In choosing not to explicitly theorize one's categories, however, one simply accepts the implicit category, and often this means a first-order category, as we will see. Confusing between first-order and second-order categories, which we have seen over and again in these case studies, leaves us operating within the episteme we should be critiquing. In so doing, we risk defending, rather than critiquing, the dominant episteme, and thus mystifying, rather than revealing, hegemonic power. Not explicitly addressing the criteria for the data you are using makes it easy to then manipulate that data to fit the category – or sometimes, vice versa.

The post-theoretical turn is a rejection not only of the need for theorizing but also of any attempt to consciously consider our theoretical models, and in doing so potentially changing them. It is a rejection of challenges to business as usual in the study of religion, because it is this business as usual which these scholars are interested in – salvific, transformational and transcendent. And it goes beyond Religious Studies – religion as a category in governance, in the media, in medicine, and in other discourses acts as a legitimizer of certain kinds of special knowledge, while demonizing others.[6] Where Religious Studies should (and could) be a discipline in which systems of knowledge and non-scientific truth claims are analysed, too often it is functioning as a gatekeeper of which types of special knowledge we are permitted to think with.

Despite Gnosticism's historical non-existence, scholars, the public and contemporary Gnostics mutually construct Gnosticism – just as with most of the terminology in this hotly contested field, religion. It is striking that we find similarities between terms such as Gnosticism, Shamanism and religion in the introductions of the textbooks where the issue of definitions comes up, such as the lip-service to critical or postcolonial deconstruction, and the framing of the issue as finding a definition for a very complex but nevertheless real thing, rather than finding alternative ways of conceptualizing and writing about the data. This involves a simple shift of emphasis – a move from first-order to second-order, not making any ontological claims but rather analysing the ontological claims of others – but this confusion between first-order and second-order is so deeply ingrained in contemporary Religious Studies that such a shift seems radical to many and impossible to some. Indeed, for some it may even seem to miss the point, as these ontological claims are the very things that interest them.

Why then are these contemporary gnostic religions ignored by scholars who wish to find modern-day Gnosticism? I have suggested that this is because these scholars already have an idea of what Gnosticism is before they even begin. Apostolic and Weorite Gnosticisms are rejected because they don't fit the scholar's opinion of what the essence of Gnosticism is – ignoring any data which does not fit, just as the Messina Congress did. Rather, these scholars prefer to envisage ancient Gnostics who somehow parallel and illuminate our own time, a theme that has been there since the rediscovery of Gnosticism in the nineteenth century. Jonas saw the Gnostics as precursors to Existentialism; Jung saw the Gnostics as the forerunners of psychology; Hanegraaff, the forerunners of Esotericism; Voegelin saw Gnosticism in modern political movements; Harold Bloom saw it in contemporary American Protestantism; DeConick in the New Age movement. For Kripal, it is the very future of the discipline of Religious Studies. Always, however, the connection between ancient and modern Gnosticism is based upon philosophical parallels – often vague and sometimes outright conjecture – rather than specific historical connections.

To repeat – what gnosis is, or who are real Gnostics, is a first-order insider claim (remember Irenaeus's 'gnostics, falsely so-called'). Typological definitions of Gnosticism say more about normative constructions of Christianity, or of 'true religion', than about the beliefs and practices of any actual group of people. But Gnosticism problematizes the distinction – it is by definition a second-order category, an *ism*, a categorical abstraction created by scholars for their own purposes, yet it is one which is entirely reliant upon first-order ontological claims – gnosis. Like the undead, it belongs fully to neither world, but rather exists in the shadows, made of rumour and folk tales, yet still with the power to fascinate and repulse.

But as with some other polemical constructions – Shamanism, witchcraft, Hinduism, maybe even religion itself – Gnosticism has taken on a life of its own (or perhaps an afterlife, to extend the metaphor). In this way, we might usefully compare Gnosticism with other zombie categories in contemporary Religious Studies, which remain alive in discourse even though they are dead in reality.[7] In this case, the Nag Hammadi discovery was the death knell for the category Gnosticism – or more accurately, showed that it had never in fact been alive at all. Yet the category lumbers on, consuming more and more ideas.

The clearest comparison with Gnosticism, perhaps, is to Shamanism. Both were specific cases which were essentialized into ahistorical sui generis categories by scholars. In Eliade's *Shamanism: Archaic Techniques of Ecstasy* (1951; expanded English translation 1964), the shaman is transformed from a Siberian specific to a universal category found everywhere, in which a shaman is anyone who uses trance to travel through the axis mundi to other worlds. Both are imbricated in an Orientalizing critique of modernity and modern religion. Both were later adopted as emic self-identifiers. Both processes of reification were fueled by psychiatry and psychology. The relationship between Shamanism and psychiatry was present from the late nineteenth century, often in a reductionist narrative which explained the Shaman's visions as a pathology, termed 'Arctic Hysteria' by Maria Czaplicka.[8] It became increasingly prominent from the mid-twentieth century, however, with a move towards a psychoanalytic model which stressed the shaman's role in relation to the well-being of their community.[9] Claude Lévi-Strauss, for example, went as far as to state that psychoanalysis was 'the modern version of shamanistic techniques' and shamans the precursors to psychoanalysts.[10] Gnosticism's psychoanalytic credentials came from Jung and remain highly visible today. Finally, phenomenological History of Religions provided the theoretical support to both.

The difference between Gnosticism and Shamanism, perhaps, is that *no one owns Gnosticism*. There are no native communities to reclaim the category, no monuments to be competed over and, for a long time, no texts. Just a free-floating signifier. No texts, no history.

Jonas stated in his 'farewell speech' in 1973:

> Sometimes I find cause for believing that I was right in the way I saw it at the time when we did not have the new evidence yet. At other times I see that I probably guessed wrong … it is a question of competence in the particular fields of knowledge. It is the coptologist's day. It is the iranologist's day. The philosopher, the historian of religion, and the explorer of the history of ideas will have to defer, for a time now, to what the specialists and those working with the texts come up with.

Wise words, but sadly, not heeded.

What we have in effect are, on the one hand, biblical scholars who overreach into comparative work (Quispel, DeConick) and, on the other hand, comparativist Religious Studies scholars using categories derived from Biblical Studies as though they were universals (Kripal, Jonas). It is a curious result of Religious Studies' emergence as a discipline that it tends not to consider early Christianity, or indeed classical religion at all, as these are considered the domain of Biblical Studies and Classics or Archaeology, respectively. Comparatively few theoretically focused Religious Studies scholars started with a focus on Christianity; conversely, those with training in Biblical Studies and other area studies tend not to be so concerned with broader theoretical concerns. As a result, the theological and colonial issues with certain categories have yet to trickle down, and grand essentializing theories remain a particular problem there. The weeds take root in the dirt that accumulates in the cracks between the disciplines; the no man's land between the populated areas is roamed by zombie categories.

Such categories – like Gnosticism – potentially offer a rich seam of data for the critical scholar of religion on how knowledge is produced and how that then affects the field as a whole. However, this would require the shift from scholar-as-caretaker to scholar-as-critic to spread from those with a focus on theory and methodology to those operating in particular area studies. This is especially problematic, as in the twenty-first century, Religious Studies departments have increasingly become 'balkanized' – organized by coverage of 'World Religions', rather than by methodological focus, favouring area studies scholars over those with a Religious Studies disciplinary background. Already we see a predominance in such areas for scholarship with a methodological focus on 'material' or 'lived religion', which often obscures a phenomenological paradigm in which religion is an at best self-evident and at worst sui generis entity that we must simply observe all around us. Clearly, such a shift will present particular problems for scholar-practitioners, and indeed already is in disciplines which tend to be dominated by insiders, such as Pagan Studies and Islam.[11]

Interdisciplinary work needs to be more than strip mining other disciplines for terms and approaches while ignoring the third-order analysis of the use of such terms, as DeConick does. Religious Studies stands to benefit as much from the hermeneutic and historical skills of Biblical Studies as Biblical Studies could benefit from a keener awareness of the political implications of comparative categories. More than this, Religious Studies needs to become more than a humanistic exercise in the religions of Others if it deserves a place in the post-colonial university.

Contemporary scholarship on gnostic religion is above all an artefact of the broader debate on the nature of – and reason for – the social-scientific study of religion. It demonstrates that the sui generis legacy of the History of Religions remains active – indeed, popular – within today's academy and indeed that these perspectives may be hardwired into the discipline. The strange charm of the field remains confessional and normative claims, bolstered by phenomenological sui generis models, and appeals to special knowledge.

Notes

Introduction: A strange charm

1 Jonas, 'A Retrospective View', 13.
2 DeConick, *The Gnostic New Age*, 350.
3 *An Unnatural History of Religions*, 65, 88, 122–40. Perennialism (also called the *philosophia perennis* or Traditionalism) is an esoteric meta-religious doctrine that posits a single, shared truth or origin from which all religious and esoteric knowledge has sprung. A popular version of perennialist thinking is the current idea that all religions are, despite outer trappings, at their core teaching the same capital-T Truth. In the History of Religions, perennialism permitted scholars to perform great comparative leaps of time and context, as the ultimate equivalency of traditions and teachings was assumed. Perennialism (and especially Traditionalism) also appealed to the superiority of pre-modern societies, and frequently presented contemporary Western society and culture as in decline, and heading inevitably toward crisis. See Ambasciano, *Unnatural History of Religions*, 107.
4 Ambasciano, *Unnatural History of Religions*, 1–2.
5 Hanegraaff, *Dynamic Typological Approach*, 39.
6 Green, 'Gnosis and Gnosticism: A Study in Methodology', 133; emphasis added.
7 *Rethinking 'Gnosticism'*, 52.
8 This is not simply replacing one term with another, as Williams's critics sometimes suggest. While the majority of Irenaeus's data set would fall into biblical demiurgical traditions, *not all of it would*. Rather, it is a second-order category build up from commonalities in the data set. As such, it is essentially an application of the 'building-block' methodology proposed by Ann Taves (*Religious Experience Reconsidered*; 'Reverse Engineering Complex Cultural Concepts'). The 'complex cultural category' Gnosticism can be broken down into discrete building blocks such as 'protest exegesis', 'emanationist cosmologies' or indeed 'biblical demiurgical traditions' which overlap Gnosticism – but also other complex cultural categories to varying degrees.
9 E.g. Brakke, *The Gnostics*; Denzey Lewis, *Introduction to 'Gnosticism'*; Schenke, 'The Problem of Gnosis'.
10 'Sexuality and Sexual Symbolism in Hermetic and Gnostic Thought and Practice', 2.

11 *Gnostic Religion in Antiquity*, 13.
12 Wasserstrom, *Religion after Religion*; Hakl, *Eranos*; Styfhals, *No Spiritual Investment in the World*; Lazier, *God Interrupted*; Williams, *Rethinking 'Gnsoticism'*; King, *What Is Gnosticism?*
13 Tite, 'Transgression and Countercultural Gnosticism', 8.
14 King, *What Is Gnosticism?*, 1.
15 Translated from Sacco, 'Neosciamanesimo e New Age', 280. In the excerpt, the author is referring to Eliade.

1 Against all heresies: Gnosticism before modern scholarship

1 Osborn, *Irenaeus of Lyons*, 2–7.
2 Gr.:Ἔλεγχος καὶ ἀνατροπὴ τῆς ψευδωνύμου γνώσεως. This is more commonly translated as *Exposure and Refutation of Gnosis Falsely So-Called*, but Osborn's more neutral translation makes it clearer that 'Gnosis' does not here carry the essentialist connotations it later would.
3 Osborn, *Irenaeus of Lyons*, 1.
4 Valleé, *Anti-Gnostic Polemics*, 6; c.f. Williams, *Rethinking 'Gnosticism'*, 33.
5 Behr, *Irenaeus of Lyons*, 2–4; c.f. Binns, *Irenaeus*.
6 Jorgensen, 'Irenaeus of Lyons and the Rhetoric of Interpretation', 127–8.
7 Le Boulluec, *Le Notion d'hérésie*; c.f. King, *What Is Gnosticism?*, 22–5.
8 Winterberg, 'Remembering the Gnostics', 50.
9 King, *What Is Gnosticism?*, 30.
10 Barnabas, 1.5; Smith, 'Post-Bauer Scholarship on Gnosticism(s)', 79.
11 Markschies, *Gnosis*, 8–9.
12 1 Tim 6.20–21; c.f. Smith, 'Post-Bauer Scholarship on Gnosticism(s)', 79; italics in original.
13 King, *What Is Gnosticism?*, 165; Markschies, *Gnosis*, 8–9.
14 King, *What Is Gnosticism?*, 26–7.
15 Magris, 'Gnosticism: Gnosticism from Its Origins to the Middle Ages (Further Considerations)', 3518.
16 Thomassen, *The Spiritual Seed*.
17 C.f. 2.31.1; 3.10.4; 4.35.1; 5.26.2, etc.
18 *Adversus Haereses*, 4.33.8
19 2.23.8–10; 2.31.1; 2.35.2; 4.6.4; 4.35.1, etc; c.f. Williams, *Rethinking 'Gnosticism'*, 36.
20 King, *What Is Gnosticism?*, 32.
21 Also known as the *Philosophumena*, the text was not discovered until 1842. It was published in Latin in 1851, by M. G. Schwartze, in German in 1892 by C. Schmidt and in French in 1895 by E. Amélineau. The first English translation was in 1921, by

the lawyer and amateur antiquarian Francis George Legge. Legge published several other works on non-canonical and 'lost' early Christian texts, and although he was a Christian, he published in Theosophical and 'occult' journals, making him an interesting, if little-known, popularizer of this material in the pre-Nag Hammadi twentieth century.

22 *Refutatio Omnium Haeresium*, 5.2; 5.6.4; 5.8.29; 5.9.22; 5.11.1.
23 *Refutatio Omnium Haeresium*, 5.23.3.
24 Williams, *Rethinking 'Gnosticism'*, 38-9.
25 *Panarion*, 25, 2, 1; 26, 3, 7.
26 *Panarion*, 31.1.1; 31.1.5; 31.7.8; 31.36.4.
27 Williams, *Rethinking 'Gnosticism'*, 40.
28 Smith, 'History of the Term Gnostikos', 803.
29 *Stromata*, 3.30.1.
30 *Contra Celsum* 5.61-2; c.f. Williams, *Rethinking 'Gnosticism'*, 40-1.
31 Also referred to as *Ennead* 2.9.
32 Cited in Burns, *Apocalypse of the Alien God*, 2-3.
33 Burns, *Apocalypse of the Alien God*, 1-2.
34 *Magia Sexualis*, 23; c.f. Cohn, *Europe's Inner Demons*, 259; Frankfurter, *Evil Incarnate*.
35 *Panarion*, 26.8.2-3.
36 *Panarion*, 26.5.4-6.
37 147.
38 43.
39 DeConick, 'Conceiving Spirits'; Urban, *Magia Sexualis*, 41.
40 Urban, *Magia Sexualis*, 41.
41 *What Is Gnosticism?*, 32.
42 Hanegraaff, *Esotericism and the Academy*, 101-2.
43 *A Modest Enquiry into the Mystery of Iniquity*, 452; *Divine Dialogues Containing Sundry Disquisitions*, 270; for 'Gnosticism' already being in circulation before this, see Williams, 'Gnosticism Emergent', 9-10.
44 *An Exposition of the Seven Epistles to the Seven Churches*, preface.
45 Hanegraaff, *Esotericism and the Academy*, 102-7.
46 *Histoire Critique de Manichée*, II, 11-13.
47 *Decline and Fall of the Roman Empire*, 442-3.
48 Published as *The Gnostic Heresies of the First and Second Centuries* in 1875.
49 Mansel, *The Gnostic Heresies of the First and Second Centuries*, 15.
50 Neill and Wright, *Interpretation of the New Testament*, 29. On Baur's work more generally, 20-9.
51 Baur, *Die Christliche Gnosis*, 25-9.

52 Baur, *Die Christliche Gnosis*, vi. 'Ist daher die Gnosis schon innerhalb ihrer eigenen Sphäre nicht als geschichtliche Erscheinung im wahren Sinne aufgefasst, wenn nicht nicht die einzelnen Systeme, als die nothmendigen sich selbst gegenfeitig bedingenden Momente, in welche der Begriff in seiner innern Iebendigen Bewegung sich selbst auseinanderlegt, hervortreten, so muss dieselbe Bewegung auch in der weitern Sphäre, auf welche sie sich erstreft, in der Polemik, die sich gegen die Gnosis erhob.'
53 Baur, *Die Christliche Gnosis*, 675–81.
54 Baur, *Die Christliche Gnosis*, 544–740.
55 MS Bruce 96, Bodleian Library, Oxford.
56 The books of Jeu have not received much scholarly attention, but Johnston has recently established similarities in the cosmology of Jeu and book four of *Pistis Sophia* which might suggest some commonality. See 'Proximité littéraire'.
57 British Library add. MS 5114.
58 There are several texts of this title. This is not the same text as the later Nag Hammadi one.
59 King, *What Is Gnosticism?*, 81–2.
60 See Williams, *Rethinking 'Gnosticism'*, 94.
61 King, *What Is Gnosticism?*, 81.
62 *History of Dogma*, 243.
63 *History of Dogma*, 226, 230.
64 King, *What Is Gnosticism?*, 55–61.
65 *History of Dogma*, 253.
66 *History of Dogma*, 222–3; c.f. Grimstad, *The Modern Revival of Gnosticism*, 20.
67 King, *What Is Gnosticism?*, 56–66.
68 Harnack, *What Is Christianity?*, 200–1; c.f. King, *What Is Gnosticism?*, 62–3.
69 Molendijk, 'At the Cross-roads'.
70 See Cotter and Robertson, 'The World Religions Paradigm in Contemporary Religious Studies', for a short introduction; for more detail, see Chidester, *Empire of Religion*; Masuzawa, *Invention of World Religions*.
71 Masuzawa, *In Search of Dreamtime*, 21.
72 E.g. DeConick, *The Gnostic New Age*; Hanegraaf, *New Age Religion*.
73 'erlöster Erlöer'. *Die Hellenistischen Mysterienreligionen*, 278.
74 Neill and Wright, *The Interpretation of the New Testament*, 193.
75 King, *What Is Gnosticism?*, 109.
76 Culianu, *Tree of Gnosis*, 52–3.
77 Junginger, 'Introduction', 8–9.
78 Ambasciano, *Gnostic History of Religion*, 70.
79 *The Gnostics and Their Remains*, vi.
80 *The Gnostics and Their Remains*, x.

2 The era of gnosis restored: Nineteenth-century Gnostics

1 Pearson, *Wicca and the Christian Heritage*, 46.
2 Apiryon, 'Jules Doinel and the Gnostic Church of France'.
3 Pearson, *Wicca and the Christian Heritage*, 46.
4 Gibson, *A Social History of French Catholicism*.
5 Pegg, 'On Cathars, Albigenses, and Good Men of Languedoc'.
6 Denis, *Tableau Historique*, 11.
7 Denis, *Tableau Historique*, 180–2; c.f. Hanegraaff, *Esotericism and the Academy*, 236–7.
8 Merkur, *Gnosis*.
9 Bogdan, *Western Esotericism and Rituals of Initiation*, 67–94.
10 Dachez, 'Martinist Orders and Freemasonry in France since the Time of Papus', 1; *Devil-Worship in France*, 1–7.
11 Bogdan, *Western Esotericism and Rituals of Initiation*, 120.
12 Apiryon, 'Jules Doinel and the Gnostic Church of France.' In reality, we know very little about Cathar liturgy, as very few of their texts survive. Like Gnosticism, Catharism (as generally understood, at least) was constructed first by heresy-hunting opponents, then reinvented (with a more positive spin) in nineteenth-century esoteric circles. See Zbíral, *Největší hereze*.
13 Female bishops are called Sophias. William Behun, current Primate of the Apostolic Johannite Church, suggests that there may have been a plan at one time for each diocese to have a Sophia and a Tau, which would certainly match the later arrangement of the Ecclesia Gnostica Catholica and perhaps the sexual magic of the Aun Weor groups.
14 It is interesting to note how many of the major figures in fin de seiclé occultism were medical doctors.
15 See Dachez, 'Martinist Orders and Freemasonry in France since the Time of Papus', 4–6.
16 Apiryon, 'Jules Doinel and the Gnostic Church of France'.
17 Pearson, *Wicca and the Christian Heritage*, 47.
18 'Wandering Bishops'.
19 See Brandreath, *Episcopi Vagantes*.
20 Pearson, *Wicca and the Christian Heritage*, 39. The archbishop of the Independent Catholic Church of Ceylon, Frater Alvares, was raised by the patriarch of the Syrian Jacobite Church in 1888. His consecration is therefore invalid because Syrian Jacobite patriarchs do not have the authority to create autonomous patriarchies (Anson, *Bishops at Large*, 35–6; Plummer, *The Many Paths of the Independent Sacramental Movement*, 28–9).
21 Or Reuß.

22 Pearson, *Wicca and the Christian Heritage*, 46–7.
23 Theodor Reuss, Franz Hartmann and Henry Klein. Klein (1842–1913) was a composer, musician and publisher; Hartmann (1838–1912) was another doctor and, like Carl Jung, of wealthy Bavarian stock with a history of occult experiences (Kaczynski, *Forgotten Templars*, 1–32, 49–66).
24 Urban, *Magia Sexualis*, 100.
25 Urban, *Magia Sexualis*, 81–108.
26 Reuss, 'Parsival und das Enthüllte Grals-Geheimnis', 72.
27 Urban, *Magia Sexualis*, 25.
28 Urban, *Magia Sexualis*, 123–8.
29 AKA *Liber XV*. See Pearson, *Wicca and the Christian Heritage*, 47; Urban, *Magia Sexualis*, 121.
30 Pearson, *Wicca and the Christian Heritage*, 46–7.
31 Hanegraaff, *Esotericism and the Academy*, 244.
32 For an account of the development of the Theosophical Society, see Godwin, *The Theosophical Enlightenment*; Washington, *Madame Blavatsky's Baboon*; and Campbell, *Ancient Wisdom Revised*.
33 Poller, 'Under a Glamour', 86.
34 *The Gnostics and Their Remains*, 2nd ed., ix.
35 *Isis Unveiled*, I, 271, f.n. †.
36 *Isis Unveiled*, II, 38.
37 Tillett, *Charles Webster Leadbeater*, 476.
38 Butler, *Victorian Occultism and the Making of Modern Magic*, 116.
39 Original: 'Un très grand nombre de lecteurs orientalistes et théosophes, qui ne sont point familiarisés avec les termes sanscrits de la Théosophie, du Gnosticisme et de l'Esotericisme, nous ont manifesté, à diverses reprises, le désir de posséder un ouvrage leur donnant la signification exacte de nombreux termes en usage aujourd'hui dans les ouvrages théosophiques, c'est pourquoi nous nous sommes décidés á la publication du présent Glossaire, auquel nous avons ajouté l'explication des termes du Gnosticisme, car beaucoup de personnes s'occupent aujourd'hui de l'Eglise Gnostique et de ses cérémonies' (Translation by the author).
40 Blavatsky, *Isis Unveiled II*, 163.
41 *The Gnosis or Ancient Wisdom*, 11; emphasis in original.
42 *The Gnosis or Ancient Wisdom*, 107.
43 Goodrick-Clarke and Goodrick-Clarke, *G.R.S. Mead*, 2.
44 Goodrick-Clarke and Goodrick-Clarke, *G.R.S. Mead*, 2–4; Mead, '"The Quest" – Old and New', 298.
45 The first two chapters, at least, in *Lucifer* vols 6–8, 1890–1.
46 'Pistis Sophia: Commentary and Notes'.

47 Manuscript M 275 in the Ritman Library collection in Amsterdam. At https://embassyofthefreemind.com/nl/collectie/online-catalogus/detail/e6b9045e-48cb-afd5-0272-5efd5014a0a3/media/6b710348-a0a2-de2e-0337-e18c1fd74f99?mode=detail&view=horizontal&q=M%20275&rows=1&page=5 (accessed 12 March 2019).
48 *Fragments*, 144, 35.
49 *Fragments*, 570–3.
50 *Fragments*, 577.
51 *Fragments*, 458.
52 *Fragments*, 474.
53 *The Gnosis of the Mind*, 42.
54 *The Gnosis of the Mind*, 5; emphasis added.
55 *Fragments*, 5.
56 *How Theosophy Came to Me*, 18–47; Pearson, *Wicca and the Christian Heritage*, 33.
57 *How Theosophy Came to Me*, 156–60.
58 Poller, 'Under a Glamour', 83; c.f. Tillett, 864–5.
59 Poller, 'Under a Glamour', 80.
60 Tillett, *Charles Webster Leadbeater*, 242–60.
61 Tillett, *Charles Webster Leadbeater*, 383–4, 386.
62 Goodrick-Clarke and Goodrick-Clarke, *G.R.S. Mead*, 19–21.
63 I have been unable to track down Mead's papers. After correspondence with Clare Goodrick-Clarke, Jerry Heijka-Ekins and Ken Small during 2018, it seems that upon Mead's death, the library and his personal papers were dispersed, likely to individual members of the Quest Society. One possibility is that some or all went to William Kingsland's 'Blavatsky Group', but Kingsland died shortly after Mead and there is no record of Kingsland's papers and library either.
64 Vol. 17, nos 2 and 3, 1926.
65 '"The Quest" – Old and New', 297.
66 Richardson, 'Psychoanalysis and the Occult Periodical'.
67 Vol. 4, no. 4 (July), 1913 (676–97), 696, 676–7.
68 Vol. 5, no. 1, 58–78; vol. 5, no. 2, 247–69.
69 Poller, 'Under a Glamour', 86.
70 For example, her 1914 book *Mysticism* ends with the words, 'So alone shall appear in us the likeness of the Son, and so alone shall we compass Atonement with the Father, the Life of all that lives' (143).
71 Pert, *Red Cactus*, 115–31.
72 Tillett, *Charles Webster Leadbeater*, 560.
73 Tillett, *Charles Webster Leadbeater*, 430, 560–77.
74 Anson, *Bishops at Large*, 29.

75 Plummer, *The Many Paths of the Independent Sacramental Movement*, 20–1; Tillett, *Charles Webster Leadbeater*, 581–3.
76 Poller, 'Under a Glamour', 88; Plummer, *The Many Paths of the Independent Sacramental Movement*, 20.
77 At that point suspended from the OCC for 'gross indecency', that is, homosexuality (J. Pearson, *Wicca and the Christian Heritage*, 32–3), for which he had previously been suspended from the Catholic Church (Plummer, *The Many Paths of the Independent Sacramental Movement*, 20).
78 Tillett, *Charles Webster Leadbeater*, 588–93.
79 Poller, 'Under a Glamour', 88; c.f. Tillett, *Charles Webster Leadbeater*, 598–605.
80 Tillett, *Charles Webster Leadbeater*, 622–3.
81 Tillett, *Charles Webster Leadbeater*, 635–8.
82 Tillett, *Charles Webster Leadbeater*, 633, 671–9. Krishnamurti's father made similar accusations in court in 1912 (Tillett, *Charles Webster Leadbeater*, 531).
83 Tillett, *Charles Webster Leadbeater*, 659.
84 Tillett, *Charles Webster Leadbeater*, 904–18.
85 Tillett, *Charles Webster Leadbeater*, 923–5.
86 Poller, 'Under a Glamour', 89.
87 Tillett, *Charles Webster Leadbeater*, 817, 842–3.
88 http://www.lcci-gbie.org.uk/ministry.html (accessed 24 August 2020).
89 Hanegraaff, *Esotericism and the Academy*, 335–7.

3 The alien god: Gnosticism as existentialism

1 Casadio, 'Historiography (Further Considerations)', 4046–7.
2 Safranski, *Martin Heidegger*, 75.
3 It included Edith Stein (who would die in Auschwitz), Hans-Georg Gadamer and Adolf Reinach.
4 Safranski, *Martin Heidegger*, 71–2.
5 Ott, *Martin Heidegger*, 44–79.
6 Sheehan, 'Reading a Life', 73–4.
7 In Safranski, *Martin Heidegger*, 78.
8 Sheehan, 'Reading a Life', 75–6.
9 Sheehan, 'Reading a Life', 80.
10 Tuckett, 'Clarifying Phenomenologies in the Study of religion', 83.
11 Or 'numinöse'. Otto, *Das Heilige*, 13.
12 *Das Heilige*, 5–7.
13 *Das Heilige*, 2.

14 *Das Heilige*, 4. 'dann wenn überhaupt auf einem Gebeite menschlichen Erlebens etwas diesem Gebeite Eigenes und so nur in ihm Vorkommendes zu bemerken ist, so auf dem religiösen.'
15 *Das Heilige*, 4. 'dann wenn überhaupt auf einem Gebeite menschlichen Erlebens etwas diesem Gebeite Eigenes und so nur in ihm Vorkommendes zu bemerken ist, so auf dem religiösen.'
16 In Dadosky, *The Structure of Religious Knowing*, 13.
17 Caputo, 'Heidegger and Theology', 275.
18 Lowith, 'The Political Implications of Heidegger's Existentialism', 121–2.
19 Sheehan, 'Reading a Life', 76–7.
20 Sheehan, 'Reading a Life', 84.
21 'in Verehrung und Freundschaft zugeeignet'.
22 *Sein und Zeit*, 19.
23 Grimstad suggests that, in fact, Heidegger's use of this word may have come from his reading of Bultmann's papers and Jonas's doctoral work, rather than inspiring them (*The Modern Revival of Gnosticism*, 59–60).
24 *Sein und Zeit*, 128.
25 Safranski, *Martin Heidegger*, 152; emphasis mine.
26 *Sein und Zeit*, 129. 'Wenn das Dasein die Welt eigens entdeckt und sich nahebringt, wenn es ihm selbst sein eigentliches Sein erschließt, dann vollzieht sich deises Entdecken von 'Welt' und Erschließen von Dasein immer als Wegräumen der Verdeckungen und Verdunkelungenn, als Zerbrechen der Verstellungen, mit denen sich das Dasein gegen es selbst abriegelt' (translation from *Being and Time*, 129).
27 Caputo, 'Heidegger and Theology', 274–5.
28 'Neues Testament und Mythologie', 26; c.f. Hopland, 'Hans Jonas and the History of Gnosis und *spätantiker Geist*', 58; Segal, *The Existentialist Reinterpretation of Myth*, 120.
29 Safranski, *Martin Heidegger*, 134.
30 Styfhals, *No Spiritual Investment in the World*, 39.
31 Safranski, *Martin Heidegger*, 135–6.
32 Wolin, 'Ethics after Auschwitz', 2.
33 Lazier, 'Pauline Theology in the Weimar Republic', 109.
34 Jonas, *Memoirs*, 61.
35 Jonas, *Memoirs*, 63; c.f. Brumlik, 'Ressentiment', 88–9.
36 Jonas, *Gnostic Religion*, 334.
37 Jonas, *Memoirs*, 66.
38 Brumlik, 'A Few Motifs in Hans Jonas's Early Book on Gnosticism', 73–5.
39 Levy, *The Integrity of Thinking*, 16.
40 E.g. Williams, *Rethinking 'Gnosticism'*, 96–115; Filoramo, *A History of Gnosticism*, 55; Rudolph, *Gnosis*, 60.

41 Rudolph, 'Hans Jonas and Research on Gnosticism', 101.
42 *The Gnostic Religion*, 42.
43 Jonas, *The Gnostic Religion*, xvi.
44 Wasserstrom, *Religion after Religion*, 49–51.
45 See Koonz, *The Nazi Conscience*, 46–68.
46 In Sheehan, 'Reading a Life', 85.
47 Lazier, 'Pauline Theology in the Weimar Republic', 109–10.
48 Caputo, 'Heidegger and Theology', 276–7.
49 Sheehan, 'Reading a Life', 86–7.
50 Safranski, *Martin Heidegger*, 270–2.
51 Since the publication of Heidegger's *Black Notebooks* (Schwarze Hefte) in 2014 (edited by Peter Trawny and published by Verlag Vittorio Klostermann), there has been a sweeping reassessment of the depth of Heidegger's anti-Semitism and Nazi beliefs, and the degree to which they were embedded in his philosophical work. For an overview, see Donatella di Cesare, *Heidegger and the Jews: The Black Notebooks* (Cambridge: Polity Press, 2017).
52 Culianu, *The Tree of Gnosis*, 52–3; Junginger, 'Introduction', 7–18.
53 Desjardins, 'Bauer and Beyond,' 67–8; Robinson, 'Bauer Thesis Examined', 15–18; Decker, 'The Bauer Thesis: An Overview', 9.
54 Hartog, *Orthodoxy and Heresy in Early Christian Contexts*, 2.
55 Hartog, *Orthodoxy and Heresy in Early Christian Contexts*, 4. For a helpful overview of critiques of Bauer's book, see Decker, 'The Bauer Thesis: An Overview', 17–32.
56 Rudolph, 'Hans Jonas and Research on Gnosticism from a Contemporary Perspective', 94.
57 'A Retrospective View', 8.
58 'A Retrospective View', 11; c.f. Wolin, *Heidegger's Children*, 1.
59 E.g. 'Judaism and Gnosticism', 6.
60 *Kabbalah*, 15–18.
61 *Major Trends*, 75; c.f. Biale, *Gershom Scholem*, 130–4.
62 *Jewish Gnosticism*, 1; emphasis added.
63 Weise, 'Zionism, the Holocaust, and Judaism in a Secular World'; Jonas, *Memoirs*, 88.
64 J. Polotsy, Jonas, H. Lewy, G. Lichtheim, Sholem and Sh. Sambursky (Scholem, Smith and Stroumsa, *Morton Smith and Gershom Scholem, Correspondence 1945–1982*, 5, f.n. 30).
65 *Major Trends*, 280; 'Der Nihilismus als religioses phanomen', 7–10.
66 Extensively in 'Redemption through Sin', 133–4; c.f. Wasserstrom, *Religion after Religion*, 65–8.
67 Wasserstrom, *Religion after Religion*, 63; emphasis in original.
68 Smith, 'Post-Bauer Scholarship on Gnosticism(s)', 81.

4 A crack in the universe: Jung and the Eranos circle

1. Stark, *Entrepreneurs of Ideology*; c.f. Noll, *Jung Cult*, 69; c.f. Goodrick Clarke, *The Occult Roots of Nazism*, 265–87.
2. Goodrick-Clarke, *The Occult Roots of Nazism*, 1–6.
3. Goodrick-Clarke, *The Occult Roots of Nazism*, 91–7.
4. In Kershaw, *Hitler, 1889–1936*, 187.
5. Ball, *Flight out of Time*, 66.
6. Corngold, *Lambent Traces*.
7. Letter of Carl G. Jung to E. Meier, 24 March 1950; Bernardini, *Jung a Eranos*, 181, note 58; also see Feitknecht, *Herman Hesse*.
8. Grimstad, *The Modern Revival of Gnosticism*. Gilles Quispel also wrote about the Faustus tales, equating Faustus with the arch-proto-Gnostic, Simon Magus ('Faust: Symbol of Western Man').
9. See Green, *Mountain of Truth*, for a history of the Monté Verita community.
10. Kaczynski, *Forgotten Templars*, 249. Olga Fröbe-Kapteyn mentioned the existence of an esoteric cult devoted to the 'Oriental Templars' on Monte Verità in a letter sent to Jung on 1 September 1935 (in Bernardini, *Jung a Eranos*, 257, note 55).
11. Noll, *The Jung Cult*, 108.
12. Bernardini, *Jung a Eranos*, 250.
13. Albertus Philippus Kapteyn (or Kapteijn, 1848–1927) was director general of the English Westinghouse Brake & Signal Co., and he had a residence in Bloomsbury, London, where Olga was born (Bernardini, *Jung a Eranos*, 247–8).
14. Hakl, *Eranos*, 12–17, 25–8; Hayman, *Life of Jung*, 315; Bernardini, *Jung a Eranos*, 253; Mellon, *Reflections in a Silver Spoon*, 163.
15. Bailey, *Unfinished Autobiography*, 216.
16. Hakl suggests that this was because Jung had reacted to Alice Bailey in strongly negative terms (*Eranos*, 30–1), though her autobiography suggests that she had withdrawn before Jung was involved, put off by her belief that the area had been 'the centre of the Black Mass in Central Europe' (*Unfinished Autobiography*, 222–3; c.f. Hayman, *A Life of Jung*, 316). Bailey also stated that 'the place had been overrun by German professors', however (*Unfinished Autobiography*, 225).
17. *Aryan Christ*, xv. For a counter-challenge to Noll's polemical critiques, see Shamdasani, *Cult Fictions*.
18. Noll, *Jung Cult*, 19–20.
19. Published in *Psychiatric Studies* (1970) and *Experimental Researches* (1973), vols 1 and 2 of the *Collected Works*.
20. Noll, *Jung Cult*, 107.
21. For Jung's later modifications and deliberate alterations to the story, see Noll, *The Aryan Christ*, 268–71.

22 Noll, *The Jung Cult*, 148.
23 Jung, 'New Paths in Psychology', 260.
24 Noll, *The Jung Cult*, 6.
25 Noll, *The Aryan Christ*, 159.
26 Noll, *The Jung Cult*, 7; Wulff, 'Psychological Approaches', 262–3.
27 Shamdasani, *Cult Fictions*, 4.
28 *New Age Religion*, 509.
29 Noll, *The Jung Cult*, 202–7.
30 *Memories, Dreams, Reflections*, 184–6; Noll, *The Jung Cult*, 209–15; Noll, *The Aryan Christ*, 143.
31 Noll, *The Aryan Christ*, 265–74.
32 Hayman, *A Life of Jung*, 178.
33 Robinson, *Nag Hammadi Story 2*, 620.
34 Hayman, *A Life of Jung*, 119.
35 Noll being a notable exception (*The Jung Cult*, 69, 326 note 28). This may be in part because of Mead's relative obscurity and the lack of easily available archives. However, it may also be because of a desire to obscure the *volkisch* and esoteric influences of his earlier work (Noll, *The Jung Cult*, 181–4) and therefore create a hagiographical Jung.
36 *C. G. Jung Manuskripte-Katalog* 49–50. *Fragments of a Faith Forgotten* is the 1906, 2nd ed., incorrectly listed as part of the Echoes of the Gnosis series.
37 Goodrick-Clarke and Goodrick-Clarke, *G.R.S. Mead*, 28–9; Noll, *The Jung Cult*, 181–4.
38 It is widely reported that they met towards the end of Mead's life. Noll reports that Mead in return made several trips to visit Jung towards the end of his life (Noll, *The Jung Cult*, 69), and less reliably, Hoeller has Jung visiting Mead in London to thank him for his translation of *Pistis Sophia* (Hoeller, 169; c.f. Goodrick-Clarke and Goodrick-Clarke, *G.R.S. Mead*, 31).
39 'A Word on Psychoanalysis', *The Quest*, vol. 9, no. 2 (1918), 240–61. The book mentioned is probably *The Psychology of the Unconscious* (English translation by Beatrice Hinkle (London: Keegan Paul)).
40 241. He does not ask Jung for the German original, but rather 'Dr. Eder', and has read 'a certain number of books and some articles here and there' on psychoanalysis generally.
41 He did contribute some articles on the Mandaeans as Gnostics in vol. 15, however (1923–4).
42 Dated 19 November 1919. The opening line reads, 'My dear Jung, You may remember that among the many interesting subjects we discussed in what were to me most pleasant talks together'.
43 Segal, 'Jung and Gnosticism', 304–8.
44 Segal, *The Gnostic Jung*, 15–17.

45 Segal argues that Jung misconstrues Gnosticism, by equating the divine with the unconscious and matter with the conscious ego. Jungian therapy aims to elevate the unconscious into the conscious mind, to balance the two, for the individual to become more whole. Yet the goal of the Gnostic as put forth in the classical texts is not to unite the divine and the material world, but to identify entirely with the divine, rejecting the material completely. So the aim of the Gnostic, given Jung's schema, is not integrated wholeness, but a rejection of the ego and a return to undifferentiated unconsciousness. This would be, in fact, a more unbalanced psychological state than to begin with, and the individual would not risk malaise, but psychosis ('Jung and Gnosticism', 314–18).
46 Grimstad, *The Modern Revival of Gnosticism*, 44.
47 Hayman, *A Life of Jung*, 284.
48 Jung, 'Religion and Psychology', 60.
49 Jung, *Psychological Types*, 445.
50 *C. G. Jung Manuskripte-Katalog*; Noll, *The Jung Cult*, 326–7.
51 Jung, 'The Spiritual Problem of Modern Man', 83–4.
52 Hanegraaff, *Esotericism and the Academy*, 288–9.
53 Hayman, *A Life of Jung*, 316. See Hakl, *Eranos*, for details of the various meetings.
54 Goodrick-Clarke and Goodrick-Clarke, *G.R.S. Mead*, 26–7.
55 Hakl, *Eranos*, 49. Intriguingly, Otto was also involved with theosophy, being involved with prominent Theological figures in Göttingen and having contact with Annie Besant and Krishnamurti in India (Hakl, *Eranos*, 53).
56 After Jung read *Das Heilige* in 1917, he began to refer to the experience of the 'numinosum' (Noll, *The Jung Cult*, 282).
57 *The Aryan Christ*, 151, 277.
58 O. Fröbe-Kapteyn, 'Vorwort', *Eranos-Jahrbuch*, vol. 2 (1934), 7. Translation from Sorge, 'Love as Devotion', 396. Original: 'Wenn sich diese Vermutung als begründet erweisen sollte, dann hätten wir damit die Anfänge eines Heilwegs für unsere Zeit aufgedeckt, der heute, inmitten der allgemeinen Desorientierung, des Suchens nach neuen Wertungen der alten ewigen Werte, besonders nottut.'
59 His final lecture was in 1951, however, on 'synchronicity', which would become a highly influential idea in the New Age milieu.
60 Hayman, *A Life of Jung*, 316. For a history of Eranos from Fröbe-Kapteyn's point of view, see Sorge, 'Love as Devotion'.
61 Hayman, *A Life of Jung*, 341–2.
62 Mellon, *Reflections in a Silver Spoon,* 159–67.
63 Mellon, *Reflections in a Silver Spoon*, 163.
64 Mellon, *Reflections in a Silver Spoon*, 164–7, 171–7; c.f. Hakl, *Eranos*, 109–10.
65 Graphologist Max Pulver and philologist Károly Kerenyi both spoke on it in 1941 (Hakl, *Eranos*, 123).

66 One notable exception was Eric Voegelin, who perhaps for this reason spoke only once, in 1977; his political conceptualization of Gnosticism is described in Chapter 6.
67 Wasserstrom, *Religion after Religion*, 30; Hakl, *Eranos*, 267–9.
68 Wasserstrom, *Religion after Religion*, 23.
69 Wasserstrom, *Religion after Religion*, 239–41.
70 Hanegraaff, *Esotericism and the Academy*, 296.
71 Biale, *Kabbalah and Counter-History*, 145.
72 Scholem, Smith and Stroumsa, *Morton Smith and Gershom Scholem, Correspondence 1945–1982*, 27.
73 *Kabbalah and Counter-History*, 146–7.
74 'Mut auch, durch die symbölische Fläche, die Wand der Historie hindurchzusetzen' (Biale, *Kabbalah and Counter-History*, 75 [translation], 216 [original]).
75 Hanegraaff, *Esotericism and the Academy*, 296–7.
76 *Cyclical Time and Ismaili Gnosis*, 151–2. This chapter, 'From the Gnosis of Antiquity to Ismaili Gnosis', was originally presented as a conference paper in 1956 and is here translated by James W. Morris.
77 *Cyclical Time*, 161.
78 *Cyclical Time*, 153; emphasis in original.
79 Wasserstrom, *Religion after Religion*, 31.
80 Wasserstrom, *Religion after Religion*, 128.
81 Wasserstrom, *Religion after Religion*, 146.
82 Casadio, '*NVMEN*, Brill and the IAHR in Their Early Years', 308.
83 Campbell, *Man and Time*, 40–54.
84 Campbell, *Man and Time*, 55.
85 Campbell, *Man and Time*, 38; emphasis added.
86 Gilles Quispel, 'La Conception de l'Homme dans la Gnose Valentinienne', 249–86.
87 Given, 'Nag Hammadi at Eranos', 91.
88 Quispel, 'Remembering Jung'.
89 Farmer, 'An Interview with Gilles Quispel', 28.
90 Quispel, 'Remembering Jung'.
91 Quispel, 'Inleiding', 9; c.f. Hakl, *Eranos*, 143.
92 Farmer, 'An Interview with Gilles Quispel', 27.
93 Ambasciano, *Unnatural History of Religions*, 99, 122–36.
94 *Religion after Religion*, 234.

5 No texts, no history: Nag Hammadi

1 xiii.
2 Decker, 'The Bauer Thesis: An Overview', 10.
3 *Das Evangelium des Johannes*.
4 Rudolph, 'Hans Jonas and Research on Gnosticism from a Contemporary Perspective', 92–3.
5 King, *What Is Gnosticism?*, 105–7.
6 Robinson, 'Theological Autobiography – 1988', 11.
7 The account in the following paragraphs is drawn from Robinson, *Nag Hammadi Story 1*, 20–70.
8 Muhammad 'Ali's original account contains a number of further mythological flourishes.
9 Schwartz's report of this incident to Jean Doresse informed the 1948 announcement in the CRAI by Puech and Doresse, the first publication about the find (Robinson, *Nag Hammadi Story 1*, 49).
10 Robinson speculates the leaves had been removed by one of the 'Ali brothers, Raghib, or by one of the many dealers involved in the deal.
11 Robinson, 'Introduction', 25.
12 Letter from Daumas to James Robinson, 29 November 1977, text and translation in Robinson, *Nag Hammadi Story 1*, 178.
13 Robinson, *Nag Hammadi Story 1*, 1–2, 130–1.
14 Robinson, *Nag Hammadi Story 1*, 267.
15 Robinson, *Nag Hammadi Story 1*, 92.
16 Robinson, *Nag Hammadi Story 1*, 168–70.
17 Robinson, *Nag Hammadi Story 1*, 334–7.
18 Robinson, *Nag Hammadi Story 1*, 267–9.
19 Robinson, *Nag Hammadi Story 1*, 208.
20 Robinson, *Nag Hammadi Story 1*, 3–16.
21 Goodacre, 'How Reliable Is the Story of the Nag Hammadi Discovery?', 315–16; Denzey Lewis and Blount, 'Rethinking the Origins of the Nag Hammadi Codices', 402.
22 Denzey Lewis and Blount, 'Rethinking the Origins of the Nag Hammadi Codices', 416.
23 Dillon, *The Heretical Revival*, 2–3.
24 See Williams, *Rethinking 'Gnosticism'*, 47–8, for a synoptic comparison.
25 Codices I, VII and XI were produced by a group of three scribes working together and include Christian materials (e.g. the *Prayer of Paul*, the *Apocryphon of James*), Sethian Christian texts (e.g. the *Apocalypse of Peter*, the *Three Steles of Seth*), Valentinian texts (the *Gospel of Truth*, a *Valentinian Exposition*, the *Tripartite Tractate*) and a Sethian text with Neoplatonic influence (*Allogenes*). Codices II and

XIII are the work of a pair of different scribes and contain more or less Christian texts (the *Apocryphon of John, the Gospel of Thomas, Trimorphic Protennoia, On the Origin of the World*, etc.). Codices IV and VIII, containing the *Apocryphon of John*, along with the *Gospel of the Egyptians*, the *Letter of Peter to Philip* and the Sethian/Neoplatonic text *Zostrianos*, are grouped together due to their paleographical style, as are codices V, VI and IX, which also have a similar style of binding and contain apocalypses of Paul, James and Adam; Hermetic texts; the letter of Eugnostos the Blessed and the aforementioned section of Plato's *Republic*. Codices III, XII and X show no relationship to each other, nor to the other groups, and contain a number of texts duplicated elsewhere. See Burke, 'What Do We Talk about When We Talk about the Nag Hammadi Library', 34; c.f. Williams, *Rethinking 'Gnosticism'*, 242.

26 Denzey Lewis and Blount, 'Rethinking the Origins of the Nag Hammadi Codices', 407.
27 Burke, 'What Do We Talk about When We Talk about the Nag Hammadi Library', 35.
28 Lim, *Dead Sea Scrolls*, 111–16.
29 Williams, *Rethinking 'Gnosticism'*, 32.
30 Robinson, *Nag Hammadi Story 1*, 356–60.
31 Robinson, *Nag Hammadi Story 2*, 615. None of the accounts I have read mention that Mary Mellon had died of an asthma attack in October 1946, so this was a *different* Mrs Mellon – Rachel, usually known as 'Bunny'. It is worth considering if the reason that the Bollingen Foundation seemed somewhat less keen on financially supporting Jung and his circle by the late 1940s may be a result of this.
32 Pagels, *The Gnostic Gospels*, xxvi; Robinson, *Nag Hammadi Story 1*, 374–7.
33 Robinson, *Nag Hammadi Story 1*, 381–3.
34 The English version, *Gnosis as World Religion*, was published in 1972.
35 Quispel and van Oort, *Gnostica, Judaica, Catholica*, 142.
36 'Eine Weltreligion ist neu entdeckt. So darf man vielleicht schon jetze die Bedeutung der neuen Funde gnostischer Manuskripte zusammenfassen. Bisher bestand in der Schatzung und Einreihung dieser merkwürdigen Stromung eine gewisse Unsicherheit und Verlegenheit, die sich aus der Dürftigkeit des Materials und der Schwierigkeit der Deutung erklären lasst. Jetzt sehen wir klar, und die zeit ist nicht fern, dass wir ganze Gnosis von der Quelle bis zur Mündung überblicken, ihre phanomenologischePhysiognomie Wurzeln herausarbeiten konnen' (Quispel 1951, 1; translation by the author).
37 Robinson, *Nag Hammadi Story 2*, 624–6.
38 Quispel's argument for the Jung Codex proving a Jewish origin, and disproving an Eastern origin, is found in Cross, *The Jung Codex*, 62–76.
39 *Gnosis als Weltreligion*, 39.

40 *Gnosis als Weltreligion*, 38.
41 'Die Gnosis ist ein geheimes Wissen um die verborgenen Zusammenhänge des Universums, um eine esoterische Tradition der Urweisheit, die von Göttern den Menchen offenbart ist, es ist die Enthüllung des Sinnes seines Seins in der Welt' (*Gnosis als Weltreligion*, 38, translation by the author).
42 *Gnosis als Weltreligion*, 2nd ed. (1972), 37.
43 Robinson, *Nag Hammadi Story 1*, 403–4.
44 Robinson, *Nag Hammadi Story 1*, 398–425.
45 The papers were signed on the following day, however, which became the official date of the purchase. See Robinson, *Nag Hammadi Story 1*, 429.
46 Robinson, *Nag Hammadi Story 1*, 446.
47 Cross, *The Jung Codex*, 19.
48 Robinson, *Nag Hammadi Story 1*, 384–90.
49 Robinson, *Nag Hammadi Story 1*, 454–78.
50 In Cross, *The Jung Codex*, 27. Note that 'him' in these passages refers to 'Man' in the sexist mid-twentieth-century sense of 'humanity'.
51 In Cross, *The Jung Codex*, 27
52 In Robinson, *Nag Hammadi Story 1*, 474
53 Robinson, *Nag Hammadi Story 1*, 468
54 Robinson, *Nag Hammadi Story 1*, 483
55 Robinson, *Nag Hammadi Story 1*, 528–38
56 Robinson, *Nag Hammadi Story 2*, 635–57. Queen Juliana was already very 'interested in the phenomenology of religion', and on 19 October 1951, she invited Olga Fröbe-Kapteyn to her residence for a tea, to know more about Eranos over the course of a two-hour meeting. (Letter from Olga Fröbe-Kapteyn to Henri Corbin, in Bernardini, *Jung a Eranos*, 52.)
57 Robinson, *Nag Hammadi Story 2*, 686–700.
58 Guillaumont, Puech, Quispel, Till and al-Masih, *The Gospel According to Thomas*.
59 Robinson, 'Theological Autobiography – 1988', 11–12.

6 A revolt against history: Gnostic scholarship, after Nag Hammadi

1 'The Secret Books of the Egyptian Gnostics', 293. Part of a discussion on Jean Doresse's *The Secret Books of the Egyptian Gnostics* (1960).
2 Styfhals, *No Spiritual Investment in the World*, 12.
3 'The Spiritual Problem of Modern Man', 83–4.
4 Hayman, *A Life of Jung*, 411.
5 'Answer to Job', 383.

6 'Answer to Job', 397–411, 408.
7 Buber, 'Religion and Modern Thinking'. Heidegger and Sartre were also singled out for criticism.
8 Wasserstrom, *Religion after Religion*, 190.
9 Buber, 'Rejoiner to Jung', 70.
10 Wasserstrom, *Religion after Religion*, 233, 234.
11 *Memories, Dreams, Reflections*, 303.
12 *Memories, Dreams, Reflections*, 303.
13 *Religion und Spatantiker Geist 2*, 224; 'A Retrospective View', 11–12.
14 *Gnostic Religion*, xvii.
15 *Gnostic Religion*, xvii.
16 *Gnostic Religion*, xvii; emphasis mine.
17 Brumlik, 'A Few Motifs in Hans Jonas's Early Book on Gnosticism', 75.
18 *Gnostic Religion*, 327.
19 Lazier, 'Pauline Theology in the Weimar Republic', 127–9.
20 Jonas, 'Heidegger and Theology'; *Memoirs*, 190–3.
21 Styfhals, *No Spiritual Investment in the World*, 30. This paper was later included in the paperback edition of *The Gnostic Religion*.
22 Jonas, *Memoirs*, 66.
23 E.g. Hotam, 'Gnosis and Modernity'; Wolin, *Heidegger's Children*.
24 Jonas, 'A Retrospective View', 13.
25 Chahana, *A Gnostic Critic of Modernity*, 174.
26 *Gnostic Religion*, 338.
27 Wasserstrom, *Religion after Religion*, 40.
28 Hakl, *Eranos*, 265.
29 Jonas, 'The Concept of God after Auschwitz'.
30 *Gnosticism and Early Christianity*, 35–8.
31 Pearson, *Gnosticism, Judaism, and Egyptian Christianity*, 130; Rudolph, *Gnosis*, 277–82.
32 Scholem, *Jewish Gnosticism*, 259.
33 'Gnosticism and the New Testament', 259–60.
34 Jonas, 'Response by Hans Jonas', 289.
35 Jonas, 'Response by Hans Jonas', 290–1.
36 Jonas, 'Response by Hans Jonas', 293; emphasis in original.
37 As well as Eliade, whose *Myth of the Eternal Return* he notes was unusual in that it was a response to the defeat of the Axis powers (and, implicitly, Romanian legionary and theocratic fascism), rather than its ascendency (2010, 318). On Eliade's political past, see Ambasciano, *Unnatural History of Religions*, 97–9, 117–20.

38 'Nightmare and Flight', 134.
39 Rabinbach, *In the Shadow of Catastrophe*, 11.
40 *Summa Theologica*, 1.1.
41 *Negative Dialetics*, 361.
42 *Gnosticism, Judaism, and Egyptian Christianity*, 93; emphasis mine. Williams notes that the only reference to the failure of God in the passage is Birger's own insertion: '(and done, failed to do)' (*Rethinking 'Gnosticism'*, 78).
43 'The Problem of God after Auschwitz', 10.
44 Styfhals, *No Spiritual Investment in the World*, 63.
45 Styfhals, *No Spiritual Investment in the World*.
46 *Meaning in History*, 2.
47 Styfhals, *No Spiritual Investment in the World*, 63.
48 Wolin, *Heidegger's Children*, 78; c.f. Styfhals, *No Spiritual Investment in the World*, 75.
49 *Abendländische Eschatologie*.
50 Styfhals, *No Spiritual Investment in the World*, 78.
51 'Die Geschichte Jacob Taubes-Carl Schmitt', 305. My use of it comes from Styfhals, *No Spiritual Investment in the World*.
52 Styfhals, *No Spiritual Investment in the World*, 86.
53 *Gnostische Politik*, 316. 'Der pathologische Versuch, ein Reich transzendenter Vollendung geschichtlich immanent zu verwerklichen.'
54 'Ein krankhaftes Gewächs' (*Gnostische Politik*, 317).
55 *New Science*, 163.
56 Nieli, 'Eric Voegelin: Gnosticism, Mysticism, and Modern Radical Politics', 337, 340; Hanegraaff, *On the Construction*, 31–3.
57 *Science, Politics and Gnosis*, 7.
58 'On the Construction', 31.
59 'The Oxford Political Philosophers', *Philosophical Quarterly* vol. 11, no. 3 (1953), 111.
60 *The Legitimacy of the Modern Age*, 127–60.
61 *The Legitimacy of the Modern Age*, 126.
62 Lincoln, *Discourse and the Construction of Society*, 32.
63 'Taubes, Vorwort', 5. Translation from Styfals, *No Spiritual Investment in the World*, 162.
64 *Eternity*, 23; *Eternal Return*, 141.
65 Wasserstrom, *Religion after Religion*, 241.
66 Ginzburg, 'Mircea Eliade's Ambivalent Legacy', 318.
67 Biale, *Gershom Scholem*, 86.

7 Tongues and misunderstandings: Messina 1966

1 Letter originally published in Spineto, *Mircea Eliade-Raffaele Pettazzoni*, 179–81; c.f. Gandini, 'Raffaele Pettazzoni 1948', 118–20.
2 Gandini, 'Raffaele Pettazzoni 1949–1950', 222.
3 Cassadio, '*NVMEN*, Brill and the IAHR in Their Early Years', 307–21.
4 Letter to Lucy Heyer, 31 August 1951: 'Sono stato ad Ascona nel 1950, ho partecipato per tre giorni alle riunioni dell'ERANOS, e ne ho riportato una impressione duratura. Non so quanta parte vi abbia la bellezza naturale del luogo, la serenità del paesaggio che rasserena gli spiriti e li dispone al raccoglimento. Ma più che la cornice e lo sfondo è la luce spirituale che dà vita al quadro, è la corrente di simpatia che circola tra i convenuti, conferenzieri e uditori, tutti raccolti non per dissertare e discutere, non per imporre le proprie idee, ma per esporle e proporle in tutta semplicità e schiettezza, nel sentimento dell'aspirazione comune ad intendere e a fare intendere i gravi problemi dello spirito umano, della condizione umana, della vita umana.'
5 The 'S' was dropped by the second congress in 1955.
6 Cited in Cassadio, '*NVMEN*, Brill and the IAHR in Their Early Years', 307.
7 Molendijk, 'Early Dutch Science of Religion in International Perspective', 5.
8 *The Meaning of Religion*, 13.
9 'Clarifying Phenomenologies in the Study of Religion', 92.
10 See Alles, 'Introduction', 2.
11 While Rijk held a doctorate, he was not a scholar of religion. He did the accounts for the IAHR as well as several other professional organizations. Armin Geertz in 1985 was the first scholar of religion to hold the post of honorary treasurer.
12 Pettazzoni, 1954, 'Aperçu Introductif'. Translation from *Essays in the History of Religions*, 218.
13 Weibe, *Politics of Religious Studies*, 175.
14 See Capps, *Religious Studies*, 130.
15 Capps, *Religious Studies*, 129.
16 Dadosky, *The Structure of Religious Knowing*, 17.
17 Van der Leeuw, *Religion in Essence and Manifestation*, 646; c.f. Dadosky 2014, *The Structure of Religious Knowing*, 20–1; Weibe, *Politics of Religious Studies*, 173; Ake Hultkranz described his work as 'too speculative, in some places, even incomprehensible, to be of much use to the seriously working empirical religious researcher' (cited in Capps, *Religious Studies*, 131). Capps goes further, stating that his 'liturgical … attitude' was his primary influence (Capps, *Religious Studies*, 132).
18 Van der Leeuw, *Religion in Essence and Manifestation*, 23–4.
19 *Religion in Essence and Manifestation*, 684.
20 *Religion in Essence and Manifestation*, 694.

21 Bleeker, 'The Future Task of the History of Religions', 228–9; c.f. Bleeker, 'The Contribution of the Phenomenology of Religion to the Study of the History of Religions'.
22 Bleeker, 'The Contribution of the Phenomenology of Religion to the Study of the History of Religions', 41; c.f. Tuckett, 'Clarifying Phenomenologies in the Study of Religion'.
23 Bleeker, 'The Relation of the History of Religions to Kindred Religious Sciences', 147–9.
24 Bleeker, 'The Future Task of the History of Religions', 226–7.
25 Bleeker, 'The Future Task of the History of Religions', 227.
26 Cassadio, 'NVMEN, Brill and the IAHR in Their Early Years', 312, f.n. 23.
27 Eliade, *The Quest*, 8; c.f. McCutcheon 1997, 37.
28 Dubuisson, 'The Poetical and Rhetorical Structure of the Eliadean Text', 139.
29 Hakl, *Eranos*, 170.
30 Ambasciano, *Sciamanesimo senza sciamanesimo*, 194–5; Ambasciano, *Unnatural History of Religions*, 107; cf. Hakl, *Eranos*, 170. Eliade cites Mead *en passant* in his published diary just once, on 16 June 1952, as he reports that Olga Fröbe-Kapteyn told him in Ascona some amusing yet unspecified gossip concerning 'Mead, Waite, Robert Heisler' and others (Eliade, *Giornale*, 136).
31 Ginzburg, 'Mircea Eliade's Ambivalent Legacy', 314–15.
32 On the difference between Eliade and Jung's notions of the archetype, see Spineto, 'The Notion of Archetype in Eliade's Writings'; Ambasciano, 'Politics of Nostalgia, Logical Fallacies, and Cognitive Biases'.
33 Dubuisson, *Twentieth Century Mythologies*, xvii–xviii; Faivre, 'Modern Western Esoteric Currents in the Work of Mircea Eliade'.
34 Ambasciano, *An Unnatural History of Religions*, 93–103; Ambasciano, *Sciamanesimo senza sciamanesimo*.
35 Eliade, *Yoga. Essai sur les Origines de la Mystique Indienne*.
36 *Shamanism*, 11.
37 Eliade, *Shamanism*, xiv.
38 *The Sacred and the Profane*, 7.
39 Otto, *Das Heilige*, 8. 'Wir fondern auf, sich einen Moment starker und möglichst einseitger religiöser Erregtheit zu besinnen. Wer das nicht kann oder solche Momente überhaupt nich hat, ist gebeten, nicht weiter zu lesen.'
40 McCutcheon, *Manufacturing Religion*, 51.
41 'The Poetical and Rhetorical Structure of the Eliadean Text', 137.
42 'The Sacred in a Secular World', 62.
43 McCutcheon, *Manufacturing Religion*, 58.
44 http://easr.info/wp-content/uploads/2018/02/EASR-IAHR-joint-statement-about-the-EuARe.pdf (accessed 19 January 2021).

45 The need for these seems to have waned with the growth of regional sub-organizations like the British Association for the Study of Religion and later the European Association for the Study of Religion, whose annual conference is considered a 'special meeting of the IAHR' also.
46 Robinson, 'Theological Autobiography – 1988', 204.
47 The second edition version (1971) was translated by Birger Pearson with additional notes from *Religionsphanomenologie* and published as a monograph entitled *The Gnostic Attitude* in 1973. I have worked from this, most comprehensive, version.
48 E.g. *Gnostic Attitude*, 17–18.
49 *Gnostic Attitude*, 45–52.
50 *Gnostic Attitude*, 1–3.
51 'Le problème des origines du gnosticisme et l'histoire des religions', 162–3. Original: 'Depuis le commencement de ce siècle la question historico-religieuse des origines du gnosticisme est donc posée, surtout dans les milieux de l'école *religionsgeschichtlich*. D'ailleurs, les études de cette école sur les origines du gnosticisme (et ses rapports avec le christianisme) ont puissamment relevé de la situation du milieu culturel allemand des trois premières décades de ce siècle; c'est pourquoi on a maintenant tout l'intérêt à ne pas identifier ces deux choses, historiquement liées mais distinctes: la problématique et les théories *religionsgeschichtlich* de Bousset, Reitzenstein, Dieterich, Norden, Clemen, si méritoires qu'elles aient pu s'avérer, et le problème tout court historico-religieux des origines du gnosticisme, tel qu'il est impose par les connaissances d'aujourd'hui. Il est vrai que la discussion continue parfois à s'orienter dans d'autres directions aussi: ou bien on continue de rechercher les origines de la gnose dans le sillon de la tradition judaïque et chrétienne, ou bien on se cantonne dans une hypothèse historique extrême, réduisant la gnose au "syncrétisme". Mais il faut remarquer qu'une interprétation "judaïque" de la gnose, une fois qu'elle soit sensible aux problèmes poses par les connaissances actuelles sur le milieu judaïque, ne cesse pourtant pas d'être une recherche "historico- religieuse" (qui n'équivaut pas à dire *religionsgeschichtlich* au sens classique et historiquement conditionne du mot). La solution syncrétiste, à son tour, présente le danger de dissimuler et, pratiquement, nier le problème comparatif: justement le contraire d'une analyse historico-religieuse réelle; ce qui est pire, elle tend à vanifier trop hâtivement le contenu spécifique de la pensée et du mouvement gnostiques.'
52 His conference paper, 'Delimitation of the Gnostic Phenomenon – Typological and Historical', was replaced with a paper entitled *Makarius und das Leid von der Perle* in the published proceedings.
53 'A Retrospective View', 12.
54 Neither Quispel nor Rudolph attended in person.

55 In Bianchi, *Origins of Gnosticism*, 651–67. Conze's 1979 memoir was entitled *Memirs of a Modern Gnostic*.
56 Cited in Robinson, *Nag Hammadi Story 2*, 985–6.
57 See Bianchi, *Origins of Gnosticism*, xx–xxxii.
58 Robinson, *Nag Hammadi Story 2*, 1006.
59 Bianchi, *Origins of Gnosticism*, xxvi; emphasis in original.
60 This is even clearer in the German text, which reads 'in diese Welt des Schicksals, der Geburt und des Totes gefallen ist' (*Origins of Gnosticism*, xxix).
61 *Origins of Gnosticism*, xxvii. Also, Carston Colpe's Messina presentation argued that the spiritual beings of Gnosticism should not be interpreted literally but rather understood as names for different aspects of the 'self' (Hakl, *Eranos*, 265).
62 *Origins of Gnosticism*, xxvi–xxvii.
63 As cited by Mead in the *Quest*, vol. 6, 677.
64 Quispel, 'Review of Jewish Gnosticism, Merkabah Mysticism and Talmudic Tradition by Gershom G. Scholem', 117.
65 *Origins of Gnosticism*, xxvii.
66 *Origins of Gnosticism*, xxvii; emphasis added.
67 Robinson, 'Introduction', 4.
68 It dismisses the Bruce and Askew codices as not similar enough to the heresiological descriptions, 'and so posed more problems than they solved' (we might ask what problem needed to be solved – not a lack of sources, presumably, but rather, evidence which bolsters certain preconceptions?), but goes to great lengths to connect the Nag Hammadi finds with groups named by the heresiologists, equating the *Hypostasis of the Archons* with the *Book of Norea* mentioned by Epiphanius (534).

8 Takes a Gnostic to find a Gnostic: Contemporary gnostic groups

1 E.g. Doherty, 'The Neo-Gnostic Synthesis of Samael Aun Weor'; Winterberg, *Remembering the Gnostics*; Urban, 'The Knowing of Knowing'.
2 Leyton, *The Gnostic Scriptures*, 335.
3 Doherty, 'The Neo-Gnostic Synthesis of Samael Aun Weor'.
4 In the interests of fairness, DeConick's 2019 paper 'The Sociology of Gnostic Spirituality' does mention the Ecclesia Gnostica (54), suggesting that some of these groups will be considered in her ongoing work on 'Gnostic Spirituality'. However, they are included alongside the I AM movement and the Church Universal and Triumphant, neither of which identifies as Gnostic religions, so the issue of the scholar deciding the dataset for their own interests remains.

5 I might also have included the Ecclesia Catholica Gnostica. It has its roots in the French 'gnostic' churches and German OTO, but is today devoted to Aleister Crowley's Law of Thelema. I have decided to exclude them from this chapter due to constraints on space, as they are smaller than the other two groups, and effectively a subgroup of the OTO. As such, they tend to regard themselves as primarily Thelemites, rather than Gnostics per se. I intend to include them in my future book on contemporary Gnostic groups, however, due to these historical connections and some other structural similarities.
6 *No Spiritual Investment in the World*, 12–13.
7 *What Is Gnosticism?*, 3.
8 *The Gnostic Jung*, 15.
9 https://web.archive.org/web/20110819030143/http://jordanstratford.blogspot.com/2008/01/gnosticism-102-gnostic-world-view.html (accessed 20 August 2020).
10 http://www.gnosis.org/ecclesia/ecclesia.htm (accessed 21 July 2020). This claim relies upon him denying that the Ecclesia Gnostica Catholica are a legitimate Gnostic sacramental body.
11 https://www.amazon.co.uk/s?k=gnosticism (accessed 4 August 2020 and 18 June 2010).
12 Interview with Hoeller, 10 April 2019; c.f. Dillon, *The Heretical Revival*, 65–6.
13 Hoeller, *The Gnostic Jung*, xxvii.
14 Hill, 'Exile in Godville'.
15 'Wandering Bishops'.
16 'Wandering Bishops', 4.
17 Smith, 'The Revival of Ancient Gnosis', 206.
18 Hoeller told me that they had reconciled following his death after du Palatine visited him in a dream.
19 Hoeller, *The Gnostic Jung*, 33.
20 Hoeller, *The Gnostic Jung*, 31.
21 *Isis Unveiled*, II, 124.
22 Hoeller, *The Gnostic Jung*, 22.
23 Hoeller, *The Gnostic Jung*, 33.
24 Hoeller, *Gnosticism*, viii, 16.
25 *The Gnostic Jung*, 15.
26 *Gnosticism*, 16.
27 Hoeller, *Gnosticism*, viii.
28 Hoeller, *Jung and the Lost Gospels*, 244; emphasis mine.
29 Hoeller, *Jung and the Lost Gospels*, 6.
30 *Gnosticism*, 37–53; http://www.gnosis.org/ecclesia/calendar.htm (accessed 24 August 2020).
31 Hammer, 'Jungian Gnosticism of the Ecclesia Gnostica', 47.

32 Hoeller, *Gnosticism*, 225; 'Position Paper Concerning the Thelemite or Crowleyan Gnostic Churches'; Pagels, *The Gnostic Gospels*.
33 Smith, 'The Revival of Ancient Gnosis', 209–10.
34 XXI, 4–5. At http://www.tertullian.org/anf/anf03/anf03-24.htm#P3125_1133921 (accessed 24 August 2020).
35 *Gnosticism*, 178.
36 Originally, the Catholic Church of the Holy Grail. https://johannite.org/response.pdf (accessed 17 March 2021); Dillon, 'The Impact of Scholarship on Contemporary 'Gnosticism(s)'', 58.
37 The Temple of Set was formed in 1975 as an offshoot of Anton LaVey's Church of Satan, reproducing much of its theology and practice, though significantly, the Egyptian god Set replaced Satan at the top of the hierarchy. Importantly, Set was regarded as an actual deity, whereas for LaVey, Satan was an antinomian symbol of the individual will. Rather than the playful naturalism of the Church of Satan, then, the Temple of Set was a fully-fledged, committed esoteric religion. See Dyrendal, Lewis and Petersen, *The Invention of Satanism*, 67–70.
38 https://sites.google.com/site/gnostickos/bishopsfoster (accessed 12 March 2020).
39 https://nacgb.org/ (accessed 12 March 2020).
40 The most recent activity I can find is the 2010 'State of the College Address' delivered by Mar Iohannes, patriarch of the Apostolic Johannite Church and president of the North American College of Gnostic Bishops. https://www.johannite.org/state-of-the-college-address-2010/ (accessed 17 March 2021).
41 'Position Paper Concerning the Thelemite or Crowleyan Gnostic Churches', 194; emphasis added.
42 https://www.johannite.org/all-saints-accord/ (accessed 12 March 2020).
43 https://www.johannite.org/governance/ (accessed 12 March 2020).
44 *Living Gnosticism*, 17; c.f. 15–32, 119. The quote is from Allen Ginsberg's 'Howl'.
45 Stratford, *Living Gnosticism*, 16.
46 *The Gnostic Jung*, 33.
47 Dillon, 'The Impact of Scholarship on Contemporary "Gnosticism(s)"', 61, f.n. 14. The term is also used as the title of a 1999 volume edited by Jungian psychologist June Singer, to which Hoeller contributed. Hanegraaff suggests that the term may have derived from Quispel's Dutch Pietist *bevindelijken* Protestantism (http://wouterjhanegraaff.blogspot.com/2020/07/the-third-kind-gilles-quispel-and-gnosis.html, accessed 20 August 2020).
48 Email communication dated 25 May 2011.
49 *Living Gnosticism*, 45–7.
50 A modified version of the Gospel of John allegedly discovered in 1804 by Fabré-Palaprat, written by a monk named Nicophorus of Athens. It warrants further investigation.

51. http://anthonysilvia.com/the-johannite-rosary/ (accessed 13 March 2020). Original in Clement, *Excerpta ex Theodoto*, 78. Μέχρι τοῦ βαπτίσματος οὖν ἡ Εἱμαρμένη, φασίν, ἀληθής· μετὰ δὲ τοῦτο οὐκέτι ἀληθεύουσιν οἱ ἀστρο λόγοι.Ἔστιν δὲ οὐ τὸ λουτρὸν μόνον τὸ ἐλευθεροῦν, ἀλλὰ καὶ ἡ γνῶσις, τίνες ἦμεν, τί γεγόναμεν· ποῦ ἦμεν, ἢ ποῦ ἐνεβλήθημεν· ποῦ σπεύδομεν, πόθεν λυτρούμεθα· τί γέννησις, τί ἀναγέ ννησις.
52. https://www.youtube.com/watch?v=X_8BK-dQ1Fo (accessed 17 March 2021).
53. https://www.youtube.com/watch?v=pFgxu9_6Yic&list=PLtvRkBZGjaKSLdl1RhFan BXP5Lj-3xAjT (accessed 17 March 2021).
54. https://www.youtube.com/watch?v=Rbsva9X71JI (accessed 17 March 2021).
55. 'The Creed of the Gnostic Catholic Church: An Examination – Sabazius – Hermetic Library', https://hermetic.com/sabazius/creed_egc (accessed 17 March 2020).
56. Email correspondence, 25 May 2011. Note that Stratford refuses to refer to him as Aun Weor; emphasis in original.
57. Puma, *This Way; How to Think Like a Gnostic*.
58. See Dillon, 'The Impact of Scholarship on Contemporary 'Gnosticism(s)'', 64; emphasis in original.
59. Dillon, *The Heretical Revival*.
60. A number of different terms are used to identify the groups in the Weor tradition, many of which are confusingly similar acronyms. I am here using Gnostic Movement for simplicity and clarity, as well as to make it distinct from the many other Gnostic churches already named in this book.
61. *Living Gnosticism*, 104.
62. In English, Winter, 'Studying the "Gnostic Bible"'; Winterberg, 'Remembering the Gnostics'; Doherty, 'The Neo-Gnostic Synthesis of Samael Aun Weor'; Dillon, *The Heretical Revival* and 'The Impact of Scholarship on Contemporary "Gnosticism(s)"'; Burns and Renger (eds.), *New Antiquities*; Andrew Dawson, *New Era, New Religions*, 54–65 and 'The Universal Christian Gnostic Church'. In Italian, PierLuigi Zoccatelli, 'Note a margine dell'influsso di G. I. Gurdjieff su Samael Aun Weor' and 'Il Paradigma Esoterico E Un Modello Di Applicazione. Note Sul Movimento Gnostico Di Samael Aun Weor'. In Spanish, Guinazu's anthropological account, *Nuevas religiosidades en América Latina*, and Marcello Campos's historical work (e.g. 'Lideranças femininas no gnosticismo samaeliano'; 'Entre contextos ediscursos' (with Ana Silva); 'Gnosticismo Samaeliano na Academia') are important contributions, though these are little known outside of South America.
63. Zoccatelli, 'Sexual Magic and Gnosis in Colombia', 141; Smith, 'The Revival of Ancient Gnosis', 211.
64. Dawson, *New Era, New Religions*, 55.
65. Known locally as Iglesia Gnostica. Kaczynski, *Forgotten Templars*, 253–4; Apiryon, 'Jules Doinel and the Gnostic Church of France'.

66 *The Three Mountains*, 29–34.
67 Köenig, 'Arnoldo Krumm-Heller – Huiracocha'.
68 Zoccatelli, 'Sexual Magic and Gnosis in Colombia', 145.
69 Dawson, *New Era, New Religions*, 55.
70 Smith, 'The Revival of Ancient Gnosis', 211.
71 Weor, *The Perfect Matrimony*, 3–4.
72 Dawson, *New Era, New Religions*, 55.
73 *The Three* Mountains, 49–53; c.f. Dawson, *New Era, New Religions*, 56.
74 http://rememberingthegnosticmovement.com/about/story/ (accessed 4 August 2020).
75 https://lumendelumine.org/ (accessed 22 June 2020).
76 Dawson, *New Era, New Religions*, 56–60.
77 https://www.gnosis.org.uk/ (accessed 4 August 2020).
78 These are outlined in throughout Weor's work, particularly *Tratado de psicología revolucionaria* (1970).
79 Dawson, *New Era, New Religions*, 60.
80 Weor, *The Perfect Matrimony*, xviii.
81 *The Perfect Matrimony*, 59. This gender imbalance is reinforced by Weor's frequent descriptions of male energies as active/producing and female as passive/receiving. Dawson's research suggests that such an imbalance was played out in the institutional roles within Weor groups, so his findings that the groups were predominantly male (68 to 32 per cent female) is perhaps understandable ('The Gnostic Church of Brazil', 23).
82 Weor, *The Perfect Matrimony*, 147; Dawson, *New Era, New Religions*, 59.
83 Weor, *The Perfect Matrimony*, 63.
84 Weor, *The Perfect Matrimony*, 71–2.
85 Krumm-Heller, *La Iglesia Gnostica*, 13; c.f. Winter, 'Studying the "Gnostic Bible"', 98.
86 Krumm-Heller, *La Iglesia Gnostica*, 40.
87 Winter, 'Studying the "Gnostic Bible"', 98–103.
88 Robertson, 'Diversification in Samael Aun Weor's Gnostic Movement'; c.f. Dawson, *New Era, New Religions*, 63.
89 Dillon, *The Heretical Revival*, 6–7; c.f. Winterberg, 'Remembering the Gnostics', 47.
90 Dillon, *The Heretical Revival*, 9.

9 The third way: Gnosticism in Western esotericism

1 Given, 'Nag Hammadi at Eranos', 96–7.
2 Neugebauer-Wölk, 'From Talk about Esotericism to Esotericism Research', 136.

3 Junginger, 'Introduction', 4.
4 Hanegraaff, 'On the Construction', 14.
5 Vickers, 'Frances Yates and the Writing of History'.
6 See Hanegraaff, 'Beyond the Yates Paradigm'.
7 Stausberg, 'What Is It All about?', 219; Faivre 'From Paris to Amsterdam and Beyond', 123–4.
8 See *Religion after Religion*, 271, n. 37.
9 *Religion after Religion*, 42; Eliade, 'Some Notes on *Theosophia perennis*', 173; Hanegraaff, *Esotericism and the Academy*, 341–4. A full list of Centre International du Recherche Spirituelle Comparée publications can be found at https://henrycorbinproject.blogspot.com/2008/12/cahiers-de-luniversit-saint-jean-de.html (accessed 12 May 2020).
10 Faivre, *Access to Western Esotericism*, 19–20; c.f. Faivre, 'Renaissance Hermeticism and the Concept of Western Esotericism', 119–20.
11 Hanegraaff, *New Age Religion*, 387–8.
12 'Renaissance Hermeticism and the Concept of Western Esotericism', 10.
13 *Access to Western Esotericism*, 20.
14 *Access to Western Esotericism*, 19–20.
15 *Access to Western Esotericism*, 19.
16 *Access to Western Esotericism*, 19, 113–34.
17 *Access to Western Esotericism*, 21–2.
18 *A History of Religious Ideas, Vol II*, 369; c.f. *A History of Religious Ideas, Vol III*, 162–71, in which he restates Scholem's 'Jewish Gnosticism' thesis.
19 Hakl, *Eranos*, 240–1.
20 See Ambasciano, *Unnatural History of Religions*, 128–30, 169.
21 Culianu, *The Tree of Gnosis*, xv.
22 Culianu, *The Tree of Gnosis*, 46.
23 Faivre, 'From Paris to Amsterdam and Beyond', 124–6.
24 *New Age Religion*, 520.
25 Hanegraaff, *Esotericism and the Academy*, 334–55.
26 *New Age Religion*, vii.
27 See http://wouterjhanegraaff.blogspot.com/2020/07/the-third-kind-gilles-quispel-and-gnosis.html for a more recent account by Hanegraaff of this discovery (accessed 20 August 2020).
28 van den Broek, *Gnostic Religion in Antiquity*, 2–3.
29 van den Broek, 'Gnosticism I: Gnostic Religion', 405.
30 van den Broek, 'Gnosticism I: Gnostic Religion', 404.
31 This model is repeated in 'A Dynamic Typological Approach'; 'The Problem of "Post-Gnostic" Gnosticism'; 'On the Construction of "Esoteric Traditions"', 372–3;

Dictionary of Gnosis and Western Esotericism, 138–40; 'The New Age Movement and Western Esotericism', 40–2.
32 Hanegraaff, 'The New Age Movement and Western Esotericism', 40.
33 *New Age Religion*, 497–504, 510.
34 *New Age Religion*, 507–9.
35 *New Age Religion*, 4–7.
36 A model suggested by Dan Merkur, in *Gnosis*. See the next chapter.
37 'On the Construction', 42.
38 'On the Construction', 47–8.
39 'On the Construction', 43; emphasis added.
40 *Esotericism and the Academy*, 372; emphasis added.
41 'On the Construction', 54; 'Reason, Faith and Gnosis', 138.
42 Held from its founding in 2006 until Goodrick-Clarke's death in 2012. At the time of writing, it seems that the chair will remain vacant. http://centres.exeter.ac.uk/exeseso/ (accessed 4 August 2018).
43 Stausberg, 'What Is It All About?'
44 van den Broek, 'The Birth of a Chair', 11–13.
45 van den Broek, 'The Birth of a Chair', 14.
46 Hanegraaff, Forshaw and Pasi, *Hermes Explains*, 19–20.
47 Details from personal correspondence with Hanegraaff, 28 August 2019.
48 In the first issue with Roland Edighoffer and Faivre, and then with Faivre and Nicholas Goodrick-Clarke.
49 Something that has not typically been the case in academic studies of stigmatized traditions (see Davidsen, 'What Is Wrong with Pagan Studies?').
50 'Discursive Study of Religion'; 'Western Esotericism'.
51 *Western Esoterisicm*, 10; emphasis in original.
52 'Esotericism Disputed', 171–5.
53 'Esotericism Disputed', 180.
54 *Esotericism and the Academy*, 362–7.
55 *Esotericism and the Academy*, 366–7.
56 *Esotericism and the Academy*, 365; emphasis in original.
57 *Esotericism and the Academy*, 355.
58 https://www.esswe.org/resources/pdf/newsletter/ESSWE_Newsletter_2019_Vol_10_No_1_2_Summer_Winter_2019.pdf (accessed 20 January 2021).
59 See Asprem and Strube, *New Approaches to the Study of Esotericism*, for reflections of these issues and the future of the field from those working in it.
60 *Hermes Explains*, 10.

10 Knowledge of the heart: The gnostic New Age

1. Lazier, *God Interrupted*, 29.
2. Sutcliffe, *Children of the New Age*, 55–83.
3. See Hanegraaff, 'Kabbalah in Gnosis Magazine'.
4. Robertson, *UFOs, Conspiracy Theories and the New Age*, 125–36; Robertson, 'David Icke's Reptilian Thesis'.
5. Robertson, 'Transformation'.
6. Gilhus, 'The Gnostic Myth and the Goddess Myth', 130.
7. *Eternity*, 242.
8. *Eternity*, 20–1.
9. Versluis, *The New Inquisitions*, 108; c.f. Dyrendal, Lewis and Petersen, *The Invention of Satanism*, 102–4.
10. *Omens of the Millennium*, 24–5.
11. *Omens of Millennium*, 26–7.
12. Pakenham, 'In Full Bloom'.
13. Bloom and Meyer, *The Gospel of Thomas*.
14. Beginning with Yeats in 1970 and most clearly argued in *Agon* (1982).
15. *Agon*, 87.
16. *Omens of the Millennium*, 16.
17. *The American Religion*, 31.
18. Jones, *The Gnostic Empire Strikes Back*, 7.
19. Jones, *The Gnostic Empire Strikes Back*, 72. To me, this sounds just like today's (2020) populist discourse about 'cultural Marxism'.
20. Carette and King, *Selling Spirituality*; Bruce, 'Good Intentions and Bad Sociology'.
21. Heelas, *The New Age Movement*; York, *The Emerging Network*.
22. See Sutcliffe and Gilhus, *New Age Spirituality*, 6–8. Examples include Hanegraaff, *New Age Religion*; Sutcliffe, *Children of the New Age*; Gilhus, Kraft and Lewis, *New Age in Norway*; Robertson, *UFOs, Conspiracy Theories and the New Age*; Wood, *Possession, Power and the New Age*; etc.
23. I have previously suggested that 'popular millennialism' could be used for a particular set of post-war teleological discourses, including New Age *sensu strictu*, Ascension, and 2012 (see Robertson, *UFOs, Conspiracy Theories and the New Age*, 39–42) – and perhaps QAnon might also fit).
24. Hanegraaff, *New Age Religion*, 98–103.
25. *Gnostic New Age*, 350.
26. Sutcliffe, *Children of the New Age*.
27. Wasserstrom, *Religion after Religion*, 238.
28. DeConick, *Gnostic New Age*, 349.
29. Ambasciano, *Unnatural History of Religions*, 116–17.

30 *The Gnostic Attitude*, iii.
31 E.g. Filoramo, *A History of Gnosticism*; Markschies, *Gnosis: An Introduction*; Pearson, *Ancient Gnosticism: Traditions and Literature*; Rudolf, *Gnosis: The Nature and History of Gnosticism*.
32 *Gnostic Gospels*, 34.
33 *Gnostic Gospels*, 38.
34 Townsend, 'Explorations at the Edges of Orthodoxy', 1.
35 *The Tripartite Tractate, The Dialogue of the Savior, The Interpretation of Knowledge* and *A Valentinian Exposition*, all texts considered Valentinian.
36 Townsend, 'Explorations at the Edges of Orthodoxy', 6; emphasis in original.
37 'Paul and Women', 538–49; 'What Became of God the Mother?', 301.
38 *Gnostic Gospels*, 48–69.
39 *Gnostic Gospels*, 102.
40 *Gnostic Gospels*, 124–5, 133, 144.
41 *Gnostic Gospels*, 143.
42 *Beyond Belief*, 5.
43 Quispel and van Oort, *Gnostica, Judaica, Catholica*, xv–xvii.
44 '"Finding" the Gospel of Thomas in Edessa', 523.
45 Kripal, *Secret Body*, 132.
46 https://reli.rice.edu/GEM (accessed 28 July 2018).
47 http://booksandjournals.brillonline.com/content/journals/2451859x (accessed 28 July 2018).
48 'Gnostic Spirituality at the Crossroads of Christianity', 149. This position is also developed in 'Crafting Gnosis: Gnostic Spirituality in the Ancient New Age'.
49 The second volume is, as I write, a work-in-progress entitled *The Gnostic Awakening: How an Ancient Countercultural Spirituality Migrated into Modern America*.
50 DeConick, *Gnostic New Age*, 5.
51 DeConick, *Gnostic New Age*, 9, 11.
52 DeConick, *Gnostic New Age*, 196, 180; c.f. DeConick, 'The Sociology of Gnostic Spirituality'.
53 DeConick, *Gnostic New Age*, 343.
54 DeConick, *Gnostic New Age*, 348.
55 Tite, 'Transgression and Countercultural Gnosticism', 7.
56 *Gnostic New Age*, 21.
57 Tite, 'Transgression and Countercultural Gnosticism'.
58 Brakke, review of *Gnostic Religion in Antiquity*, 147–8.
59 Merkur, *Gnosis*, 14–20.
60 Merkur, *Gnosis*, 16–17.

61 Tite, 'Theoretical Challenges in Studying Religious Experience in Gnosticism', 10; c.f. Taves, *Religious Experience Reconsidered*; Taves, *Revelatory Events*; McCutcheon, *Manufacturing Religion*, 115–20.
62 DeConick, 'The Sociology of Gnostic Spirituality', 10; emphasis added.
63 DeConick, 'The Sociology of Gnostic Spirituality', 10.
64 DeConick, 'The Sociology of Gnostic Spirituality', 56.
65 *Gnostic New Age*, 1–4.
66 https://aprilDeConick.com/the-gnostic-awakening (accessed 5 November 2019).
67 Wasserstrom, *Religion after Religion*, 239–41.
68 *Gnostic New Age*, 350.

11 The greatest heresy: Jeffrey Kripal's gnostic scholarship

1 *The Secret Life of Puppets*, 16.
2 *No Spiritual Investment in the World*, 27, 29.
3 *Religion in Essence and Manifestation*, 52, 645.
4 *Gnostic New Age*, 5.
5 Tite, 'Transgression and Countercultural Gnosticism', 2–3.
6 McCutcheon, 'Beyond Cynicism', 4.
7 Ambasciano, 'Mind the (Unbridgeable) Gaps', 161.
8 Kripal, 'Gnosisssss'.
9 Wasserstrom, *Religion after Religion*, 195; emphasis in original.
10 Kripal, *Secret Body*, 131; https://www.chronicle.com/article/Embrace-the-Unexplained/145557 (accessed 18 March 2021).
11 *Secret Body*, 104.
12 Kripal, 'The Future Human', 187.
13 *Secret Body*, 30–3.
14 Recounted in *Secret Body*, 53–5.
15 *Serpent's Gift*, 1.
16 *Secret Body*, 101.
17 *Secret Body*, 104.
18 Kripal, 'Gnosisssss', 278.
19 *Secret Body*, 363.
20 *The Serpent's Gift*, 11.
21 *The Serpent's Gift*, 12.
22 *Esalen*, 4; *Secret Body*, 121.
23 *Secret Body*, 104.
24 *Secret Body*, 122–3.
25 *Secret Body*, 104.

26 *Roads to Excess*, 109; *Secret Body*, 116.
27 *Secret Body*, 315–16.
28 Hanegraaff makes the same observation, adding that Kripal seems to be unable to plainly state the difference ('Leaving the Garden (in search of religion)', 263).
29 *Secret Body*, 126.
30 *Serpent's Kiss*, 171–2; c.f. *The Sacred and the Profane*, 7; Otto, *Das Heilige*, 8.
31 *Secret Body*, 371–2.
32 *Secret Body*, 123.
33 See Kripal, *Secret Body*, 402–9; Ambasciano, 'Comparative Religion as a Life Science', 144.
34 *Secret Body*, 400.
35 *Secret Body*, 353; 'The Future Human'; *Serpent's Gift*, 107, 153; see Ambasciano, *Mind the Unbridgeable Gaps*, for more on Kripal's reliance on Eliade.
36 Kripal, *Authors*, 199.
37 *Secret Body*, 353; emphasis in original.
38 Hanegraaff, 'Leaving the Garden (in search of religion)', 269.
39 *Secret Body*, 400; emphasis added.

12 Elite knowledge: Gnosticism and the study of religion

1 Culianu, 'The Gnostic Revenge', 290.
2 Dillon makes the same point in *The Heretical Revival*, 7–9, 12.
3 *Gnostic New Age*, 1–2.
4 Hanegraaff is the exception – see, for example, the acceptance of Williams's conclusions in the introduction to the *Dictionary of Gnosis and Western Esotericism*, vii.
5 McCutcheon, *Manufacturing Religion*, 67.
6 A point I argued at more length in my 2020 Temenos Lecture (publication forthcoming).
7 Beck and Beck-Gernsheim, *Theory, Culture & Society*.
8 Znamenski, 'Adventures of the Metaphor', xxxvii.
9 see Alberts, *Shamanism, Discourse, Modernity*, 26–7.
10 Lévi-Strauss, *Structural Anthropology*, 204.
11 Davidsen, 'What Is Wrong with Pagan Studies?'; Hughes, *Islam and the Tyranny of Authenticity*.

Bibliography

Adorno, Theodor. 1973. *Negative Dialectics*. E. B. Ashton (trans.). New York: Continuum.

Alberts, Thomas K. 2015. *Shamanism, Discourse, Modernity*. Farnham: Ashgate.

Alles, Gregory. 1996. 'Introduction'. In Rudolf Otto (ed.) and Gregory D. Alles (trans.), *Autobiographical and Social Essays*. Berlin: Mouton de Gruyter, 1–49.

Ambasciano, Leonardo. 2014. *Sciamanesimo senza sciamanesimo le radici intellettuali del modello sciamanico di Mircea Eliade; evoluzionismo, psicoanalisi, te(le)ologia*. Roma: Edizioni Nuova Cultura.

Ambasciano, Leonardo. 2016. 'Mind the (Unbridgeable) Gaps'. *Method & Theory in the Study of Religion* 28(2), 141–225.

Ambasciano, Leonardo. 2018. 'Politics of Nostalgia, Logical Fallacies, and Cognitive Biases: The Importance of Epistemology in the Age of Cognitive Historiography'. In A. K. Petersen, G. I. Sælid, L. H. Martin, J. S. Jensen and J. Sørensen (eds), *Evolution, Cognition, and the History of Religion: A New Synthesis*. Leiden: Brill, 280–96.

Ambasciano, Leonardo. 2018. 'Comparative Religion as a Life Science: William E. Paden's Neo-Plinian New Naturalism'. *Method & Theory in the Study of Religion* 30(2), 141–9.

Ambasciano, Leonardo. 2019. *Unnatural History of Religion: Academia, Post-Truth and the Quest for Scientific Knowledge*. London: Bloomsbury.

Anson, Peter F. 1964. *Bishops at Large*. London: Faber & Faber.

Apiryon, Tao. 1995. 'Jules Doinel and the Gnostic Church of France'. https://www.oto-uk.org/egchistory.html.

Arendt, Hannah. 1945. 'Nightmare and Flight'. *Partisan Review* 12(2), 259–60, reprinted in Kohn, Jerome (ed.). 1994. *Essays in Understanding, 1930–1954*. San Diego, CA: Harcourt Brace, 133–5.

Arnold, Gottfried. 1699–1700. *Unparteyische Kirchen- und Ketzer-historie*. Frankfurt am Main: Ey Thomas Fritsch.

Asprem, Egil, and Julian Strube. 2021. *New Approaches to the Study of Esotericism*. Leiden: Brill.

Bailey, Alice A. 1951. *The Unfinished Biography*. London: Lucis Trust.

Ball, Hugo. 1996. *Flight out of Time: A Dada Diary*. Berkeley: University of California Press.

Baur, Ferdinand Christian. 1835. *Die Christliche Gnosis oder die christliche Religions-Philosophie in ihrer geschichtlichen Entwicklung*. Tübingen: Verlag von C. F. Osiander.

Beausobré, Isaac de. 1734. *Histoire Critique de Manichée et du Manicheisme.* Amsterdam: Chez J. Frederic Bernard.

Beck, Ulrich, and Elisabeth Beck-Gernsheim. 2002. *Theory, Culture & Society: Individualization: Institutionalized Individualism and its Social and Political Consequences.* London: SAGE.

Behr, John. 2013. *Irenaeus of Lyons: Identifying Christianity.* Oxford: Oxford University Press.

Bernardini, Riccardo. 2011. *Jung a Eranos: Il progetto della psicologia complessa.* Milano: FrancoAngeli.

Besant, Annie. 1912. 'Growth of the T.S.' *Theosophist* 33(10), 497–510.

Besant, Annie. 1914. *Mysticism.* London: Theosophical Publishing Society.

Biale, David. 1979. *Gershom Scholem: Kabbalah and Counter-History.* Cambridge, MA: Harvard University Press.

Bianchi, Ugo. (ed.). 1967. *Le Origini dello Gnosticismo: Colloquio di Messina 13–18 April 1966* (NUMEN Supplement 12). Leiden: Brill.

Bianchi, U. 1965. 'Le problème des origines du gnosticisme et l'histoire des religions'. *NUMEN* 12(3), 161–78.

Binns, Denis. 2010. *Irenaeus: An Introduction.* London: Bloomsbury.

Blavatsky, Helena P. 1877. *Isis Unveiled: A Master-Key to the Mysteries of Ancient and Modern Science and Theology,* vols 1–2. New York: J. W. Bouton.

Blavatsky, Helena P. 1982. 'Pistis Sophia: Commentary and Notes'. In *Helena P. Blavatsky: Collected Writings,* vol. 13. Wheaton, IL: Theosophical Publishing House, 1–81.

Bleeker, Claas. J. 1954. 'The Relation of the History of Religions to Kindred Religious Sciences, Particularly Theology, Sociology of Religion, Psychology of Religion and Phenomenology of Religion'. In 'Bulletin', 141–55. *NVMEN* 1, 147–9.

Bleeker, C. J. 1960. 'The Future Task of the History of Religions'. *NVMEN* 7, 221–34

Bleeker, C. J. 1972. 'The Contribution of the Phenomenology of Religion to the Study of the History of Religions'. In U. Bianchi, C. J. Bleeker and A. Bausani (eds), *Problems and Methods of the History of Religions.* Leiden: Brill, 35–54

Bloom, Harold. 1979. *The Flight to Lucifer: A Gnostic Fantasy.* New York: Farrar, Straus, Giroux.

Bloom, Harold. 1982. *Agon: Towards a Theory of Revisionism.* New York: Oxford University Press.

Bloom, Harold. 1992. *The American Religion.* New York: Simon & Schuster.

Bloom, Harold. 1996. *Omens of Millennium: The Gnosis of Angels, Dreams, and Resurrection.* New York: Riverhead Books.

Bloom, Harold. 1998. 'Preface'. In Henry Corbin (ed.), *Alone with the Alone: Creative Imagination in the Sufism of Ibn 'Arabi.* Princeton: Princeton University Press, ix–xx.

Blumenberg, Hans. 1966. *Die Legitimität der Neuzeit.* Frankfurt am Main: Suhrkamp.

Blumenberg, Hans. 1985. *The Legitimacy of the Modern Age.* Robert M. Wallace (trans.). Cambridge, MA: MIT Press.

Bod, Rens. [2010] 2015. *A New History of the Humanities: The Search for Principles and Patterns from Antiquity to the Present*. L. Richards (trans.). Oxford: Oxford University Press.

Bogdan, Henrik. 2007. *Western Esotericism and Rituals of Initiation*. Albany: State University of New York Press.

Bogdan, Henrik. 2010. 'New Perspectives on Western Esotericism'. *Nova Religio: Journal of Alternative and Emergent Religions* 13(3), 97–105.

Bousset, Wilhelm. 1973. *Hauptprobleme der Gnosis*. Göttingen: Vandenhoeck & Ruprecht.

Brakke, David. 2010. *The Gnostics Myth, Ritual, and Diversity in Early Christianity*. Cambridge, MA: Harvard University Press.

Brakke, David. 2017. 'Review: Roelof Van den Broek, *Gnostic Religion in Antiquity*'. *Journal of Religion* 97(1), 147–8.

Brandreth, Henry R. T. 1961. *Episcopi Vagantes and the Anglican Church*. 2nd rev. edn. London: S.P.C.K.

Broek, Roelef van den. 2005. 'Gnosticism I: Gnostic Religion'. In Wouter J. Hanegraaff with Antoine Faivre, Roelof van den Broek and Jean-Pierre Brach (eds), *Dictionary of Gnosis & Western Esotericism*. Leiden: Brill, 403–16.

Broek, Roelef van den. 2009. 'The Birth of a Chair'. In Wouter Hanegraaff and Joyce Pijnenburg (eds), *Hermes in the Academy: Ten Years' Study of Western Esotericism at the University of Amsterdam*. Amsterdam: Amsterdam University Press.

Broek, Roelef van den. 2011. 'Sexuality and Sexual Symbolism in Hermetic and Gnostic Thought and Practice (Second to Fourth Centuries)'. In W. J. Hanegraaff and Jeffrey J. Kripal (eds), *Hidden Intercourse: Eros and Sexuality in the History of Western Esotericism*. Leiden: Brill, 1–22.

Broek, Roelef van den. 2013. *Gnostic Religion in Antiquity*. Cambridge: Cambridge University Press.

Bruce, S. 1998. 'Good Intentions and Bad Sociology: New Age Authenticity and Social Roles'. *Journal of Contemporary Religion* 13(1), 22–33.

Brumlik, Micha. 2008. '*Ressentiment* – A Few Motifs in Hans Jonas's Early Book on Gnosticism'. In Hava Tirosh-Samuelson and Christian Wiese (eds), *The Legacy of Hans Jonas: Judaism and the Phenomenon of Life*. Leiden: Brill, 73–90.

Buber, Martin, and Judith Buber Agassi (eds). [1952] 1999. *Martin Buber on Psychology and Psychotherapy: Essays, Letters, and Dialogue*. New York: Syracuse University Press, 34–59.

Buber, Martin. [1952] 1999. 'Rejoiner to Jung'. In Martin Buber and Judith Buber Agassi (eds), *Martin Buber on Psychology and Psychotherapy: Essays, Letters, and Dialogue*. New York: Syracuse University Press, 67–71.

Buber, Martin. [1952] 2016. 'Religion and Modern Thinking'. In *Eclipse of God: Studies in the Relation between Religion and Philosophy*. Leora Batnitzky (trans.). Princeton: Princeton University Press, 53–82.

Bultmann, Rudolf. 1925. 'Die Bedeutung der neuerschlossenen mandaischen und manichaischen Quellen fur das Verstandnis des Johannesevangeliums'. *Zeitschrift für die Neutestamentliche Wissenschaft* 24, 100–46.

Bultmann, Rudolf. 1948. 'Neues Testament und Mythologie'. In Hans-Werner Bartsch (ed.), *Kerygma und Mythos; Teile 1: Ein Theologische Gespräch*. Hamburg-Bergstedt: Reich, 15–48.

Bultmann, Rudolf. 1941. *Das Evangelium des Johannes*. Göttingen: Vandenhoeck und Ruprecht.

Burke, Tony. 2016. 'What Do We Talk about When We Talk about the Nag Hammadi Library'. *Bulletin for the Study of Religion* 45(2), 33–7.

Burns, Dylan M. 2014. *Apocalypse of the Alien God: Platonism and the Exile of Sethian Gnosticism*. Philadelphia: University of Pennsylvania Press

Burns, Dylan M., and Almut-Barbara Renger (eds). 2019. *New Antiquities: Transformations of Ancient Religion in the New Age and Beyond*. Sheffield: Equinox.

Butler, Alison. 2011. *Victorian Occultism and the Making of Modern Magic: Invoking Tradition*. London: Palgrave.

Campbell, Bruce F. 1980. *Ancient Wisdom Revived: A History of the Theosophical Movement*. Berkeley: University of California Press.

Campbell, Joseph (ed.). 1957. *Man and Time: Papers from the Eranos Yearbooks*. Bollingen Series, vol. 3, no. 30. New York: Princeton University Press.

Campos, Marcelo Leandro de. 2016. 'Gnosticismo Samaeliano Na Academia: O Estado Da Arte'. *Melancolia* 1, 7–29

Campos, Marcelo Leandro de. 2018. 'Lideranças femininas no gnosticismo samaeliano: uma análise a partir da biografia de Arnolda Garro de Gomez (1920–1998)'. *Melancolia* 3, 92–107.

Capps, Walter. 1995. *Religious Studies: The Making of a Discipline*. Minneapolis, MN: Fortress Press.

Caputo, John D. 1993. 'Heidegger and Theology'. In Charles B. Guignon (ed.), *The Cambridge Companion to Heidegger*. Cambridge: Cambridge University Press, 270–88.

Carbonneau, Richard, and Robin Simon. 2010. *The Marvel: A Biography of Jack Parsons*. Portland: Cellar Door.

Carrette, Jeremy, and Richard King. 2004. *Selling Spirituality: The Silent Takeover of Religion*. London: Routledge.

Carter, John. 2004. *Sex and Rockets: The Occult World of Jack Parsons*, 2nd ed. Port Townsend: Feral House.

Cassadio, Giovani. 2016. '*NVMEN*, Brill and the IAHR in Their Early Years: Glimpse at Three Parallel Stories from an Italian Stance'. In T. Jensen and A. W. Geerz (eds), *NVMEN, the Academic Study of Religion, and the IAHR: Past, Present and Prospects*. Leiden: Brill, 303–41.

Casadio, Giovanni. 2005. 'Historiography (Further Considerations)'. In L. Jones (ed.), *Encyclopedia of Religion*, vol. 6. Detroit: Thomson Gale–MacMillan, 4042–52.

Castro, Giovanni de. 1864. *Il Mondo Secreto*. Milan: G. Daelli e C. Editori.

Chahana, J. 2018. 'A Gnostic Critic of Modernity: Hans Jonas from Existentialism to Science'. *Journal of the American Academy of Religion* 86(1), 158–80.

Chidester, David. 2014. *Empire of Religion: Imperialism and Comparative Religion*. Chicago: University of Chicago Press.

Cohn, Norman. 1972. *Europe's Inner Demons: The Ddemonization of Christians in Medieval Christendom*. London: Pimlico.

Corngold, Stanley. 2004. *Lambent Traces: Franz Kafka*. Princeton: Princeton University Press.

Cotter, Christopher R., and David G. Robertson. 2016. 'Introduction: The World Religions Paradigm in Contemporary Religious Studies'. In Christopher R. Cotter and David G. Robertson (eds), *After World Religions: Reconstructing Religious Studies*. London: Routledge, 1–20.

Cox, James L. 2006. *A Guide to the Phenomenology of Religion: Key Figures, Formative Influences and Subsequent Debates*. London: Continuum.

Cross, Frank L. (trans. and ed.). 1955. *The Jung Codex: A Newly Recovered Gnostic Papyrus*. London: A. R. Mowbray.

Crowley, Aleister. [1918] 1997. 'Liber XV: Ecclesiæ Gnosticæ Cathilicæ Canon Missæ'. In A. Crowley, M. Desti, H. Beta and L. Waddell (eds), *Magick: Book 4 (Liber ABA)*, 2nd rev. ed. York Beach, ME: Red Wheel, Weiser, 584–97.

Culianu, Ioan P. 1992. *The Tree of Gnosis: Gnostic Mythology from Early Christianity to Modern Nihilism*. H. S. Wiesner and I. P. Culianu (trans.). New York: HarperCollins.

Culianu, Ioan. P. 1984. 'The Gnostic Revenge: Gnosticism and Romantic Literature'. In Jacob Taubes (ed.), *Gnosis und Politik*. Munich: Wilhelm Fink, 290–306.

Dachez, Roger. 2008. 'Martinist Orders and Freemasonry in France since the Time of Papus'. In *The Canonbury Papers Vol 5: Knowledge of the Heart*. Hersham: Lewis Masonic, 1–7.

Dadosky, John Daniel. 2004. *The Structure of Religious Knowing: Encountering the Sacred in Eliade and Lonergan*. Albany: State University of New York Press.

Darlés, Jean. 1910. *Glossaire Raisonné de la Théosophie du Gnosticisme et de l'Esotérisme*. Paris: Bibliothéque de la Curiosité.

Dart, John. 1988. *The Jesus of Heresy and History: The Discovery and Meaning of the Nag Hammadi Gnostic Library*. San Francisco: Harper & Row.

Davidsen, Markus Altena. 2012. 'What Is Wrong with Pagan Studies? A Review Essay on the Handbook of Contemporary Paganism'. *Method and Theory in the Study of Religion* 24(2), 183–99.

Dawson, Andrew. 2007. *New Era, New Religions: Religious Transformation in Contemporary Brazil*. Aldershot: Ashgate.

Dawson, Andrew. 2005. 'The Gnostic Church of Brazil: Contemporary Neo-Esotericism in Late-Modern Perspective'. *Interdisciplinary Journal of Research on Religion* 1(8), 1–28.

Decker, Rodney. 2014. 'The Bauer Thesis: An Overview'. In Paul A. Hartog (ed.), *Orthodoxy and Heresy in Early Christian Contexts: Reconsidering the Bauer Thesis.* Eugene, OR: Pickwick, 6–33.

DeConick, April. 2008. 'Conceiving Spirits: The Mystery of Valentinian Sex'. In W. J. Hanegraaff and Jeffrey J. Kripal (eds), *Hidden Intercourse: Eros and Sexuality in the History of Western Esotericism.* Leiden: Brill, 23–48.

DeConick, April. 2013. 'Gnostic Spirituality at the Crossroads of Christianity: Transgressing Boundaries and Creating Orthodoxy'. In Eduard Iricinschi, Lance Jenott, Nicola Denzey Lewis and Philippa Townsend (eds), *Beyond the Gnostic Gospels: Studies Building on the Work of Elaine Pagels.* Tübingen: Mohr Siebeck, 148–84.

DeConick, April. 2013. 'Crafting Gnosis: Gnostic Spirituality in the Ancient New Age'. In Kevin Corrigan and Tuomas Rasimus, in collaboration with Dylan M. Burns, Lance Jenott and Zeke Mazur (eds), *Gnosticism, Platonism and the Late Ancient World: Essays in Honour of John D. Turner.* Leiden: Brill, 285–305.

DeConick, April. 2016. *The Gnostic New Age: How a Countercultural Spirituality Revolutionized Religion from Antiquity to Today.* New York: Columbia University Press.

DeConick, April. 2019. 'The Sociology of Gnostic Spirituality'. *Gnosis: Journal of Gnostic Studies* 4, 9–66.

Denis, Ferdinand. 1830. *Tableau Historique, Analytic et Critique des Sciences Occultes.* Paris: Decourchant.

Denzey Lewis, Nicola, and Justine Ariel Blount. 2014. 'Rethinking the Origins of the Nag Hammadi Codices'. *Journal of Biblical Literature* 133, 399–419.

Denzey Lewis, Nicola. 2013. *Introduction to 'Gnosticism': Ancient Voices, Christian Worlds.* New York: Oxford University Press.

Deveny, John P. 1997. *Paschal Beverly Randolph: A Nineteenth-Century Black American Spiritualist, Rosicrucian, and Sex Magician.* Albany: State University of New York Press.

Dillon, Matthew. 2017. 'The Heretical Revival: The Nag Hammadi Library in American Religion and Culture'. PhD thesis, Rice University.

Dillon, M. 2018. 'The Impact of Scholarship on Contemporary "Gnosticism(s)": A Case Study on the Apostolic Johannite Church and Jeremy Puma'. *International Journal for the Study of New Religions* 9(1), 57–81.

Doherty, Bernard. 2019. 'The Neo-Gnostic Synthesis of Samael Aun Weor'. In Gary Trompf, Gunner B. Mikkelsen and J. Johnston (eds), *The Gnostic World.* London: Routledge, 621–31.

Donato, Rev. Donald. 2010. *The Lévitikon: The Gospels According to the Primitive Church.* USA: Apostolic Johannite Church.

Doresse, Jean, Philip Mairet and Leonard Johnston. 1960. *The Secret Books of the Egyptian Gnostics: An Introduction to the Gnostic Coptic Manuscripts Discovered at Chenoboskion, with an English Translation and Critical Evaluation of the Gospel According to Thomas*. New York: Viking.

Dubuisson, Daniel. 2006. *Twentieth Century Mythologies: Dumézil, Lévi-Strauss, Eliade*. Sheffield: Equinox.

Dubuisson, Daniel. 2010. 'The Poetical and Rhetorical Structure of the Eliadean Text: A Contribution to Critical Theory and Discourses on Religion'. In Christian K. Wedemeyer and Wendy Doniger (eds), *Hermeneutics, Politics and the History of Religions: The Contested Legacies of Joachim Wach and Mircea Eliade*. Oxford: Oxford University Press, 133–46.

Dyrendal, Asbjørn, James. R. Lewis, and Jesper A. A. Petersen. 2016. *The Invention of Satanism*. Oxford: Oxford University Press.

Eliade, Mircea. 1936. *Yoga. Essai sur les Origines de la Mystique Indienne*. Bucharest: Fundatia pentru literatura si arta «Regele Carol II» – Librairie orientaliste Paul Geuthner.

Eliade, Mircea. 1958. *Patterns of Comparative Religion*. London: Sheed & Ward.

Eliade, Mircea. 1964. *Shamanism: Archaic Techniques of Ecstasy*. W. R. Trask (trans.). London: Routledge & Kegan Paul.

Eliade, Mircea. 1970. 'Some Notes on *Theosophia perennis:* Ananda K. Coomaraswamy and Henry Corbin'. *History of Religions* 19, 167–760.

Eliade, Mircea. [1973] 2006. 'The Sacred in the Secular World'. In B. Rennie (ed.), *Mircea Eliade: A Critical Reader*. London: Equinox, 57–67.

Eliade, Mircea. 1976. *Giornale*. Liana Aurigemma (trans.). Turin: Bollati Boringhieri.

Eliade, Mircea. 1951. *Le Chamanisme: et les Techniques Archaïques de L'extase*. Paris: Payot.

Eliade, Mircea. 1957. *The Sacred and the Profane: The Nature of Religion*. W. R. Trask (trans.). New York: Harvest/HBJ.

Eliade, Mircea. 1957. *Das Heilige und das Profane: vom Wesen des Religiösen*. Hamburg: Rowohlt.

Eliade, Mircea. 1971. *The Myth of the Eternal Return: Cosmos and History*. Princeton: Princeton University Press.

Eliade, Mircea. 1984. *The Quest: History and Meaning in Religion*. Chicago: University of Chicago Press.

Eliade, Mircea. 1982. *A History of Religious Ideas, vol. II, From Gautama Buddha to the Triumph of Christianity*. W. Trask (trans.). Chicago: University of Chicago Press.

Eliade, Mircea. 1985. *The History of Religious Ideas, vol. III, From Muhammad to the Age of the Reforms*. A. Hiltebeitel and D. Apostolos-Cappadona (trans.). Chicago: University of Chicago Press.

Fabré-Palaprat, Bernard Raymond. 1831. *Lévitikon: ou exposé des principles fondamentaux de la doctrine des Chrétiens-Catholiques-Primitifs; suivi de leurs évangiles, d'un extrait de la table d'or et du rituel cérémoniaire pour le service religieux, etc. et précédé du statut sur le gouvernement de l'église, et la hiérarchie lévitique.* Paris: Librairie des Chrétiens Primitifs.

Faivre, Antoine. 1994. *Access to Western Esotericism*. Albany: State University of New York Press

Faivre, Antoine. 1998. 'Renaissance Hermeticism and the Concept of Western Esotericism'. In R. van den Broek and W. Hanegraaff (eds), *Gnosis and Hermeticism from Antiquity to Modern Times*. Albany: State University of New York Press, 109–24.

Faivre, Antoine. 2009. 'From Paris to Amsterdam and Beyond: Origins and Development of a Collaboration'. In Wouter Hanegraaff and Joyce Pijnenburg (eds), *Hermes in the Academy: Ten Years' Study of Western Esotericism at the University of Amsterdam*. Amsterdam: Amsterdam University Press, 123–7.

Faivre, Antoine. 2010. 'Modern Western Esoteric Currents in the Work of Mircea Eliade: The Extent and Limits of Their Presence'. In Christian K. Wedemeyer and Wendy Doniger (eds), *Hermeneutics, Politics and the History of Religions: The Contested Legacies of Joachim Wach and Mircea Eliade*. Oxford: Oxford University Press, 147–57.

Farmer, Christopher. 1985. 'An Interview with Gilles Quispel'. In *Gnosis* 1 (Autumn/Winter), 27–9.

Feitknecht, Thomas. 2006. *Herman Hesse. Die dunkle und wilde Seite der Seele: Briefwechsel mit seinem Psychoanalytiker Josef Bernhard Lang 1916–1944*. Berlin: Suhrkamp.

Filoramo, Giovanni. 1990. *A History of Gnosticism*. Cambridge, MA: Basil Blackwell.

Frankenburg, Abraham von. 1703. *Theophrastia Valentiniana*. Frankfurt: Bey Thomas Fritschen.

Frankfurter, David. 2006. *Evil Incarnate: Rumors of Demonic Conspiracy and Ritual Abuse in History*. Princeton: Princeton University Press.

Frick, Karl Richard. 1978. *Licht und Finsternis. Gnostisch-theosophische und freimaurerisch-okkulte Geheimgesellschaften bis an die Wende zum 20. Jahrhundert. Wege in die Gegenwart. Teil 2: Geschichte ihrer Lehren, Rituale und Organisationen*. Graz: Akademische Druck- und Verlagsanstalt.

Gandini, Mario. 2005. 'Raffaele Pettazzoni nel 1948: Materiali per una biografia'. *Strada Maestra* 59, 51–207.

Gandini, Mario. 2006. 'Raffaele Pettazzoni negli anni 1949–1950: Materiali per una biografia'. *Strada Maestra* 60, 19–237.

Gibbon, Edward. 1910. *Decline and Fall of the Roman Empire*. Oliphant Smeaton (ed.). London: J.M. Dent.

Gibson, Ralph. 1989. *A Social History of French Catholicism, 1789–1914*. London: Routledge.

Gilhus, Ingvild S. 2001. 'The Gnostic Myth and the Goddess Myth: Two Contemporary Responses to Questions about Human Identity'. In Mikael Rothstein (ed.), *New Age Religion and Globalisation*. Aarhus: Aarhus University Press, 113–32.

Gilhus, Ingvild S., Siv Ellen Kraft, and James Lewis. 2017. *New Age in Norway*. Sheffield: Equinox.

Ginzburg, Carlo. 2010. 'Mircea Eliade's Ambivalent Legacy'. In Christian K. Wedemeyer and Wendy Doniger (eds), *Hermeneutics, Politics and the History of Religions: The Contested Legacies of Joachim Wach and Mircea Eliade*. Oxford: Oxford University Press, 307–23.

Given, J. Gregory. 2017. '"Finding" the Gospel of Thomas in Edessa'. *Journal of Early Christian Studies* 25(4), 501–30.

Given, J. Gregory. 2019. 'Nag Hammadi at Eranos: Rediscovering Gnosticism among the Historians of Religions'. In Kambiz Ghanea Bassiri and Paul Robertson (eds), *All Religion Is Inter-Religion: Engaging the Work of Steven M. Wasserstrom*. London: Bloomsbury, 87–97.

Godwin, Joscelyn, Christian Chanel, and John P. Deveney. 1995. *The Hermetic Brotherhood of Luxor: Initiatic and Historical Documents of an Order of Practical Occultism*. York Beach, ME: S. Weiser.

Godwin, Joscelyn. 1994. *The Theosophical Enlightenment*. Albany: State University of New York Press.

Goodacre, Mark. 2013. 'How Reliable Is the Story of the Nag Hammadi Discovery?' *Journal for the Study of the New Testament* 35, 303–22.

Goodrick-Clarke, Nicholas, and Clare Goodrick-Clarke. 2005. *G.R.S. Mead and the Gnostic Quest*. Berkeley, CA: North Atlantic Books.

Goodrick-Clarke, Nicholas. 1985. *The Occult Roots of Nazism: the Ariosophists of Austria and Germany, 1890–1935*. Wellingborough: Aquarian Press.

Grant, Robert M. 1959. *Gnosticism and Early Christianity*. New York: Columbia University Press.

Green, Henry. 1977. 'Gnosis and Gnosticism: A Study in Methodology'. *NUMEN* 24(2), 95–134.

Green, Martin. 1987. *Mountain of Truth: The Counterculture Begins, Ascona, 1900–1920*. Hanover, New Hampshire: University Press of New England.

Grimstad, Kirsten J. 2002. *The Modern Revival of Gnosticism and Thomas Mann's Doktor Faustus*. Rochester, NY: Camden House.

Guignon, Charles B. (ed.), *The Cambridge Companion to Heidegger*. Cambridge: Cambridge University Press.

Guillaumont, A., Henri-Charles Puech, Gilles Quispel, Walter Till, and Yassah ʻAbd Al Masih. 1959. *The Gospel According to Thomas*. Leiden and London: Brill and Collins.

Guiñazu, Veronica Samanta. 2012. *Nuevas religiosidades en América Latina: una etnografía sobre la escuela gnóstica de Samael Aun Weor en Buenos Aires*. Saarbrücken: Editorial Académica Española

Gurdjieff, George. I. [1950] 1976. *Beelzebub's Tales to His Grandson: An Objectively Impartial Criticism of the Life of Man*. London: Routledge & Kegan Paul.

Hakl, Hans Thomas. 2012. *Eranos: An Alternative Intellectual History of the Twentieth Century*. Christopher McIntosh (trans.). Montréal: McGill-Queen's University Press.

Hammer, Olav. 2018. 'The Jungian Gnosticism of the Ecclesia Gnostica'. *International Journal for the Study of New Religions* 9(1), 33–56.

Hanegraaff, Wouter J., and Jeffrey J. Kripal (eds). 2008. *Hidden Intercourse: Eros and Sexuality in the History of Western Esotericism*. Leiden: Brill.

Hanegraaff, Wouter J., Antoine Faivre, R. van den Broek, and Jean-Pierre Brach (eds). 2005. *Dictionary of Gnosis & Western Esotericism*. Leiden: Brill.

Hanegraaff, Wouter J. 1992. 'A Dynamic Typological Approach to the Problem of "Post-Gnostic" Gnosticism'. *ARIES* 16, 5–43.

Hanegraaff, Wouter J. 1994. 'The Problem of "Post-Gnostic" Gnosticism'. In Ugo Bianchi (ed.), *The Notion of 'Religion' in Comparative Research: Selected Proceedings of the XVI IAHR Congress, Rome 1994*. Rome: 'L'Erma' di Bretschneider, 625–32.

Hanegraaff, Wouter J. 1996. *New Age Religion and Western Culture: Esotericism in the Mirror of Secular Thought*. Brill: Leiden.

Hanegraaff, Wouter J. 1998. 'On the Construction of "Esoteric Traditions"'. In Antoine Faivre and Wouter Hanegraaff (eds), *Western Esotericism and the Science of Religion*. Leuven: Peeters, 11–62.

Hanegraaff, Wouter J. 2001. 'Beyond the Yates Paradigm: The Study of Western Esotericism between Counterculture and New Complexity'. In *ARIES* 1(1), 5–37.

Hanegraaff, Wouter J. 2007. 'The New Age Movement and Western Esotericism'. In Daren Kemp and James Lewis (eds), *Handbook of New Age*. Leiden: Brill, 25–50.

Hanegraaff, Wouter J. 2008. 'Reason, Faith, and Gnosis: Potentials and Problematics of a Typological Construct'. In Peter Meusbuger, Michael Welker and Edgar Wunder (eds), *Clashes of Knowledge: Orthodoxies and Heterodoxies in Science and Religion*. New York: Springer, 133–44.

Hanegraaff, Wouter J. 2008. 'Leaving the Garden (in Search of Religion): Jeffrey J. Kripal's Vision of a Gnostic Study of Religion'. *Religion* 38, 259–76.

Hanegraaff, Wouter J. 2011. 'Kabbalah in Gnosis Magazine (1985–1999)'. In Boaz Huss (ed.), *Kabbalah and Contemporary Spiritual Revival*. Beer-Sheva: Ben-Gurion University of the Negev Press, 251–66.

Hanegraaff, Wouter J. 2012. *Esotericism and the Academy: Rejected Knowledge in Western Culture*. Cambridge: Cambridge University Press.

Hanegraaff, Wouter J., Peter J. Forshaw, and Marco Pasi. 2019. *Hermes Explains: Thirty Questions about Western Esotericism*. Amsterdam: Amsterdam University Press.

Harman, Graham. 2007. *Heidegger Explained: From Phenomenon to Thing*. Chicago: Open Court.

Harnack, Adolf von. 1885. *Lehrbuch fur Dogmengeschichte*. Tübingen: Mohr.

Harnack, Adolf von. [1894] 1997. *History of Dogma*. Neil Buchanan (trans.). Eugene, OR: Wipf and Stock.

Harnack, Adolf von. 1921. *Marcion: Das Evangelium vom fremden Gott*. Leipzig: J. C. Hinrichs'sche Buchhandlung.

Harnack, Adolf von. 1957. *What Is Christianity?* New York: Harper Torchbooks.

Hartog, Paul. 2015. *Orthodoxy and Heresy in Early Christian Contexts: Reconsidering the Bauer Thesis*. Cambridge: James Clarke.

Hayman, Ronald. 1999. *A Life of Jung*. London: Bloomsbury.

Heckethorn, Charles William. 1875. *The Secret Societies of All Ages and Countries*. London: G. Redway.

Heelas, Paul. 1996. *The New Age Movement*. Oxford: Blackwell.

Heidegger, Martin. [1927] 1962. *Being and Time*. John Macquarrie and Edward Robinson (trans.). New York: Harper & Row.

Heidegger, Martin. [1927] 1949. *Sein und Zeit*. Tübingen: Neomarius Verlag.

Hill, Andy W. 2005. 'Exile in Godville: Profile of a postmodern Heretic'. *LA Weekly*, 19–25 May 2005.

Hippolytus of Rome. 1989. *The Refutation of All Heresies*. In Alexander Roberts, James Donaldson and A. Cleveland Coxe (eds), *Fathers of the Third Century: Hippolytus, Cyprian, Caius, Novatian*. Grand Rapids, MI: Eerdmans, 9–162.

Hobsbawm, Eric, and Terence Ranger (eds). [1983] 1992. *The Invention of Tradition*. Cambridge: Cambridge University Press.

Hoeller, Stephan. [1981] 1998. 'Position Paper Concerning the Thelemite or Crowleyan Gnostic Churches'. In P.-R. Köenig (ed.), *Ecclesia Gnostica Catholica*. Munich: Arbeitgemeinschaft fur Religions- und Weltanschauungsfragen, 194.

Hoeller, Stephan. 1982. *The Gnostic Jung and the Seven Sermons to the Dead*. Wheaton, IL: Theosophical Publishing House.

Hoeller, Stephan. 1989. 'Wandering Bishops: Not All Roads Lead to Rome'. *Gnosis: A Journal of Western Inner Traditions* 12, 20–5.

Hoeller, Stephan. 1989. *Jung and the Lost Gospels: Insights into the Dead Sea Scrolls and the Nag Hammadi Library*. Wheaton, IL: Theosophical Publishing House.

Hoeller, Stephan. 2002. *Gnosticism: New Light on the Ancient Tradition of Inner Knowing*. Wheaton, IL: Quest Books.

Hopland, Karstein. 1998. 'Hans Jonas and the History of *Gnosis und spätantiker Geist*'. *Temenos* 34, 51–72.

Hotam, Yotam. 2007. 'Gnosis and Modernity: A Postwar German Intellectual Debate on Secularisation, Religion and "Overcoming" the Past'. *Totalitarian Movements and Political Religions* 8, 591–608.

Hughes, Aaron W. 2015. *Islam and the Tyranny of Authenticity: An Inquiry into Disciplinary Apologetics and Self-Deception*. Sheffield: Equinox.

Hutton, Ronald. 1999. *The Triumph of the Moon: A History of Modern Pagan Witchcraft*. Oxford: Oxford University Press.

Introvigne, Massimo. 1993. *Il Ritorno Dello Gnosticismo*. Varese: SugarCo.

Irenaeus of Lyons. 1997. 'Against the Heresies (Detection and Overthrow of Gnosis Falsely So-Called)'. In Robert M. Grant (ed.), *Irenaeus of Lyons. The Early Church Fathers.* London: Routledge.

Jenkins, Philip. 2001. *Hidden Gospels: How the Search for Jesus Lost Its Way.* Oxford: Oxford University Press.

Johnston, Steve. 2015. 'Proximité littéraire entre les codices Askew et Bruce'. *Journal of Coptic Studies* 17, 85–107.

Jonas, Hans. 1934. *Gnosis und Spätantiker Geist. 1. Die Mythologische Gnosis.* Göttingen: Vandenhoeck & Ruprecht.

Jonas, Hans. 1954. *Gnosis und Spätantiker Geist. 2. Von der Mythologie zur Mystischen Philosophie.* Göttingen: Vandenhoeck & Ruprecht.

Jonas, Hans. [1958] 1963. *The Gnostic Religion*, 2nd rev. ed. Boston: Beacon.

Jonas, Hans. 1962. 'The Secret Books of the Egyptian Gnostics'. *Journal of Religion* 42(4), 262–73.

Jonas, Hans. 1964. 'Heidegger and Theology'. *Review of Metaphysics* 18, 208–32.

Jonas, Hans. 1965. 'Response by Hans Jonas'. In J. Philip Hyatt (ed.), *The Bible in Modern Scholarship.* London: Carey Kingsgate, 279–93.

Jonas, Hans. 1977. 'A Retrospective View'. In Geo Widengren and David Hellholm (eds), *Proceedings of the International Colloquium on Gnosticism, Stockholm, August 20–25, 1973.* Leiden: Brill, 1–15.

Jonas, Hans. 1984. *The Imperative of Responsibility: In Search of an Ethics for the Technological Age.* Chicago: University of Chicago Press.

Jonas, Hans. 1987. 'The Concept of God after Auschwitz: A Jewish Voice', *Journal of Religion* 67(1), 1–13.

Jonas, Hans. 2008. *Memoirs.* Christian Wiese (ed.), Krishna Winston (trans.). Waltham, MA: Brandeis University Press.

Jorgensen, David W. 2013. 'Irenaeus of Lyons and the Rhetoric of Interpretation'. In Eduard Iricinschi, Lance Jenott, Nicola Denzey Lewis and Philippa Townsend (eds), *Beyond the Gnostic Gospels: Studies Building on the Work of Elaine Pagels.* Tübingen: Mohr Siebeck, 124–47.

Jung, Carl Gustav. [1916] 1989. 'The Seven Sermons to the Dead Written by Basilides in Alexandria, the City Where the East Toucheth the West'. In Stephan A. Hoeller (ed., trans., commentary), *The Gnostic Jung and the Seven Sermons to the Dead.* Wheaton, IL: Quest Books, 44–58.

Jung, Carl Gustav. [1952] 2014. 'Religion and Psychology: Reply to Martin Buber'. In *Collected Works, Vol. 18: The Symbolic Life.* London: Routledge, 663–70.

Jung, Carl Gustav. 1966. 'New Paths in Psychology'. In *Collected Works, Vol. 7: Two Essays in Analytical Psychology.* Princeton: Princeton University Press, 245–68.

Jung, Carl Gustav. [1952] 1969. 'Answer to Job'. In *Collected Works, Vol 11: Psychology and Religion: West and East.* Princeton, NJ: Princeton University Press, 365–470.

Jung, Carl Gustav. [1958] 1969. 'Psychology and Religion: West and East'. *Collected Works, Vol 11*, 2nd ed. Princeton: Princeton University Press.

Jung, Carl Gustav. [1964] 1970. 'The Spiritual Problem of Modern Man'. In *Collected Works, Vol 10: Civilisation in Transition*. Princeton: Princeton University Press, 74–94.

Jung, Carl Gustav. 1970. *Collected Works, Vol 1: Psychiatric Studies*. Princeton: Princeton University Press.

Jung, Carl Gustav. 1971. *Collected Works, Vol 6: Psychological Types*. Princeton: Princeton University Press.

Jung, Carl Gustav. 1973. *Collected Works, Vol 2: Experimental Researches*. Princeton: Princeton University Press.

Jung, Carl Gustav. 1995. *C. G. Jung Manuskripte-Katalog: Verzeichnis der im C. G. Jung- Archiv der ETH-Bibliothek vorhandenen Manuskripte*. Zurich: Wissenschaftshistorische Sammlungen der ETH-Bibliothek.

Jung, Carl Gustav. [1961] 1963. *Memories, Dreams, Reflections*. Aniela Jaffe (ed.), Richard Winston and Clara Winston (trans.). London: Collins and Routledge & Kegan Paul.

Junginger, Horst. 2008. 'Introduction'. In H. Junginger (ed.), *The Study of Religion under the Impact of Fascism*. Leiden: Brill.

Kaczynski, Richard. 2012. *Forgotten Templars: The Untold Origins of the Ordo Templi Orientis*. USA: Privately Printed.

Kemp, Daren, and James R. Lewis. 2007. *Handbook of New Age*. Leiden: Brill.

Kershaw, Ian. 1999. *Hitler, 1889–1936: Hubris*. New York: W.W. Norton

King, Charles William. 1864. *The Gnostics and Their Remains, Ancient and Medieval*. London: Bell and Dalby.

King, Charles William. 1887. *The Gnostics and Their Remains*, 2nd rev. ed. London: D. Nutt.

King, Karen. L. 2003. *What Is Gnosticism?* Cambridge, MA: Belknap Press of Harvard University Press.

Kingsland, William. 1937. *The Gnosis or Ancient Wisdom in the Christian Scriptures*. London: George Allen & Unwin.

Köenig, Peter-R. 1998. *Ecclesia Gnostica Catholica*. Munich: Arbeitsgemeinschaft fur Religions- und Weltanschauungsfragen.

Köenig, Peter-R. n.d. 'Arnoldo Krumm-Heller – Huiracocha'. http://www.parareligion.ch/fra.htm (accessed 21 August 2020).

Koonz, Claudia. 2003. *The Nazi Conscience*. Cambridge, MA: Bellnap Press of Harvard University Press.

Kripal, Jeffrey J. 1995. *Kālī's Child: The Mystical and the Erotic in the Life and Teachings of Ramakrishna*. Chicago: University of Chicago Press

Kripal, Jeffrey J. 2001. *Roads of Excess, Palaces of Wisdom: Eroticism and Reflexivity in the Study of Mysticism*. Chicago: University of Chicago Press.

Kripal, Jeffrey J. 2006. *The Serpent's Gift: Gnostic Reflections on the Study of Religion*. Chicago: University of Chicago Press.

Kripal, Jeffrey J. 2007. *Esalen: America and the Religion of No Religion*. Chicago: University of Chicago Press.
Kripal, Jeffrey J. 2008. 'Gnosisssss – A Response to Wouter Hanegraaff'. *Religion* 38(3), 277–9.
Kripal, Jeffrey J. 2010. *Authors of the Impossible: The Paranormal and the Sacred*. Chicago: University of Chicago Press.
Kripal, Jeffrey J. 2011a. *Mutants and Mystics: Science Fiction, Superhero Comics, and the Paranormal*. Chicago: University of Chicago Press.
Kripal, Jeffrey J. 2011b. 'The Future Human: Mircea Eliade and the Fantastic Mutant'. *Archaus. Studies in the History of Religions* 15(1–2): 187–208.
Kripal, Jeffrey J. 2017. *Secret Body: Erotic and Esoteric Currents in the History of Religions*. Chicago: University of Chicago Press
Kristensen, William Brede. 1960. *The Meaning of Religion: Lectures in the Phenomenology of Religion*. John Braisted Carman (trans.). The Hague: Nijhoff.
Krumm-Heller, Heinrich A. [1931] 1985. *La Iglesia Gnostica*, 3rd ed. Buenos Aires: Kier.
Layton, Bentley. 1995. 'Prolegomena to the Study of Ancient Gnosticism'. In L. Michael White and O. Larry Yardbrough (eds), *The Social World of the First Christians: Essays in Honour of Wayne A. Meeks*. Minneapolis, MN: Fortress Press, 334–350.
Layton, Bentley. 1995. *The Gnostic Scriptures: A New Translation with Annotations and Introductions*. New York: Doubleday.
Lazier, Benjamin, 2008. *God Interrupted: Heresy and the European Imagination Between the World Wars*. Princeton: Princeton University Press.
Lazier, Benjamin. 2008. 'Pauline Theology in the Weimar Republic'. In Hava Tirosh-Samuelson and Christian Wiese (eds), *The Legacy of Hans Jonas: Judaism and the Phenomenon of Life*. Leiden: Brill, 107–29.
Le Boulluec, Alain. 1985. *Le Notion d'hérésie dans la literature grecque IIc-IIIc siècles*. Paris: Études Augustiniennes.
Leadbeater, Charles W. 1930. *How Theosophy Came to Me*. Adyar: Theosophical Publishing House.
Leeuw, Gerardus van der. 1933. *Phänomenologie der Religion*. Tübingen: Verlag von J.C.B. Mohr (Paul Siebeck).
Leeuw, Gerardus van der. [1933] 1938. *Religion in Essence and Manifestation*. J. Turner (trans.). London: George Allen & Unwin.
Levi-Strauss, Claude. 1963. *Structural Anthropology*. New York: Basic Books.
Levy, David J. 2002. *Hans Jonas: The Integrity of Thinking*. Columbia: University of Missouri Press.
Lewis, Nicola Denzey, and Justine Blount. 2014. 'Rethinking the Origins of the Nag Hammadi Library'. *Journal of Biblical Literature* 133, 399–419.
Lim, Timothy. 2005. *The Dead Sea Scrolls: A Very Short Introduction*. Oxford: Oxford University Press.

Lincoln, Bruce. 1989. *Discourse and the Construction of Society: Comparative Studies of Myth, Ritual, and Classification*. New York: Oxford University Press.

Löwith, Karl. 1949. *Meaning in History: The Theological Implications of the Philosophy of History*. Chicago: University of Chicago Press.

Löwith, Karl, Richard Wolin, and Melissa J. Cox. 'The Political Implications of Heidegger's Existentialism'. *New German Critique* 45, 117–34.

Magris, Aldo. 2005. 'Gnosticism: Gnosticism from Its Origins to the Middle Ages (Further Considerations)'. In Lindsay Jones, Mircea Eliade and Charles J. Adams (eds), *Encyclopedia of Religion*, 2nd ed. Detroit: Macmillan Reference, 3515–22.

Mansel, Henry Longueville. 1875. *The Gnostic Heresies of the First and Second Centuries*. London: John Murray.

Markschies, Christoph. 2003. *Gnosis: An Introduction*. London: T&T Clark.

Masuzawa, Tomoko. 1993. *In Search of Dreamtime: The Quest for the Origin of Religion*. Chicago: University of Chicago Press

Masuzawa, Tomoko. 2005. *The Invention of World Religions: Or, How European Universalism Was Preserved in the Language of Pluralism*. Chicago: University of Chicago Press.

Matter, M. Jacques. 1828. *Histoire Critique du Gnosticism*. Paris: F. G. Levrault.

Mayer, Marvin, and Harold Bloom. 1992. *The Gospel of Thomas: The Hidden Sayings of Jesus; Translation with Introduction, Critical Edition of the Coptic Text and Notes by Marvin Meyer, with an Interpretation by Harold Bloom*. San Francisco: HarperSanFrancisco.

McCutcheon, Russell T. 1997. *Manufacturing Religion: The Discourse on Sui Generis Religion and the Politics of Nostalgia*. New York: Oxford University Press.

McCutcheon, Russell T. 2017. 'Beyond Cynicism: A Sampling of Current Work in the Swiss Study of Religion'. *Bulletin for the Study of Religion* 46(1), 3–6.

Mead, George R. S. 1900. *Fragments of a Faith Forgotten. Some Short Sketches among the Gnostics, Mainly of the First Two Centuries. A Contribution to the Study of Christian Origins Based on the Most Recently Recovered Materials*. London: Theosophical Publishing Society.

Mead, George R. S. 1906. *The Gnosis of the Mind*. London: Theosophical Publishing Society.

Mead, George R. S. 1907. *The Mithraic ritual*. London: Theosophical Publishing Society.

Mead, George R. S. 1921. *Pistis Sophia; a Gnostic Miscellany: Being for the Most Part Extracts from the Books of the Saviour, to Which Are Added Excerpts from a Cognate Literature; Englished (with an Introduction and Annotated Bibliography)*. London: J.M. Watkins.

Mead, George R. S. 1926. '"The Quest" – Old and New: Retrospect and Prospect'. *Quest* 17(3), 289–307.

Mead, George R. S. 1982. 'Pistis Sophia: Commentary and Notes'. In *Helena P. Blavatsky: Collected Writings*, vol. 13. Wheaton, IL: Theosophical Publishing House, 1–81.

Mead, George R. S., Emile Amelineau, and Moeritz G. Schwartze. 1896. *Pistis Sophia; a Gnostic Gospel (with Extracts from the Books of the Saviour Appended) Originally Tr. from Greek into Coptic and Now for the First Time Englished from Schwartze's Latin Version of the Only Known Coptic Ms. and Checked by Amélineau's French Version with an Introduction by G.R.S. Mead*. London: Theosophical Publishing Society.

Mellon, Paul, and John Baskett. 1992. *Reflections in a Silver Spoon: A Memoir by Paul Mellon*. London: Murray.

Merkur, Daniel. 1993. *Gnosis: An Esoteric Tradition of Mystical Visions and Unions*. Albany: State University of New York Press.

Molendijk, Arie. 2000. 'At the Crossroads: Early Dutch science of religion in international perspective'. In S. Hjelde (ed.), *Man, Meaning and Mystery: Hundred Years of History of Religion in Norway. The Heritiage of W. Brede Kristensen*. Leiden: Brill, 19–56.

More, Henry. 1669. *An Exposition of the Seven Epistles to the Seven Churches Together with a Brief Discourse of Idolatry, with Application to the Church of Rome*. London: James Flesher.

More, Henry. 1668. *Divine Dialogues Containing Sundry Disquisitions and Instructions Concerning the Attributes and Providence of God: The Three First Dialogues Treating of the Attributes of Cod and His Providence at Large, Collected and Compiled by the Care and Industry of Franciscus Palaeopolitanus*. London: James Flesher.

More, Henry. 1664. *A Modest Enquiry into the Mystery of Iniquity*. London: James Flesher.

Nelson, Victoria. 2003. *The Secret Life of Puppets*. Cambridge, MA: Harvard University Press.

Neugebauer-Wölk, Monika. 2009. 'From Talk about Esotericism to Esotericism Research: Remarks on the Prehistory and Development of a Research Group'. In Wouter Hanegraaff and Joyce Pijnenburg (eds), *Hermes in the Academy: Ten Years' Study of Western Esotericism at the University of Amsterdam*. Amsterdam: Amsterdam University Press, 134–41.

Neill, Stephen, and Tom Wright. 1988. *The Interpretation of the New Testament 1861–1986*, 2nd rev. ed. Oxford: Oxford University Press.

Nieli, Russell. 1987. 'Eric Voegelin: Gnosticism, Mysticism, and Modern Radical Politics'. *Southern Review* 23(2), 332–48.

Noll, Richard. 1994. *The Jung Cult: Origins of a Charismatic Movement*. Princeton: Princeton University Press.

Noll, Richard. 1997. *The Aryan Christ: The Secret Life of Carl Gustav Jung*. London: Macmillan.

O'Regan, Cyril. 2001. *Gnostic Return in Modernity*. Albany: State University of New York Press.

Osborn, Eric. 2004. *Irenaeus of Lyons*. Cambridge: Cambridge University Press.
Ott, Hugo. 1988. *Martin Heidegger: Unterwegs zu seiner Biographie*. Frankfurt: Campus.
Otto, Rudolf. [1917] 1929. *Das Heilige: Über das Irrationale in der Idee des Göttlichen und sein Verhältnis zum Rationalen*. Gotha: Leopold Klotz Verlag.
Ouspensky, Pyotr D. [1949] 1987. *In Search of The Miraculous: Fragments of An Unknown Teaching*. London: Arkana.
Pagels, Elaine. 1974. 'Paul and Women: A Response to Recent Discussion'. *JAAR* 42, 538–49.
Pagels, Elaine. 1976. 'What Became of God the Mother? Conflicting Images of God in Early Christianity'. *Signs: Journal of Women in Culture and Society* 2(2), 293–303.
Pagels, Elaine. 1979. *The Gnostic Gospels*. New York: Random House.
Pagels, Elaine. 2003. *Beyond Belief: The Secret Gospel of Thomas*. New York: Random House
Pagels, Elaine. 2018. *Why Religion?: A Personal Story*. London: Harper Collins.
Pakenham, Michael. 2003. 'In Full Bloom: Guerrilla In Our Midst'. *The Baltimore Sun*. http://articles.baltimoresun.com/2003-03-23/entertainment/0303240442_1_bloom-dining-room-table (accessed 30 September 2020).
Pascal, Roy. 1973. *From Naturalism to Expressionism: German Literature and Society, 1880–1918*. New York: Basic Books.
Pearson, Birger. 1990. *Gnosticism, Judaism, and Egyptian Christianity*. Minneapolis, MN: Fortress Press.
Pearson, Birger. 2007. *Ancient Gnosticism: Traditions and Literature*. Minneapolis, MN: Fortress Press
Pearson, Joanne. 2007. *Wicca and the Christian Heritage: Ritual, Sex and Magic*. London: Routledge.
Pegg, Mark. 2001. 'On Cathars, Albigenses, and Good Men of Languedoc'. *Journal of Medieval History* 27(2), 181–90.
Pert, Alan. 2006. *Red Cactus: The Life of Anna Kingsford*. Watsons Bay, NSW: Books and Writers Network.
Pettazzoni, R. 1954, 'Aperçu Introductif'. *NUMEN* 1, 1–7.
Pettazoni, R. 1954. *Essays in the History of Religions*. H. J. Rose (trans.). Leiden: Brill, 215–19.
Plummer, John P. 2005. *The Many Paths of the Independent Sacramental Movement*. Berkeley, CA: Apocryphile Press.
Poller, Jake. 2018. '"Under a Glamour": Annie Besant, Charles Leadbeater and Neo-Theosophy'. In Christine Ferguson and Andrew Radford (eds), *The Occult Imagination in Britain, 1875–1947*. London: Routledge, 77–93.
Puech, Charles-Henri. 1983. *Cyclical Time and Ismaili Gnosis*. London: Routledge & Kegan Paul.
Puma, Jeremy. 2011. *This Way: Gnosis without Gnosticism*. Seattle: Strange Animal Publications.

Puma, Jeremy. 2013. *How to Think Like a Gnostic*. Seattle: Strange Animal Publications.
Quispel, Gilles. 1951. *Gnosis als Weltreligion*. Zurich: Origo Verlag.
Quispel, Gilles. 1961. 'Review of Jewish Gnosticism, Merkabah Mysticism and Talmudic Tradition by Gershom G. Scholem'. *Vigiliae Christianae* 15(2), 117–19.
Quispel, Gilles. 1965. 'Gnosticism and the New Testament'. In J. Philip Hyatt (ed.), *The Bible in Modern Scholarship*. London: Carey Kingsgate, 252–71.
Quispel, Gilles. [1968] 1992. 'Jung and Gnosis'. In Robert A. Segal (ed.), *The Gnostic Jung*. London: Routledge, 219–38.
Quispel, Gilles. 1972. *Gnosis als Weltreligion: Die Bedeutung der Gnosis in der Antike*, 2nd ed. Zurich: Origo Verlag.
Quispel, Gilles. 1977. 'Remembering Jung #19: Gilles Quispel, Ph.D.'. Video Interview. Suzanne Wagner (dir.), James Kirsch (interviewer). https://www.youtube.com/watch?v=jVd9sYTMXnE (accessed 21 March 2021).
Quispel, Gilles (ed.). 1988. 'Inleiding'. In *Gnosis: De Derde Component van de Europese Cultuurtraditie*. Utrecht: HES.
Quispel, Gilles. 1988. *Gnosis: De Derde Component van de Europese Cultuurtraditie*, 2nd ed. Utrecht: HES.
Quispel, Gilles. 1947. 'La Conception de l'Homme dans la Gnose Valentinienne'. *Eranos Jahrbuch* 15, 249–86.
Quispel, Gilles. 1975. 'Faust: Symbol of Western Man'. *Gnostic Studies* 2, 288–307.
Quispel, Gilles, and J. van Oort. 2008. *Gnostica, Judaica, Catholica: Collected Essays of Gilles Quispel*. Leiden: Brill.
Rabinbach, Anson. 2000. *In the Shadow of Catastrophe: German Intellectuals Between Apocalypse and Enlightenment*. Berkeley: University of California Press.
Radford, Lewis B. 1913. *Ancient Heresies in Modern Dress: The Moorhouse Lectures, 1913, Delivered in St. Paul's Cathedral, Melbourne*. Melbourne: George Robertson.
Raschke, Karl. 1980. *The Interruption of Eternity: Modern Gnosticism and the Origins of the New Religious Consciousness*. Chicago: Nelson-Hall.
Reitzenstein, Richard. [1910] 1956. *Die Hellenistischen Mysterienreligionen nach ihren Grundgedanken und Wirkungen*. Stuttgart: B.G. Teubner.
Reuss, Theodor. 2014. 'Parsival und das Enthüllte Grals-Geheimnis'. In P-R. Köenig (ed.), *Der Kleine Theodor Reuss Reader*. Munich: Arbeitsgemeinschaft für Religions- und Weltanschauungsfragen, 72.
Richardson, Elsa. 2018. 'Stemming the Black Tide of Mud: Psychoanalysis and the Occult Periodical'. In Christine Ferguson and Andrew Radford (eds), *The Occult Imagination in Britain, 1875–1947*. London: Routledge, 110–28.
Robertson, David G. 2013. 'David Icke's Reptilian Thesis and the Development of New Age Theodicy'. *International Journal for the Study of New Religions* 3(1), 27–47.
Robertson, David G. 2014. 'Transformation: Whitley Strieber's Paranormal Gnosis'. *Nova Religio* 18(1), 58–78.
Robertson, David G. 2016. *Conspiracy Theories, UFOs and the New Age: Millennial Conspiracism*. London: Bloomsbury.

Robertson, David G. 2020. '"When the Chips Are Down" (A Response to Ambasciano)'. *Religio: Revue pro religionistiku* 28(1), 21–30.

Robertson, David G. 2021. 'Diversification in Samael Aun Weor's Gnostic Movement'. In Eileen Barker and Beth Singler (eds), *Radical Change in Minority Religions*. London: INFORM/Routledge.

Robinson, James L. 2014a. *The Nag Hammadi Story, Vol 1: The Discovery and Monopoly*. Leiden: Brill.

Robinson, J. L. 2014b. *The Nag Hammadi Story, Vol 2: The Publication*. Leiden: Brill.

Robinson, J. L., C. Heil and J. Verheyden (eds) 2005. *The Sayings Gospel Q: Collected Essays by James M. Robinson*. Leuven: Leuven University Press.

Robinson, James L. 1993. 'Preface'. In Hans-Joachim Klimkeit (ed.), *Gnosis on the Silk Road: Gnostic Parables, Hymns & Prayers from Central Asia*. San Francisco: Harper, xvii–xx.

Robinson, James M. 1977. 'Introduction'. In James M. Robinson (ed.), *The Nag Hammadi Library in English*. San Francisco: Harper, 1–26.

Robinson, James. L. 2005. 'Theological Autobiography – 1988'. In Christoph Heil and Joseph Verheyden (eds), *The Sayings Gospel Q: Collected Essays*. Leuven: Peeters, 3–35.

Rudolf, Kurt. 1987. *Gnosis: The Nature and History of Gnosticism*. San Francisco: Harper.

Rudolph, Kurt. 2008. 'Hans Jonas and Research on Gnosticism from a Contemporary Perspective'. In Hava Tirosh-Samuelson and Christian Wiese (eds), *The Legacy of Hans Jonas: Judaism and the Phenomenon of Life*. Leiden: Brill, 91–106.

Sabazius. 1997. 'Dr. Arnoldo Krumm-Heller'. https://hermetic.com/sabazius/krumm (accessed 23 July 2020).

Sacco, Leonardo. 2008. 'Neosciamanesimo e New Age. Il "contributo" di Mircea Eliade'. *Archaeus: Études d'Histoire des Religions/Studies in the History of Religions* 11/12, 249–304.

Safranski, Rudiger. 1998. *Martin Heidegger: Between Good and Evil*. Ewald Osers (trans.). Cambridge, MA: Harvard University Press.

Schenke, Hans-Martin. 2012. 'The Problem of Gnosis'. In Gesine Schenke Robinson, Gesa Schenke und Uwe-Karsten Plisch (eds), *Der Same Seths: Hans-Martin Schenke's 'Kleine Schriften' zu Gnosis, Koptologie und Neuem Testament*. Leiden: Brill, 538–53.

Scholem, Gershom. 1941. *Major Trends in Jewish Mysticism*. New York: Schocken.

Scholem, Gershom. 1965. *Jewish Gnosticism, MerKabah Mysticism, and Talmudic Tradition: Based on the Israel Goldstein Lectures, Delivered at the Jewish Theol. Seminary of America, New York*. New York: Jewish Theol. Seminary of America.

Scholem, Gershom. 1974. 'Der Nihilismus als religioses Phanomen'. *Eranos-Jahrbuch* 43, 1–50.

Scholem, Gershom. 1995. 'Redemption through Sin'. In *The Messianic Idea in Judaism and Other Essays on Jewish Spirituality*. New York: Schocken Books.

Scholem, Gershom, Smith Morton, and Guy G. Stroumsa (eds). 2008. *Morton Smith and Gershom Scholem, Correspondence 1945-1982*. Leiden: Brill.

Schwartze, Moritz Gotthilf, and Jul Henr Petermann. 1851. *Pistis Sophia: Opus gnosticum Valentino adiudicatum e codice manuscripto coptico Londinensi*. Berolini: F. Duemmleri.

Segal, Robert A. (ed.). 1992. *The Gnostic Jung*. London: Routledge.

Segal, Robert A. 1987. 'Jung and Gnosticism'. In *Religion* 17, 301-36.

Segal, Robert A. 1998. 'The Existentialist Reinterpretation of Myth: Rudolf Bultmann and Hans Jonas'. In Michael Bell and Peter Poellner (eds), *Myth and the Making of Modernity: The Problem of Grounding in Early Twentieth Century Literature*. Amsterdam: Rodopi, 115-24.

Shamdasani, Sonu. 1998. *Cult Fictions: C. G. Jung and the Founding of Analytical Psychology*. London: Taylor & Francis.

Sheehan, Thomas. 1993. 'Reading a Life: Heidegger and Hard Times'. In Charles B. Guignon (ed.), *The Cambridge Companion to Heidegger*. Cambridge: Cambridge University Press, 70-96.

Silva, Ana Cloclet da, and Marccelo Leandro de Campos. 2017. 'Entre contextos ediscursos: a biografia de Samael Aun Weor e o gnosticismo colombiano'. *Revista Brasileira de História das Religiões* 9(27), 85-114.

Smith, Carl. B. 2015. 'Post-Bauer Scholarship on Gnosticism(s): The Current State of Our "Knowledge"'. In Paul A. Hartog (ed.), *Orthodoxy and Heresy in Early Christian Contexts: Reconsidering the Bauer Thesis*. Eugene, OR: Pickwick, 60-88.

Smith, Morton. 1981. 'The History of the Term Gnostikos'. In Bentley Layton (ed.), *The Rediscovery of Gnosticism: Proceedings of the Conference at Yale, New Haven, Connecticut, March 28-31, 1978. Vol. 2: Sethian Gnosticism*. Leiden: Brill, 796-807.

Smith, Richard. 1995. 'The Revival of Ancient Gnosis'. In R. A. Segal with J. Singer and M. Stein (eds), *The Allure of Gnosticism: The Gnostic Experience in Jungian Psychology and Contemporary Culture*. Chicago: Open Court, 204-23.

Sorge, Giovanni. 2012. 'Love as Devotion: Olga Fröbe-Kapteyn's relationship with Eranos and Jungian Psychology'. In Fabio Merlini, Lawrence E. Sullivan, Riccardo Bernardini and Kate Olson (eds), *Eranos Yearbook 2009/2011*. Einsiedeln: Daimon Verlag, 388-434.

Spineto, Natale. 1994. *Mircea Eliade-Raffaele Pettazzoni. L'histoire des religions a-telle un sens? Correspondance 1926-1959. Texte présenté, établi et annoté par N. Spineto*. Paris: Éditions du Cerf.

Spineto, Natale. 2008. 'The Notion of Archetype in Eliade's Writings'. *Religion* 38(4), 366-74.

Stark, Gary. 1981. *Entrepreneurs of Ideology: Neoconservative Publishers in Germany 1890-1930*. Chapel Hill: University of North Carolina Press.

Stausberg, Michael. 2013. 'What Is It All About? Some Reflections on Wouter Hanegraaff's *Esotericism and the Academy*'. Religion 43(2), 219–30.
Stratford, Jordan. 2007. *Living Gnosticism: An Ancient Way of Knowing*. Berkeley, CA: Apocryphile Press.
Strieber, Whitley, and Jeffrey J. Kripal. 2017. *The Super Natural: Why the Unexplained Is Real*. New York: TarcherPerigee.
Stuckrad, Kocku von. 2003. 'Discursive Study of Religion: From States of Mind to Communication and Action'. Method and Theory in the Study of Religion 15, 255–71.
Stuckrad, Kocku von. 2005. *Western Esoterisicm: A Brief History of Secret Knowledge*. London: Equinox.
Stuckrad, Kocku von. 2010. *Locations of Knowledge in Medieval and Early Modern Europe: Esoteric Discourse and Western Identities*. Brill's Studies in Intellectual History. Leiden: Brill, 186.
Stuckrad, Kocku von. 2014. *The Scientification of Religion: An Historical Study of Discursive Change, 1800–2000*. Berlin: De Gruyter.
Stuckrad, Kocku von. 2016. 'Esotericism Disputed: Major Debates in the Field'. In April D. DeConick (ed.), *Religion: Secret Religion*. New York: Gale Cengage Learning, 171–81.
Styfhals, Willem. 2019. *No Spiritual Investment in the World: Gnosticism and Postwar German Philosophy*. New York: Cornell University Press.
Sutcliffe, Steven J. 2003. *Children of the New Age: A History of Spiritual Practices*. London: Routledge.
Sutcliffe, Steven J., and Ingvild S. Gilhus (eds). 2014. *New Age Spirituality: Rethinking Religion*. London: Routledge.
Taubes, Jacob. 1947. *Abendländische Eschatologie*. Berlin: Matthes und Seitz.
Taubes, Jacob (ed.). 1984. 'Vorwort'. In *Gnosis und Politik*. Berlin: Willhelm Fink, 5–8.
Taubes, Jacob. 2017. 'Die Geschichte Jacob Taubes-Carl Schmitt'. In Herbert Kopp-Oberstebrink and Martin Treml (eds), *Apokalypse und Politik: Aufsätze, Kritiken und kleineren Schriften*. Munich: Wilhelm Fink, 299–307.
Taves, Ann. 2009. *Religious Experience Reconsidered: A Building-Block Approach to the Study of Religion and Other Special Things*. Princeton: Princeton University Press.
Taves, Ann. 2015. 'Reverse Engineering Complex Cultural Concepts: Identifying Building Blocks of "Religion"'. Journal of Culture and Cognition 15(1–2), 191–216.
Taves, Ann. 2016. *Revelatory Events: Three Case Studies of the Emergence of New Spiritual Paths*. Princeton: Princeton University Press.
Thomassen, Einar. 2006. *The Spiritual Seed: The Church of the 'Valentinians'*. Leiden: Brill.
Tillett, Gregory John. 1986. 'Charles Webster Leadbeater 1854–1934: A Biographical Study'. PhD thesis, University of Sydney. https://ses.library.usyd.edu.au/handle/2123/1623 (accessed 30 August 2020).
Tillich, Paul. [1965] 2017. 'Die Bedeutung der Religionsgeschichte für den systematischen Theologen'. In Ulrich Dehn, Ulrike Caspar-Seeger and Freya

Bernstorff (eds), *Handbuch Theologie der Religionen: Texte zur religiösen Vielfalt und zum interreligiösen Dialog*. Freiburg: Verlag, 93–106.

Tite, Philip. 2013. 'Theoretical Challenges in Studying Religious Experience in Gnosticism: A Prolegomena for Social Analysis'. *Bulletin for the Study of Religion* 42(1), 8–18.

Tite, Philip. 2019. 'Transgression and Countercultural Gnosticism: A Review Essay of April DeConick's *The Gnostic New Age*'. In *Studies in Religion/Sciences Religieuses* 49(2), 1–15.

Townsend, Philippa. 2013. 'Explorations at the Edges of Orthodoxy: Elaine Pagels' Study of the Early Christian World'. In Eduard Iricinschi, Lance Jenott, Nicola Denzey Lewis and Philippa Townsend (eds), *Beyond the Gnostic Gospels: Studies Building on the Work of Elaine Pagels*. Tübingen: Mohr Siebeck, 1–18.

Trompf, Gary, Gunner B. Mikkelsen, and Jay Johnston (eds). 2019. *The Gnostic World*. London: Routledge.

Tuckett, Jonathan. 2018. 'Clarifying Phenomenologies in the Study of Religion: Separating Kristensen and van der Leeuw from Otto and Eliade'. *Religion* 46(1), 75–101.

Tumber, Catherine. 2002. *American Feminism and the Birth of New Age Spirituality: Searching for the Higher Self, 1875–1915*. Lanham: Rowman & Littlefield.

Turner, Henry E. W. 1954. *The Pattern of Christian Truth: A Study in the Relations between Orthodoxy and Heresy in the Early Church (Bampton Lectures 1954)*. London: A.R. Mowbray.

Turner, James. 2014. *Philology: The Forgotten Origins of the Modern Humanities*. Princeton: Princeton University Press.

Urban, Hugh B. 2019. 'The Knowing of Knowing: Neo-Gnosticism, from the O.T.O. to Scientology'. *Gnosis: Journal of Gnostic Studies* 4, 129–46.

Urban, Hugh B. 2006. *Magia Sexualis: Sex, Magic, and Liberation in Modern Western Esotericism*. Berkeley: University of California.

Vallée, Gérard. 1981. *A Study in Anti-Gnostic Polemics: Irenaeus, Hippolytus, and Epiphanius*. Waterloo: Wilfrid Laurier University Press.

Versluis, Arthur. 2007. *Magic and Mysticism: An Introduction to Western Esotericism*. Lanham: Rowman & Littlefield.

Versluis, Arthur. 2006. *The New Inquisitions: Heretic-Hunting and the Intellectual Origins of Modern Totalitarianism*. Oxford: Oxford University Press.

Vickers, Brian. 1979. 'Frances Yates and the Writing of History'. *Journal of Modern History* 51(2), 287–316.

Voegelin, Eric. 1952. 'Gnostische Politik'. *Merkur* 50, 301–17.

Voegelin, Eric. 1952. *The New Science of Politics: An Introduction*. Chicago: University of Chicago Press.

Voegelin, Eric. 1953 'The Oxford Political Philosophers'. *Philosophical Quarterly* 11(3), 97–114.

Voegelin, Eric. [1968] 2004. 'Science, Politics and Gnosis'. In *Science, Politics and Gnosticism*. Wimington, DE: ISI Books, 1–57.
Waite, Arthur Edward. 2003. *Devil-worship in France, with, Diana Vaughan and the Question of Modern Palladism*. Boston, MA: Weiser Books.
Washington, Peter. 1993. *Madame Blavatsky's Baboon: Theosophy and the Emergence of the Western Guru*. London: Secker & Warburg.
Wasserstrom, Steven M. 1999. *Religion after Religion: Gershom Scholem, Mircea Eliade, and Henry Corbin at Eranos*. Princeton: Princeton University Press.
Wasserstrom, Steven M. 2008. 'Hans Jonas in Marburg, 1928'. In Hava Tirosh-Samuelson and Christian Wiese (eds), *The Legacy of Hans Jonas: Judaism and the Phenomenon of Life*. Leiden: Brill, 39–72.
Webb, James. 1971. *The Flight from Reason*. London: MacDonald.
Wiebe, Donald. 2019. *The Learned Practice of Religion in the Modern University*. London: Bloomsbury.
Weibe, Donald. 1999. *Politics of Religious Studies*. London: Palgrave MacMillan.
Weor, Samael Aun. [1961] 2001. *The Perfect Matrimony: The Door to Enter into Initiation*. Brooklyn, NY: Thelema.
Weor, Samael Aun. 1991. *Carpa Solari: Messaggio di Natale 1967–68*. Florence: Instituto Gnostico di Antropologia.
Weor, Samael Aun. 1970. *Tratado de psicología revolucionaria*. El Salvador: Movimiento Gnostico Cristiano Universal.
Widengren, Geo. 1973. *The Gnostic Attitude*. Birger Pearson (ed. and trans.). Santa Barbara: University of California Press.
Wiese, Christian. 2008. 'Zionism, the Holocaust, and Judaism in a Secular World'. In Hava Tirosh-Samuelson and Christian Wiese (eds), *The Legacy of Hans Jonas: Judaism and the Phenomenon of Life*. Leiden: Brill, 159–202.
Williams, Michael A. 2016. 'Gnosticism Emergent: The Beginning of the Study of Gnosticism in the Academy'. In April DeConick (ed.), *Religion: Secret Religion*. New York: Macmillan, 3–22.
Williams, Michael A. 1996. *Rethinking 'Gnosticism': An Argument for Dismantling a Dubious Category*. Princeton: Princeton University Press.
Winter, Franz. 2018. 'Studying the "Gnostic Bible": Samael Aun Weor and the Pistis Sophia'. *International Journal for the Study of New Religions* 9(1), 83–112.
Winterberg, Alberto Alfredo. 2018. 'Remembering the Gnostics: The Mnemohistorical Incorporation of Ancient Gnosticism within Neo-Gnostic Churches'. *La Rosa di Paracelso* 1(1), 47–64. http://www.larosadiparacelso.com/index.php/rosa/article/view/42 (accessed 21 March 2021).
Wolin, Richard. 2001. *Heidegger's Children: Hannah Arendt, Karl Löwith, Hans Jonas, and Herbert Marcuse*. Princeton: Princeton University Press.
Wolin, Richard. 2008. 'Ethics after Auschwitz: Hans Jonas's Notion of Responsibility in a Technological Age'. In Hava Tirosh-Samuelson and Christian Wiese (eds), *The Legacy of Hans Jonas: Judaism and the Phenomenon of Life*. Leiden: Brill, 1–15.

Wood, Matthew. 2007. *Possession, Power, and the New Age: Ambiguities of Power in Neoliberal Societies*. Aldershot: Ashgate.

Wulff, David. 2012. 'Psychological Approaches'. In F. Whaling (ed.), *Theory and Method in Religious Studies: Contemporary Approaches to the Study of Religion*. Berlin: DeGruyter, 253–320.

Yates, Frances. 1964. *Giordano Bruno and the Hermetic Tradition*. London: Routledge & Kegan Paul.

York, M. 1995. *The Emerging Network: A Sociology of the New Age and Neo-Pagan Movements*. Lanham, MD: Rowman and Littlefield.

Zbíral, David. 2007. *Největší hereze: Dualismus, učenecká vyprávění o katarství a budování křesťanské Evropy*. Praha: Argo.

Znamenski, Andrei A. 2004. 'General Introduction – Adventures of the Metaphor: Shamanism and Shamanism Studies'. In Andrei A. Znamenski (ed.), *Shamanism: Critical Concepts in Sociology*. London: RoutledgeCurzon, xix–lxxxvi.

Zoccatelli, PierLuigi 2013. 'Sexual Magic and Gnosis in Colombia: Tracing the Influence of G. I. Gurdjieff on Samael Aun Weor'. In P. Zoccatelli (ed), *Occultism in Global Context*. London: Acumen, 135–50.

Zoccatelli, PierLuigi. 2000. 'Il Paradigma Esoterico E Un Modello Di Applicazione. Note Sul Movimento Gnostico Di Samael Aun Weor'. *La Critica Sociologica* 135, 33–49.

Zoccatelli, PierLuigi. 2005. 'Note a margine dell'influsso di G. I. Gurdjieff su Samael Aun Weor'. *Aries. Journal for the Study of Western Esotericism* 5(2), 255–75.

Index

Note: Page numbers in bold indicate figures.

Abraxas 51
Acts of Peter 20
Adorno, Theodor 82, 83
Adversus Haereses (Irenaeus) 4, 11–13
Aeons (lower deities) 13, 14, 19
    Christ as 22
Against the Gnostics (Plotinus) 15
ahistoricism 2, 3, 5, 6–7, 9, 22, 35, 87, 89, 123, 129
    Bauer thesis and 47
    DeConick and 146–8
    Eranos scholars and 64, 96
    Jonas and 49
    Messina Congress and 38, 103, 132
    Shamanism and 160
    see also essentialism; historicism; phenomenology; phenomenology of religion; sui generis
AJC (Apostolic Johannite Church) 106, 107, 112–15, 146, 159, 167 n.13, 187 n.40
Albigenses, *see* Cathars
alchemy 57, 58
alienation 39, 45, 48, 49, 63, 125
    Judaism and 81
    Jung and 57, 77
    see also dualism
All Saints Accord 113
Alvares, Mar Julius (Frater Alvares) 167 n.20
Ambasciano, Leonardo 3, 152
Amélineau, Émile 19, 31, 164 n.21
American Academy of Religion 98
Anthroposophy 29, 57
anti-Semitism 44
    Gnosticism and 81–2
    Heidegger and 172 n.51
    Jung and 54
    see also Holocaust; Judaism; Jews

anticosmic dualism, *see* dualism
Apocryphon of James 72
Apocryphon of John 20
apostolic succession 27–8, 106–7, 109–10, 111–13, 114
Aquinas, Thomas 83
archetypes 54, 59, 60, 72
archons 80–1, 114
Arendt, Hannah 44, 48, 82, 84
Arnold, Gottfried 18
Ascended Masters 33, 53
Asclepius (Nag Hammadi document) 16
Askew Codex 19, 20, 70, 119, 185 n.68
Asprem, Egil 135
Augustine of Hippo 83, 86
Aun Weor, Samael (Victor Manuel Gómez Rodríguez) 8, 105, 114, 115, 116–20, 137, 146, 148
    groups 105–6, 114, 116–20, 146, 159, 167 n.13
Aurobindo, Sri 127

Bailey, Alice 33, 53, 91, 173 n.16
Ball, Hugo 51
Barbelites 14–15, 16
Barth, Karl 42
Basilides 21, 32
    Jung and 55
Basten, Rosalie 131–2, 133
Bauer, Walter 47, 65, 66, 142
Baur, Ferdinand Christian 18–19, 20–1, 24, 31, 46, 47, 57
Baynes, Charlotte 34
Beausobré, Isaac de 17
Behr, John 11
Behun, William 167 n.13
Benjamin, Walter 82, 84
Berlin Codex 20, 21, 70
Besant, Annie 31, 33–4, 35, 36–7

Bhagavad Gita 99
Biale, David 61
Bianchi, Ugo 99, 100–1
Biblical Studies 1, 2, 5, 8, 21–2, 49, 99, 142, 147
　canon 11
　demythologization 22, 43–4, 65
　exegesis 4, 65–6
　gnosis in 12, 17
　Religious Studies and 161, 162
　'Son of Man' in 23
　Tübingen School 18, 20, 46
Blake, William 63
Blavatsky, Helena Petrovna 29, 30, 31, 32, 33–4
　influence 51, 53, 57, 101, 110, 142
　see also theosophy
Blavatsky Trust 131
Bleeker, Claas Jouco 90, **90**, 93, 94–6, 101, 104
Bloom, Harold 138–9, 160
Blumenberg, Hans 84, 85, 138
Bogomils 100
Böhme, Jakob 18, 19, 29
Bollingen
　Bollingen Foundation 63, 71, 72
　Bollingen Press 59, 71, 142
　see also Mellon, Mary and Paul
Books of Jeu 16, 19, 166 n.56
Borborites 14, 16
Bousset, Wilhelm 23, 34, 100
Brach, Jean-Pierré 132, 133
Brentano, Franz 40, 41
Bricard, Jean 27, 28
Bruce Codex 19, 20, 21, 32, 70, 189 n.68
Buber, Martin 48, 78–9
Buddhism 101, 101, 115, 143
Buell, Denise 16
Bultmann, Rudolf 34, 43, 44–5, 47, 65–6, 79, 84, 95
Burkitt, F. C. 34
Burns, Dylan 15
Bustos, Teofilo (Venerable Master Lakshmi) 118

C. G. Jung Institute (Zurich) 64, 71
Caithness, Lady (Maria de Mariategui) 25
Campbell, Joseph 1, 59, 64
Capps, Walter 93–4

Castro, Giovanni de 26
Cathars 25, 26, 27, 63, 100, 142, 167 n.12
Catholicism
　contrasted with Gnosticism 18, 114
　decline in France 26
　as Gnosticism 17, 21
　modern groups modelled on 106, 108, 111, 113, 120
　phenomenology and 41
　schismatic churches 27–8, 107
　see also apostolic succession; Christianity; faith; Old (Liberal) Catholic Church
Centre International du Recherche Spirituelle Comparée 125
Chantepie de la Saussaye, Pierre Daniël 22, 92
Christianity 7, 11, 18–19, 20–2, 24, 62, 65, 74, 77, 82, 100, 158
　criticisms of New Age 139–40
　dualism and 127
　as Gnosticism 8, 33, 35, 37, 69, 111, 120, 145
　Hellenization 21, 22, 45, 82
　heresy 4, 6, 12–15, 16, 17–18, 86, 112, 142, 160
　History of Religion and 92, 93, 94
　Jung and 53, 58
　modern gnostic groups as Christian 106–7, 111
　Nazis and 46, 47, 79, 124
　nineteenth-century Gnostics and 26, 29, 30–1
　Religious Studies and 161
　see also Catholicism; faith; Protestantism
Church of Satan 187 n.37
Claremont Colloquium 1965 (IAHR) 99
Clemen, Carl 100
Clement of Alexandria 12, 15, 114
　in Gnostic Movement 119
Co-Masonic Order 35
collective unconscious 54
　see also unconscious
Colpe, Carston 99
Conner, Miguel 146
Conze, Edward 101
Corbin, Henry 59, **60**, 61, **62**, 68, 124–5, **126**, 127, 133, 149, 150

Corngold, Stanley 51
cosmogonies 13–14, 107
    see also alienation; dualism; 'systems'
        (human world)
Cross, Frank L. 73
Crowley, Aleister 29, 53, 112, 186 n.5
Culianu, Ioan 127, 157
Czaplicka, Maria 160

Daniélou, Jean 99
Darlés, Jean 30
Dart, John 143
Dasein 43, 45
Daumas, François 66
Dawson, Andrew 189 n.81
de Palatine, Duc (Richard Jean Chretien)
    110, 146
Dead Sea Scrolls 69, 111, 143
DeConick, April 1–2, 18, 74, 146–7, 149–
    50, 158, 161, 162
    Kripal and 145, 151, 153, 154, 155
    New Age movement and 7, 141–2,
        147–8, 160
    Quispel and 144–5, 150
demiurge 14, 22, 30, 104, 114, 125, 163 n.8
    Jonas and 81, 83
    Jung and 78
demythologization 22, 43–4, 65
Denis, Ferdinand 26
Dieterich, Albrecht 100
Dillon, Matthew 69, 115, 120
discourse analysis 134–5
Doniel, Jules 25–6, 27
Doresse, Jean and Marianne 68–9, 71, 72,
    73, 75, 104
dualism 4, 49, 86, 125, 127
    Jewish Gnosticism and 48
    Jonas and 45, 71
    modern Gnostic groups and 110
    as overstated 20, 148
    western esotericism and 128
    Zoroastrianism and 23
    see also alienation; Cathars;
        cosmogonies; 'systems'
        (human world)
Dubuisson, Daniel 98
Durand, Gilbert **126**
Durkheim, Émile 98

Ebionites 14

Ecclesia Gnostica Catholica (Gnostiche
    Katholische Kirche) 37, 106, 108–12,
    108, 146, 167 n.13, 186 n.5
    ceremonies 113
    DeConick and 185 n.4
    origins 28, 29
    'systems' in 107
Église Gnostique 26, 109, 116, 118
Église Gnostique Universelle 27, 116
    see also Ecclesia Gnostica Catholica
        (Gnostiche Katholische Kirche)
Egypt 13, 32, 70, 72, 101
    Bruce Codex discovered in 19
    Nag Hammadi Corpus and 66–9, 75, 82
    Oxyrhynchus 20
    Tau cross 27
Eid Codex, see Jung Codex (Eid Codex)
Eisler, Robert 34, 58
Eliade, Mircea 39–40, 57, 86–7, 92,
    96–7, 142
    Centre International du Recherche
        Spirituelle Comparée 125
    Eranos and 59, 64, 91, 96, 127
    IAHR and 89–90, 96
    Kripal and 152, 153, 155, 156
    Raschke and 138
    Sacred 97–8, 148, 155, 156
    Shamanism (1951) 160
elitism 5, 7, 37, 60, 103, 136, 152,
    155, 157
Enlightenment (historical period) 154–5
Epiphanius of Salamis 14–15, 16,
    185 n.68
Epistle of Barnabas 12
epoché (bracketing) 94, 95
Eranos 6, 7, 38, 42, 53, 58–60, **60**, 61,
    62, **62**, 63
    IAHR and 7, 91, 103
    influence on Kripal 154, 155
    Nag Hammadi and 72, 74
    Religious Studies and 64
    scholars of esotericism and 124, 125,
        126, 127, 130, 131, 150
Esalen (Big Sur) 153
eschatology 83–5
esotericism, *see* Western esotericism
essence of religion, *see* essentialism
Essenes 111

essentialism 5, 23, 38, 39–40, 128–9, 144, 145, 146–7, 158
   defining contemporary religions 105–6, 120–1, 141
   essentialization 6, 7, 24, 49, 64, 89, 103, 160–1
   Jonas and 77
   phenomenology and 7, 39, 42, 93, 94, 134, 147, 152
   Qusipel and 71
   Stratford and 114
   Western esotericism and 123, 127, 130, 131, 136
   see also ahistoricism; phenomenology; phenomenology of religion; sui generis
ESSWE (European Society for the Study of Western Esotericism) 133, 135
European Academy of Religion 99
European Association for the Study of Religions 133, 184 n.45
evolutionism 22–3
existentialism 39, 43, 45, 65, 80–1, 103, 110, 114, 142, 157, 160
   Bultmann and 44

Fabré-Palaprat, Bernard-Raymond 112, 114, 187 n.50
faith 12, 21, 36, 78, 107, 144
   phenomenology and 92
   tripartite epistemology 63, 126, 128, 129–31, 154–5, 158
   see also phenomenology of religion
Faivre, Antoine 124, 125–7, **126**, 128, 131, 133, 134
feminine 143
   see also Sophia (gnostic concept)
Findhorn 137
Folks, Jesse 115
Forshaw, Peter 132
Foster, James 112
Frankenburg, Abraham von 18
Fraternidad de Rosacruz Antiqua 116
Freemasonry 24, 26–7, 30, 100, 109, 113, 114, 116
Freud, Sigmund 54
Frick, Heinrich 90
Fröbe-Kapteyn, Olga 52–3, 58–9, 173 n.10, 179 n.56, 183 n.30

Gardner, Gerald 116
Gibbon, Edward 17
Gilhus, Ingvild 137–8
Ginzburg, Carlo 82, 87
Given, J. Gregory 123, 145
Gnosis (academic journal) 146–7
Gnosis (magazine) 137
Gnostic Movement (Aun Weor group) 105–6, 116–20, 159
Gnostic Society (Pryse) 109
Gnosticism, Esotericism, Mysticism (GEM) program 145–6
Godwin, Joscelyn 137
Goodrick-Clarke, Nicholas 131
Gospel of Mary 20
Gospel of Philip 69, 112
Gospel of Thomas 20, 69, 75, 139, 158
Gospel of Truth 69, 72, 73–4, 75, 177 n.25
Graeb, James 112
Graetz, Heinrich 48
Grant, Robert M. 81
Green, Henry 4
Grenfell, Bernard Pyne 20
Gross, Otto 54
Guénon, René 127
Guilhabert de Castres 25
Gurdjieff, George Ivanovich 116, 119

Hakl, Hans Thomas 6, 173 n.16
Hall, Manly P. 109
Hammer, Olav 132, 133
Hanegraaff, Wouter 4, 7, 58, 85, 141–2
   on Eranos 60
   esotericism and 124, 125, 127–8, 129–31, 132–3, 134–6, 140, 160
   on Kripal 156
Hanfstängl, Ernst 51
Harnack, Adolf von 20–2, 32, 45, 47
Hartmann, Franz 168 n.23
Hartog, Paul 47
Heckethorn, Charles William 26
Heelas, Paul 140
Hegel, Georg Wilhelm Friedrich 18, 19, 63
Heidegger, Martin 41–3, 44, 45, 47, 62, 76, 84, 94, 95
   anti-Semitism 172 n.51
   Bultmann and 65
   Jonas and 61, 80, 81, 102

Nazism and 46, 80
Hellenization 21, 22, 24, 45, 66, 82
heresy, Gnosticism as 4, 6, 12–15, 16, 17–18, 86, 112, 142, 160
Hermetic Order of the Golden Dawn 27, 113
Hermeticism 12, 34, 45, 63, 70, 124, 125, 148
Hesse, Herman 51–2
Hinduism 24, 30, 31, 99–100, 143, 160
 Rig Veda 23, 100
 see also India
Hippolytus of Rome 14, 35
historicism 91, 125, 134–5
 see also ahistoricism
Hoeller, Stephan 107, 108–13, 114, 116, 137, 148, 174 n.38, 187 n.47
Hofstadter, Richard 85
Holocaust 78–9, 80, 81, 82–3
 see also anti-Semitism; Nazism
homo religious 57, 59
Hunt, Arthur Surridge 20
Husserl, Edmund 39, 40–2, 43, 46, 94, 95, 127
Hutton, Ronald 116
Hypostasis of the Archons 69

IAHR (International Association for the History of Religions) 2, 7, 35, 39, 89–92, **90**, **102**
Icke, David 137
Iglesia Gnóstica Christiana Universal, *see* Gnostic Movement (Aun Weor group)
India 24, 28, 32, 47, 82, 97, 103
 Eliade in 96
 independence movement 29
 see also Hinduism
intentionality (Brentano) 40
 Eranos and 91, 103
 ESSWE and 133
 Gnosticism and 98–104
 phenomenology 91, 92–3, 94–6, 104
International Committee of Gnosticism 75
International Congress of the History of Religions 89
Iran 20, 23, 24, 34, 47, 81–2, 99, 101, 103
Irenaeus 4, 6, 11–15, 16, 71, 109, 142, 160, 163 n.8
 in Gnostic Movement 119
Islam 61, 99, 124, 162
 see also Corbin, Henry

Jaffé, Anelia 55
James, E. O. 90
Jansenism 36
Jaspers, Karl 46
Jenkins, Philip 143
Jensen, Tim 99
Jerusalem Colloquium 1968 (IAHR) 99
Jews 12, 19, 24, 79, 81, 139
 'Jewish cultural renaissance' 44
 see also anti-Semitism; Holocaust; Judaism; Zionism
Jonas, Hans 1–2, 3, 6, 9, 39, 44–6, 47–9, 62, 79, 81–2, 95, 110, 141, 161
 alienation 52, 63, 71, 77, 80
 Bloom and 13–19
 Corbin and 61
 existentialism 65, 77, 81, 83, 84, 85–6, 103, 157, 160
 IAHR and 99, 100–1, 102, 125, 136
 Hanegraaff and 128
 Nag Hammadi and 65, 77, 104, 114
 phenomenology and 79–80
Jones, Peter (Christian author) 140, 144
Judaism 48–9, 61, 63, 81–2, 85, 99, 100–1, 103, 124
 in Antiquity 12, 70
 Christianity and 21, 22, 23
 dualism and 127
 Nag Hammadi Corpus and 70, 72
 synthesized in Gnosticism 19, 24, 32
 see also Jews; Jonas, Hans; Kabbalah; Scholem, Gershom
Judge, W. Q. 29, 33
Jung 7, 39, 49, 51, 52, 53–8, 59, 60, **60**, 61, 64, 65, 91, 128, 138, 142, 147, 150
 Eliade and 96–7
 Faivre and 126
 Icke and 137
 influence on Messina Congress 101–3, 157
 Kripal and 152, 155–6
 Mead and 24, 34, 56
 modern gnostics and 109, 110, 111, 114, 120

Nag Hammadi Corpus and 72, 73, 74–5, 76, 77, 141, 142–3
phenomenology and 3, 5
problem of evil 78–9
Quispel and 56, 63, 72, 129, 144
Scholem and 60
Septum Sermones ad Mortuos 55, 78, 109
Western esotericism and 133
see also C. G. Jung Institute
Jung Codex (Eid Codex) 71, 72–5, 90

Kabbalah 48, 61
'oriental kabbalah' 26
Kafka, Franz 51
Kerényi, Károly 52, 96
King, Charles William 24, 30, 31
King, Karen 6, 16, 107, 114, 144
Kingsford, Anna 33, 35
Kingsland, William 30–1, 169 n.63
Klein, Henry 168 n.23
Koester, Helmut 65, 142
Krause, Martin 69, 101
Kripal, Jeffrey 7, 145, 152–6, 160, 161
Krishnamurti, Jiddu 35, 37
Kristensen, William Brede 92, 93
Krochmal, Nachman 48
Krumm-Heller, Arnoldo 116–17, 119
Kulturkreislehre 91

Labib, Pahor 69, 75
Lang, Joseph Bernhard 52
Latin American Christian Workers' Party (Aun Woer group) 118
LaVey, Anton 187 n.37
Layton, Bentley 105
Lazier, Benjamin 6
Leadbeater, Charles W. 33–4, 35, 36–7, 57
Legge, Francis George 165 n.21
Leibniz, Gottfried Wilhelm 83
Letter to Rheginos 73
Levi, Eliphas 124
Lévi-Strauss, Claude 161
Levinas, Emmanuel 44
Liebenfels, Jörg Lanz von 51
Lim, Timothy 70
Lincoln, Bruce 86
List, Guido 51

Löwith, Karl 42, 44, 48, 84
Lucifer (journal) 31, 34

MacRae, George 143
Malinine, Michel **73**
Manda d'Hayje 23
Mandaeans 20, 23, 45, 99
Manichaeans 17, 20, 23, 70, 99, 101
Mann, Thomas 52
Mansel, Henry Longueville 17–18
Marburg 1960 (IAHR) 94, 95, 98
Marcion 32
Martinism 27
Martyr, Justin 11
Marxism 85
Mathew, Arnold Harris 36
Matter, Jacques 124
McCutcheon, Russell T. 98, 151–2
Mead, George Robert Stow 24, 31–3, 34–5, 58, 110, 119, 142, 183 n.30
 Eliade and 96
 Jung and 24, 34, 56
Meier, Carl 73, 75
Mellon, Mary and Paul 59, 64, 71
 see also Bollingen
Memories, Dreams, Reflections (Jung) 55, 79
Menander 32
Merkur, Dan 148–9
Mesopotamia 101
Messina (town) 89
Messina Congress 1966 (IAHR) 35, 38, 39, 99–103, **102**, 159
 influence 104, 123, 125, 131, 132, 136, 147, 157
Michaelis, Johann David 17
Miller, Rosamonde 111
mimesis 16
Mina, Togo 67, 68, 69
modernity 77–9, 80–1, 83–6, 106, 139
 see also secularism
Monte Verità 52–3, 54
More, Henry 17, 21
Movimiento Gnóstica Christiano Universal, *see* Gnostic Movement (Aun Weor group)
Muhammad 'Ali (Nag Hammadi) 66–8, 69
Müller, Friedrich Max 22

Naassenes 14
Nag Hammadi corpus 2, 4, 7, 15, 16, 20, 69–71, 177 n.25
  discovery 66–9, 82, 141, 143, 160
  Judaism and 70, 72
  Jung and 72, 73, 74–5, 76, 77, 141, 142–3
  Jungian scholars and 64, 65, 71–5, **73**, 76
  Messina 1966 and 89, 101
  modern gnostic groups and 111, 114, 115, 120
  phenomenology and 72, 73–4, 77
  publication 73–5, 137
Nag Hammadi Library in English 2, 20, 104, 142, 143
Nazism 46–7, 51, 77, 79, 124, 138
  Heidegger and 46, 80
  as religion 85
  see also anti-Semitism; Holocaust
Nelson, Victoria 151, 152
Neoplatonism 12, 13, 15, 177 n.25
  modern science and 124
  Renaissance and 16–17
New Age 1, 7, 23, 115, 123, 137–8, 139–41, 142, 143, 144, 146
  antecedents 29, 52
  Aun Weor and 105, 118, 120
  cosmology 107
  critique of 'organized religion' 37–8
  DeConick and 140–1, 147–8, 150, 151, 160
  as Western esotericism 127–8, 137
New Religious Movements 138, 147
Nock, Arthur Darby 90
Noll, Richard 53, 54–5, 58, 174 nn.35, 38
nominalism 86
Norden, Eduard 100
NUMEN 90, 93, 94, 96
numinous 42, 58, 59, 64, 94

O'Regan, Cyril 139–40
Olcott, Henry Steel 29, 33–4
Old (Liberal) Catholic Church 35, 36, 37, 109
  see also apostolic succession
On the Origin of the World 69
Ophites 32

Ordo Templi Orientis (OTO) 27, 28, 37, 52, 107, 116, 146, 186 n.5
Orientalism 160
Origen 15
Otto, Rudolf 24, 42, 82, 94, 95, 148, 155
  Eliade and 97–8
  influence on Eranos 58, 59, 91
  numinous and 94
  see also numinous
Oxyrhynchus 20

Paganism 17, 18, 19, 29, 58, 116, 162
  Nazis and 47, 80
Pagels, Elaine 18, 74, 111, 142–4, 148, 150
Palaprat, Bernard-Raymond 26
Palm Tree Garden 115
pantheism 100
Papus (Gérard Encausse) 27, 28
paranormal 152
Parliament of World Religions 27, 112
Pasi, Marco 132, 133
Paul, Saint 127
Pearson, Birger 49, 81, 83, 114, 142, 147
perennialism 3, 32, 163 n.1
Pettazzoni, Raffaele 90, **90**, 91, 92, 93, 95
phenomenology 3, 5, 6, 7, 40–1, 42, 43–4, 93, 95, 110, 158
  see also psychology; sui generis
phenomenology of religion 7, 22, 24, 39, 42, 61, 82, 92–4, 134, 145–6, 152, 161, 162
  Biblical Studies and 44
  Eranos and 64, 127, 155
  IAHR and 39, 91, 92–3, 94–6, 104, 157
  Jonas and 63, 63, 79–80
  Nag Hammadi Corpus and 72, 73–4, 77
  New Age and 141, 144, 147, 150
  religious experience and 149
  see also ahistoricism; essentialism; sui generis
Philemon (spiritual teacher) 55
Philosophumena, see *Refutatio Omnium Haeresium*
Pistis Sophia 16, 19, 20, 21, 31, 32, 166 n.56
  owned by Jung 56, 174 n.38
  racial interpretation 51
  Weor's commentary 115, 119
Platonism 12, 15–16, 18, 70
  dualism of 127

Republic 69
seventeenth century 17
see also Neoplatonism
pleroma 13, 25, 48
Pleše, Zlatko 114
Plotinus 13, 15
pneuma 139
Porphyry 15
Prayer of Thanksgiving 69
Prayer of the Apostle Paul 73
'Pre-Gnosticism' (term) 103
Pre-Nicene Gnostic Catholic Church 110
problem of evil 78–9, 83, 86
  modern gnostic groups and 107
Prodicus 15
Protestantism 17, 18–19, 160
  liberal 2, 6, 21, 22
  phenomenology and 41, 92
  see also Christianity; faith
'Proto-Gnosticism' (term) 103
Pryse, James Morgan 109
psychoanalysis 34
  Jungian 54–5, 56, 58, 161
  mysticism and 153
  Shamanism and 160–1
  see also Jung, Carl
psychology
  of religion 95, 145–6, 157
  religion as 114, 120, 121, 141, 143, 144, 147, 149, 150, 160
  see also Jung, Carl; phenomenology
Puech, Henri-Charles 62–3, 138
  at IAHR 90, 91, 101
  Nag Hammadi and 66, 68, 69, 71, 72, 73–4, **73**, 75
Puma, Jeremy 115, 116

Quest (journal) 34
Quispel, Gilles 24, 63, 81–2, 101, 103, 114, 125, 137, 142, 161, 173 n.8, 187 n, 47
  DeConick and 144–5, 150
  esotericism and 125, 126, 127, 128, 129–30, 131, 132, 135, 136
  Jung and 56, 63, 72, 129, 144
  Nag Hammadi and 65, 69, 71–3, **73**, 75
  tripartite epistemology 126, 154, 157
  see also faith

Rabinbach, Anson 82–3

Ramakrishna 153
Randolph, Paschal Beverly 28
Raschke, Carl 138, 139
Rauschenbach, Emma 54
Redeemed Redeemer myth 23, 45, 61, 82, 100
Refutatio Omnium Haeresium 14, 164–5 n.21
Reitzenstein, Richard 23, 34, 65, 100, 103
religious experience 149–50, 152
Religious Studies 123, 131, 132, 133, 134–5
Renaissance 16–17, 132, 133
Reuss, Theodor 28, 29, 52
Rhys Davies, Caroline 58
Rig Veda 23, 100
Rijk, W. A. 90, 93
Robinson, James 65, 69, 73, 101, 104
Roig-Lanzillotta, Lautaro 146
Romanticism 100, 138, 154–5
Rosicrucianism 24, 26, 100, 109
Rudolph, Kurt 49, 66, 81, 101
Rune FA (Aun Woer concept) 118

sacraments 112, 113
Sacred (Eliade) 97–8, 148, 155, 156
Saddharmapundarika Sutra 100
Safranski, Rudiger 43
Saint-Martin, Louise-Claude de 27
Satanism 29, 187 n.37
Schelling, Friedrich Wilhelm Joseph von 19
Schleiermacher, Friedrich 19, 42
Schmidt, Carl 19, 31, 164 n.21
scholasticism 83, 86
Scholem, Gershom 48–9, 63, 78, 81–2, 85, 110, 124, 139, 150
  Eranos and 59, 60–1, **62**
  Hanegraaff and 130, 135
  Kripal and 155
  Merkur and 149
  messianism 84
  Quispel and 103
Schultz, Wolfgang 51
Schwartze, Moritz Gotthilf 19, 31, 164 n.21
Science of Religion 3, 6, 22, 23, 24, 45
Secret, François 124
secularism 77, 84, 86, 92
  Gnosticism as 45
  New Age as 127–8, 140

see also modernity
Segal, Robert 175 n.45
'self' (Jungian) 56–7, 72
seminal retention 119
Septum Sermones ad Mortuos (Jung) 55, 78, 109
Sethian Gnosticism 15, 32, 68, 70, 177 n.25
sex abuse allegations 34, 36
sex magic 28, 37, 116, 117, 120, 167 n.13
sexual imagery 3, 4–5, 16, 28, 29
Shamanism 29, 159, 160
Shamdasani, Sonu 55
Simon Magus 14, 17, 32
  in Gnostic Movement 119
Simonians 15
Singer, June 187 n.47
Sinnett, Alfred 33
Smith, Jonathan Z. 4
Smith, Morton 60
sociology of religion 95
SOL Key (Aun Woer concept) 118
'Solar Phallus Man' 54, 56
Sophia (gnostic concept) 13, 111, 143
Sophia (ecclesiastical title) 167 n.13
Sophia of Jesus Christ 20
Steiner, Rudolf 63–4, 137
Stratford, Jordan 107, 113–15, 116
Streiber, Whitley 137, 153
Styfhals, Willem 6, 106, 151
sui generis 6, 64, 93, 98, 128, 148
  Gnosticism and 49, 63, 66, 87, 99, 105, 147, 158
  numinous 58
  phenomenology and 3, 39, 42, 92, 141, 162
  Shamanism 160
  Western esotericism and 130, 131
  see also ahistoricism; essentialism; phenomenology; phenomenology of religion
Swedenborg, Emanuel 29
'systems' (human world) 85, 107, 114
  see also dualism

Tanos, Phokion 67, 68
Tantra 28, 37, 97, 119
  Tantrika 29
Tau (ecclesiastical title) 27, 167 n.13
Taubes, Jacob 84–5, 86, 138
Taves, Ann 149, 163 n.8

Templars 24, 25, 26, 30, 115
Temple of Set 112, 187 n.37
Tertullian 15, 112
Testimony of Truth 83
Thelema 29, 112–13, 114–15, 186 n.5
Theodicy, *see* problem of evil
Theodotus of Byzantium 14
theory 158–9, 161–2
  see also phenomenology; phenomenology of religion
theosophy 24, 25, 29–34, 35, 51, 137, 146
  contemporary Gnostic groups and 107, 108, 109, 110, 116
  Eliade and 96
  Fröbe-Kapteyn and 52, 53
  Jung's view of 57, 58
  Nag Hammadi and 76
  New Age and 137, 140, 141, 142, 146, 147
  Old Catholic Church and 36, 37
  publications 51, 52, 165 n.21
  see also Bailey, Alice; Blavatsky, Helena Petrovna; Blavatsky Trust; Mead, George Robert Stow
Thomasius, Jacob 17
Tiele, Cornelius Petrus 22, 92
Tillett, Gregory John 37
Tillich, Paul 42
Timotheos, Mar (Joseph René Vilatte) 28
Tite, Philip 148, 151
Tokyo 1958 (IAHR) 95
Toronto 2010 (IAHR) 98–9
Treatise on the Three Natures 73
Tübingen School 18, 20, 46
Tuckett, Jonathan 92
Tumber, Catherine 140
Turner, H. E. W. 65

UFOs 29, 137
unconscious 54, 56–7, 58
  God's 78, 79
Untitled Treatise 19, 32
Urban, Hugh 16, 28

Valbuena, Joaquin Amortegui (Venerable Master Rabolú) 118
Valentinians 13–14, 15, 16, 21, 70, 112, 139

Frankenburg on 18
Quispel on 63, 72–3
Valentinus 13, 14, 21
    in Bloom novel 139
    in Gnostic Movement 119
    nineteenth-century views of 25, 32
van den Broek, Roelf 5, 125, 127–8, 130, 131
van der Leeuw, Gerardus 90, **90**, 91, 92, 93–4, 97, 151
Verslius, Arthur 130, 138
Voegelin, Eric 84, 8586, 138, 139, 176 n.66
völkische movement 51, 52, 55, 58, 129
von Stuckrad, Kocku 132, 133–4, 135

Wasserstrom, Steven 6, 64, 78–9, 87, 141
Webb, James 124
Wedgwood, James 35, 36, 37
Weibe, Donald 93
Weor, Samael Aun, *see* Aun Weor, Samael (Victor Manuel Gómez Rodríguez)

Werblowski, Zwi 96
Western esotericism 124–36, 142, 149, 160
Wiccans 116
    see also Paganism
Widengren, Geo 81, 93, 90, 95, 99–100, 101, 104, 142
William of Ockham 86
Williams, Michael 4–5, 6, 15, 22, 24, 104, 115, 129, 144, 163 n.8
Willoughby, Frederick 36

Yarker, John 37
Yates, Frances 124, 131
yoga 29
York, Michael (religious studies scholar) 140

Zionism 44, 48, 49, 62
Zoccatelli, PierLuigi 115
Zoroastrianism 15, 17, 20, 23, 70, 100

www.ingramcontent.com/pod-product-compliance
Lightning Source LLC
Chambersburg PA
CBHW062215300426
44115CB00012BA/2075